CELTIC CROSS

Tammy Doherty

Xulon PRESS

Xulon Press
www.XulonPress.com

Xulon Press books are available in bookstores everywhere,
and on the Web at www.XulonPress.com.

ONE

Colorado, 1882

Rays of sunlight punctured the aspen grove, stabbing at the chill air. There was a stillness in the woods, as though even the birds were too cold to sing. Ahead the trees ended abruptly at the edge of a rolling meadow. The grass was bejeweled in sparkling frosty splendor.

The beauty of the sunrise was lost to Cristeen. She clung to consciousness with a desperation equaled only by her death grip on the saddle horn. Only vaguely aware of her upper body gently rocking with the horse's movement, at least she no longer felt the pain.

Cristeen looked down at her right leg that hung limply, flopping weakly when jostled. Her blood soaked pants appeared a dark reddish-brown color, almost black.

That's not right, her mind grappled with reason. A glance left confirmed the correct fabric color as the indigo blue of denim. She looked again at her right leg. Thoughts and memories swirled and the explanation danced just out of reach. What happened?

Blackness closed in; just as it seemed about to swallow her, Cristeen remembered. The memory snapped her eyes open, if only for a moment. She had been shot, twice. How long ago, she wondered. It had been dark, the landscape bathed in the silvery light of a full moon. Now the sun was rising. Had only one night passed? She was so tired. Then it had hurt; now she felt nothing. Not the wound nor even the cold. She tried to focus her thoughts, concentrating on moving her toes. The effort was exhausting and yielded no physical sensation at all.

She was dying.

She accepted the conclusion as logical and inevitable. Had she the supplies needed to nurse herself back to health, death would yet be inescapable. She was so tired. Merely staying conscious was becoming impossible. She should give up and give in to the blackness. Her eyelids drooped; her head bobbed.

No! Cristeen's mind screamed, *I'm not ready to die.*

* * *

Matt Donovan leaned against the porch post. Idly he noticed the steam rising from his coffee looked like the mist hanging over the lake. Soon the warmth of the sun would chase away the chill and with it the mist. The night had been a reminder of the winter now ended. But the day would be a preview of summer.

Already the frosty dew had melted. A small bunch of cattle began to graze. First-calf heifer, the term crossed Matt's mind. The older, more experienced cows ranged the far end of the valley. No matter her age, a cow was always susceptible to danger and problems during calving. The first time a heifer gave birth carried higher risks.

All this passed fleetingly through Matt's thoughts. His gaze traveled across the meadow, barely registering the barns before moving upward to the mountain peaks towering over the park. The nearest summit, a prelude to the higher mountains, bristled with the verdant green of spruce trees. Towering above, the craggy heights of the Rocky Mountains seemed to stretch all the way to heaven. This was the vision Matt carried with him whenever he was away.

Behind him the door opened with a loud complaint. He added oiling the hinges to his mental list of things to do. Matt didn't need to look to know it was Paul standing behind him. He waited for the other man to move to the porch railing before acknowledging him.

"Katie done the dishes?"

"Just finished. You'll have to wash that cup yourself."

Matt grinned, picturing his sister's flustered expression when he presented her with his coffee cup.

"Will you be coming out to the house?"

"Later. I am curious to see how it's coming along."

"Now don't get all foreman-like on me. I get enough of that from Ty." He scrunched his face, attempting to look stern as he mimicked Ty. *"Put more nails in that board, boy. An' don'cha think that window should be a wee bit more to the left?"*

"Was he right?"

Paul's smile was sheepish. "Isn't he always."

"I'll ride out and be the judge of that."

"Ride? You been in the city too long, Matt. Can't be more 'n half, three-quarters of a mile from here to the house. Walkin' would do you good."

Though he knew it was said in jest, Matt took the bait. "Two weeks could hardly be considered too long. If you must know, I will be riding out to check the herd. Comin' on time to head 'em up to spring pasture."

"Whoa, don't get your back up. I was just joshin' ya'." Paul's typically puckish expression became serious as he stared down the length of the valley. The herd was too far to be seen; yet he saw them in his mind's eye. "The herd did well this winter. Grass down here gonna be needin' a break, and most of the snow has melted up on the hills. Yup, it's about that time."

Matt snorted a chuckle and was about to comment on his friend's ability to understate things when his eye caught movement in the complex of barns. Matt recognized the wizened figure of Ty leading a harnessed team to a large wagon.

"So, riding out to the house would be city of me?" It was his turn to rib Paul. "I suppose taking the wagon out would be downright lazy."

Paul had the decency to flush, seeing the hole he had dug for himself. His stammered response was cut off by Matt's hearty laugh.

"Well, just don't think Katie and me don't appreciate you fetching those supplies for us."

Matt shrugged. "I had business in Fort Rossiter anyway. Be senseless to pay a freighter to haul it up here."

"Ya', well you could've been an' back a lot quicker on horseback. 'Specially coming home. Drivin' a wagon load of glass is slow business."

"You're telling me. If even one pane is so much as cracked Katie will never let me forget."

By this time the wagon had reached them. Ty swung the team in a graceful arc so that when they stopped the wagon was parallel to the porch. The old Irishman spoke a few words Matt did not understand, in a tone meant to both praise and settle the horses. Since he was a young boy, Matt heard Ty speak the language of the gone-by ones. The speech of the ancient Celts, Gaelic was a nearly forgotten tongue. Despite hearing the words for so many years, Matt never learned the language himself. Still he delighted in the poetic quality of the words.

"Well, Mattie-boy, returned home at last. Bin dull here widout ye. Sure an' Paul missed ye a might, almost as much as wee Katie."

"Mattie-boy is what you called me when I really was a boy. Shall I always be nine years old?"

Not so long ago Matt bristled at being called boy, even by the likes of Ty. With the passage of time comes wisdom. For Matt it was the wisdom to recognize Ty's gruff tenderness, and realize that Mattie-boy was a title of honor. A sign of affection from one man to another.

"Aye, and I shall forever be twenty-seven." Ty's smile crinkled the corners of his eyes and brightened an otherwise harsh complexion. "For time may make a man wise, but it also makes a man auld!"

"Truer words you have never spoken, old man," Paul swung up onto the wagon seat beside the foreman.

Ty gave him a sidelong look as he remarked, "Mother Nature cain't hold a candle to a wife for making a man aulder."

"Oh, now don't start up on that again!"

The pair continued to banter as the wagon rolled across the yard. Matt chuckled and shook his head. Two weeks really was a long time. He missed the quasi-adversarial relationship between Ty and Paul.

Katie was nowhere to be seen in the kitchen. Her handiwork, however, was apparent. The table that had hosted breakfast was now pushed up against the wall, under a window. A doily runner adorned with a vase of wildflowers disguised its utilitarian role. Plates had been washed and put away behind the closed doors of the cabinets.

The cook stove emanated heat, keeping a pot of coffee warm. Through an open door to the left Matt glimpsed the large oak table that was Katie's work place. In that larger room Katie kept her pantry supplies, for in there she would labor over meals. The massive table bore scars from use as a chopping block, and a shiny smoothness had been worn into the surface from the many piecrusts and bread dough that had been rolled and kneaded on it.

Katie was not in this room, either. Matt heard her humming from somewhere down the hallway and correctly deduced she was in the parlor. He stood silently for a moment, soaking up the picture of contentment presented as she looked through a book of wallpaper samples. Her dark hair, so much like his own, had defied all efforts to secure it, the brown strands falling over her shoulders, shrouding her face. A page slowly turned, as if Katie were unwilling to part with the beauty of the sample. When at last she noticed his presence, she greeted him with a wide smile.

"How will I ever choose from all these beautiful patterns?"

Matt strode to the chair beside the sofa. Sinking into the cushions, he said, "You'll be able to pick out just the right one for each room. You have good taste."

"Well, I'd better decide quickly. Paul says that the windows and the decorative trims you brought back are the last of the structural work to be done. The rest is up to me."

Work on the house began the summer before. It was to be Paul's wedding gift to Katie, although the land was actually Matt's gift to them both. At first only Paul worked on the building, while Ty and Matt kept the ranch running smoothly. As summer waned, Matt hired two local boys to tend the herd, freeing both Matt and Ty to work with Paul. Even Katie pitched in, handing out nails and tools like a skilled surgeon's assistant. Only the harsh reality of winter slowed their pace. Spring's warm sunshine renewed the fervent drive to complete the house.

"How are the wedding plans coming along?"

Katie groaned. "One thing at a time, please. When I've chosen the wallpaper, then I'll think about the wedding."

"You have at least settled on a date, haven't you?"

Katie's response was curtly silenced by Matt's raised hand. He turned slightly towards the window and tilted his head, listening. The dogs were barking. He listened a moment longer, expecting to hear the sound of a carriage crossing the bridge or crunching up the gravel drive.

Whatever had stirred up the dogs seemed to be out back.

Matt's long stride swiftly carried him to the porch. His gaze swept the yard, seeing nothing amiss. Far in the distance to his right he could just make out the rooftop of Paul and Katie's new house. Between there and Matt's own home, the heifers grazed undisturbed. But for the dogs, he detected no movement amongst the barns. Then he noticed the horses in the corral standing in rigid alertness, ears pricked forward, heads held high. Their attention was riveted towards the western hills.

Three shallow steps led from the porch to the ranch yard. Matt stepped to the ground in one fluid stride, moving to the side of the house. At last he saw what the horses and dogs saw. A rider had emerged from the tree line and was headed in his direction.

The horseman in Matt critiqued the horse, an eye-catching deep golden palomino mare. She walked with a smooth, clean gait, fore feet moving just in time to be missed by the rear hooves. The angle of shoulder to leg was nearly perfect, indicating a pleasurable ride. Her neck was somewhat short, but not disproportionate; together with well-muscled haunches the mare bore all the qualities of a fine cutting horse.

That the horse was tired he also recognized. Her neck extended in a horizontal line even with her back. But her ears were pricked forward, wary of the dogs that had stopped barking at a command from Matt. Her stride faltered a moment as she changed course to come directly toward him. Matt took two more long strides to shorten the distance between them. Now the mare raised her head, just slightly. Tired but not exhausted; she had been ridden long but not hard.

As he soaked in the details of the scene before him, Matt couldn't shake the feeling that something was not quite right. He had never seen this particular horse before he was sure. While palomino coloring was not rare, it was uncommon. Many men did not favor horses that are noticeable, preferring the relative anonymity afforded by a bay or chestnut. Palominos were often held aside for special occasions, when a showy mount was desirable.

He walked past the garden. Horse and rider closed the distance, allowing Matt to assess the situation better. Only when he studied the rider did he realize what was awry. Initially Matt thought the visitor rode with an easy casualness. Sitting ramrod straight in the saddle could be tiring, especially after long hours. A man often slouched when riding horseback just as he would hunch over while driving a wagon.

Now he realized this rider was actually slumped in the saddle, head lolling. Matt had seen men doze while riding. He'd done it himself a time or two. But he would never sleep when riding into a new or unfamiliar place. And there was something about the way the rider's body moved with the rhythm of the mare's gait. Loose, rag-doll like, yet restrained as well. That's when he spotted the ropes, binding hands to pommel.

Looking closer, Matt noticed something else. With no hat to cover it, coppery hair dangled in limp ringlets where it escaped from the braid. The canvas coat that draped from shoulders to knee could not hide the slender frame. And the delicate, smooth features of the rider's face, devoid of whiskers. The stranger was a woman.

That in itself was not amazing. It was not uncommon to find women filling traditionally male roles, especially here in the West. It took a dauntless spirit to endure and persevere the hardships that accompanied homesteading. Even on well-established ranches, wives and daughters might be found riding alongside the men folk. Why, Matt's own sister Katie often leant a hand in the tasks of the day.

No, Matt was not amazed that a woman sat astride the horse. Nor did her attire surprise him. Proper dress meant wearing clothing that did not hinder the work at hand. An oiled-canvas coat draped her shoulders, covering down to her knees, shedding the cold rain of the previous night before it could soak with penetrating iciness into flesh. The heavy twill of her denim pants was effective protection against shrubs and bushes that would otherwise easily scratch. Trousers themselves made riding easier rather than skirts divided over the saddle, especially for long distances. And of course the heeled boots were a necessity, both as protection and to prevent the foot from getting caught in a stirrup should the rider be thrown. The only thing missing was a hat, protection from rain and sun alike.

What stunned Matt was her condition. To say she was riding the horse was to push the definition of the term. She was on horseback, in a mostly upright position. Her body slouched in the seat. Her chin rested on her chest, head bobbing in rhythm with the horse's stride.

What made the strongest impression were her hands. Protruding from the coat sleeves only at the wrists, as if the garment were too large, her fingers were clamped tightly around the saddle horn with the rigidity of rigor mortis.

"Is she...dead?"

Katie's hesitant question broke Matt's concentration.

"I don't think so." He glanced at his sister. Katie was nearly as pale as the stranger. "Least we can give her a decent burial."

"Matthew!" Indignant color flushed Katie's cheeks.

Matt chuckled and patted Katie's arm reassuringly. "C'mon, you know me better 'n that."

Turning back to the horse, he reached for a rein. Briefly he noticed the bridle was a hackamore. Before he could give it more attention the mare shied away from his hand, tossing her head and stepping back. The jarring movement set the rider to sliding sideways. Matt moved quickly to catch her.

To his surprise, she caught herself. Startled into alertness, her head jerked up. Arm muscles contracted convulsively, pulling her back into the center of the saddle. All the while her lips moved, forming words Matt could not hear. She never looked at him, did not seem to notice Katie. For a moment after righting herself, her glazed stare remained fixed on her horse's ears. Her silent chant lost its fervency. At the last Matt deciphered the one word mantra - no. Energy waned quickly; her eyelids drooped even before her mouth stopped forming words. Her body slumped again.

"She must be exhausted," Katie exclaimed, "if every time she sleeps she is jolted awake. Why not stop and rest somewhere?"

Matt was wondering that himself until the answer presented itself. He had reached up to support the woman before she fell. Finding this gesture unnecessary, his arm fell and his hand brushed her leg. The fabric was cold with wet. *That's how it is with slickers, body keeps dry and legs get drenched*, Matt laughed to himself. He reached again for the rein.

He momentarily froze as he saw his left hand. A brownish red streak ran across the back of his fingers. He recognized it at once. Blood. With a feeling of unease, he looked back at the leg he just touched.

What he saw sickened him. It was not rain water that soaked the fabric but blood. So much blood that the denim was discolored to an almost blackened appearance. There seemed to be some sort of a bandage tied around her midcalf; it, too, was drenched in blood. Her leg hung limply, foot dangling beside the stirrup.

Exhaustion dogging at her heels, this young woman was not simply clinging to her saddle. She was clinging to life. Mere physical ability could not keep her body astride the horse. Here was a woman driven by sheer will power. Having reached death's very door, still terror drove her onward. Was it the frightening thought of dying that pushed her, or something even more horrific?

"Matt?"

"Katie, go ring the bell."

"The bell? But that's to call Paul and Ty back to the house," she paused. "Is this an emergency?"

"Go!"

His almost imperceptible nod eased the severity of the command. Katie turned heel, gathered her skirt to keep her legs unhindered and ran to the porch. The bell was a small brass ship's bell, used for years by the Donovans as a means of communication. Its peal could be heard throughout the park. Katie tugged the pull three times, paused, then again. She repeated the designated signal, all the while wondering why. What had made Matt pale so?

Meanwhile, Matt had convinced the palomino to trust him. He led the mare to the house. Katie stopped ringing; her curiosity demanded an answer.

"Why the urgency?"

Matt held up his blood-covered hand in answer. "Her leg is soaked."

Katie moved to examine the leg. When Matt tried to stop her she pushed him aside. "Can't be any worse than fetal extraction," she quipped, referring to the grisly procedure required to remove a stillborn calf from the birthing canal.

Matt conceded the point. Katie had assisted with a number of such extractions. It was a gory and bloody task, yet necessary to save the life of the cow. This gore was entirely different. It had the taste of something evil. No accidental cause could possibly explain this situation. Someone had inflicted injury on this woman; someone she perceived as akin to the devil. Nothing else could explain her flight.

Henry appeared as the rumbling sounds of the buckboard coming on fast to the house could be heard. The boy had been hired to keep the barns clean and tend to the animals in general. He lived a few miles down the road, closer to the little town of Glenpark, in a small cabin with his mother, father and four siblings. Henry was the middle child, neither skilled nor old enough to go out on his own, but ambitious enough to help out with supporting the family.

The day began at sun-up for Henry. By this time he had already milked the cows, collected all the eggs, and cleaned two box stalls. His boots were caked with a mixture of manure and straw. A few wisps of hay worked their way into his hair. But his eyes were wide and his cheeks red with excitement. He never heard the bell ring before; surely here was adventure to be had.

"Henry," Matt turned to look the boy squarely in the eye. "I need you to go find Doc Roberts. Take Dragon, and be quick about it."

The solemn tone was not entirely lost on the boy. To be given such responsibility might have weighed on him but for the carrot of riding Dragon. The gelding was a much sleeker and faster mount than the mule he customarily rode. A man's horse.

Henry charged off to the barn. As he disappeared from sight, so Matt ceased to think about him. Although still a boy, and prone to the reckless and carefree ways of childhood, Henry had proven many times over that he was dependable. And for all that Henry worshipped Dragon, the gelding was trustworthy.

The wagon hurtled into the backyard. Ty drove the team hard; hauling back on the lines he leaped from the seat. Paul launched himself off the wagon as it began to slow. Fear hardened his features until he saw Katie unharmed. His paced slowed as he eyed the stranger.

Is this what all the commotion's for?"

"I'm gonna need your help, Paul, getting her inside. Ty, I think this mare could benefit from your special attentions."

Ty looked the horse over. "She bin ridden like the banshees were after her."

"Could be they were."

It took little for them to understand Matt's sense of urgency. Ty moved to grasp the rein, freeing Matt, at the same time turning on his Irish charm and wooing the mare. The horse rested her head against the old man's chest.

"Whatever was chasin' her, she knew what to expect." Paul was examining the rope tightly wound around the saddle horn and looping her wrists. "Seems like she prepared for everything - pressure bandage for the wound, slicker for the weather, and straps to keep from falling."

"And an iron will." Matt was trying to pry her hands loose from the saddle horn. He forced each finger upwards as gently as possible. Her hands were so cold he was fearful of snapping a bone with the ease of breaking an icicle. He shivered.

Once her grip released, Matt gave a gentle tug on her arm to start her sliding towards him. As soon as the motion began her eyes fluttered open, arms flailing as she grasped for the saddle horn. And her chant started again. Matt wrapped an arm under her shoulders for support at the same time continuing to slide her from the saddle. Her gray-blue eyes, glazed with pain and exhaustion, held his gaze. He leaned his head down to catch her words.

"I am not ready to die."

TWO

Surgeon General William Hammond once referred to medicine prior to 1861 as the middle ages. With advancements in aseptic technique, anesthesia, and sutures, the latter years of the nineteenth century were indeed a medical renaissance.

Doc Roberts said a prayer of thanks for every one of those advances as he examined the patient before him. Katie efficiently prepared for his arrival and he was able to get a good look at the wounds. She had suffered two gunshots; the first and most apparent was to her lower right leg, the second through her left shoulder. In addition to the damage caused by these bullets there were multiple bruises and welts.

The open wounds intrigued Doc; the bruises troubled him. A certain degree of contusional evidence was to be expected around both entry and exit wounds. The worrisome bruises were not near either wound, although he could distinguish what appeared to be the shape of a boot heel in one of the leg bruises.

He might have missed the contusions at her throat if her pulse had been stronger. When he placed two fingers just under her jaw line to check for a pulse, the purple welt on her left cheek distracted him. Failing to detect a pulse, Doc looked down. He had inadvertently placed his fingers under her chin; her pulse was forgotten at the discovery of the distinct imprint. The unmistakable shape of a thumb and fingers straddling her windpipe. With a growing sense of dread, Doc expanded his examination.

Katie saw her own fears reflected in Doc's grim expression. "Her shirt was torn nearly in two."

Her voice trailed off. Doc raised an eyebrow in question. What Katie hesitated to say was exactly what he needed to know. "I appreciate your unease, but this is very important. Were the trousers damaged in any way?"

She shook her head negatively, quickly adding, "Except where she was shot of course."

"Of course," Doc concluded his general examination and moved to better assess the leg wound. "Do the others know about this evidence of impropriety?"

"No, I sent them away when I discovered the torn shirt."

"For the best."

"Do you think she was molested?" Katie whispered.

Doc stopped to consider both his patient and Katie. It was a disturbing topic, as uncomfortable for him to discuss as it was for Katie to question. Yet the more Katie knew, the better she understood, the greater would be her compassion.

"Given the evidence, I do not believe the act was completed." Katie looked relieved. "That does not lessen the crime, nor the defilement she is likely to feel."

Katie sat heavily in the nearby chair. "What kind of horrible monster commits such atrocity?"

Doc agreed wholeheartedly with that sentiment. "Let this be her secret for as long as she needs to keep quiet."

"Doc?" He looked into her anxious eyes. "The bruises, that welt, they can't be kept secret."

"The bodily wounds will heal. When she is ready to discuss it, I am afraid the chore of listening and counseling will fall to you as a woman."

Katie mutely accepted this as she rose to assist him in treating the leg wound. Although he told Katie the wounds would heal, Doc had his doubts. Enough blood had been lost to significantly lower cardiac function. Her level of shock was too great to even consider anesthetic or anything for the pain.

Careful examination was not required to see that her leg was broken. The tibia, the larger of the two lower leg bones, could easily be manipulated side to side. Doc could realign the halves and healing would occur so long as the leg remained immobile.

The immobility posed an interesting quandary. A plaster bandage would accomplish that task, but would inhibit the healing of the external wound. Internally fixating the bone would be ideal; moreover, Doc sorely wanted to attempt the procedure. In all likelihood his patient would not live, yet when would he again have such an opportunity?

The process was time consuming. As the shoulder injury was a simple penetration wound, Katie treated that while Doc set the leg. He was almost gladdened when his work caused an increase in his patient's breath rate. Some pain reaction at least indicated she was still willing to fight for life.

Katie assisted with bandaging. "That," Doc pointed to the shoulder wound, "needs only a light bandage, which you should plan to change this evening, as there will be much drainage."

Katie kept the leg elevated to allow bandaging to be wrapped around the limb. "This will also need changing?"

"Tomorrow; it would be best to disturb this leg as little as possible."

When they finished, Doc stepped out onto the porch. He eased into the rocking chair, so exhausted he almost feared rocking himself to sleep. The thought brought a brief smile as he looked at Matt. The younger man was leaning against the house, one leg bent slightly so that his weight rested on the other. Matt seemed to be casually studying the horses in the nearby meadow.

In reality Matt hardly noticed the horses. He had been contemplating the situation. When the doctor first arrived,

Matt left the house and turned his attention to the stranger's horse. The palomino had been ridden past exhaustion. The mare was easy to handle as Ty stripped off the saddle and bridle. The bridle itself was intriguing. It was bitless, a hackamore. The bosal noseband was made of braided rope, each strand a different color. A very personal touch.

A cowhand spent his entire day, sun-up to sundown, on horseback. Despite this, these men seldom owned their horse. When a cowhand did own his mount, it was not one like this palomino mare. No cowhand could afford a horse like that. Least ways, no honest cowhand.

Then again, this horse had not been ridden by a cowhand. Well, this woman might have worked cattle, but not as a hired hand. If she had her own ranch then she should be there being tended to by the doctor. If she was a drifter of sorts, how had she afforded such a magnificent horse? And there could be no mistake that this horse and this woman belonged together.

As he waited patiently outside his own house, Matt considered that idea. This woman had spent much time with this horse. Time well spent, he chuckled, as the animal had now saved its rider's life. Even without any medical training, Matt knew she had lost a lot of blood and sustained life threatening injuries. Had they all wasted their time and efforts?

"Well Doc, what's your assessment?"

Doc took a deep breath, ran his hand across the top of his head and let the air back out of his lungs. He took another deep breath before answering. "She lost a lot of blood. By rights she should be dead already. She has an amazing will to survive."

The doctor was talking in circles, avoiding a direct answer. A direct answer was what they needed at this point. "So do we find a comfortable bed for her, or send for Reverend Polchek?"

"Paul Whitcomb!" Katie was appalled. On consideration

she realized he was right. She held her breath waiting for the doctor to speak.

"Find a bed. A very comfortable bed; she may be in it for a long while. But I can't really give you a prognosis until tomorrow. Now that the wounds have been tended to it's up to her, and God. If she lives till tomorrow I'll assess the situation better."

They went inside; still no one moved the young lady.

Matt looked intently at this stranger lying in his kitchen. Her breathing was slow and regular. A good sign, he thought. Her boots stood in the corner, beside the chair that held the slicker. Her gun belt hung there, as well. In the holster was a .44 caliber Colt Cavalry pistol. The outfit spoke of someone used to hard work. The denim trousers would stand up to hours in the saddle and were fair protection against brush. Her hair was plaited, neat and out of the way. This was a lady who could take care of herself.

Yet here she lay, so weak and vulnerable. Matt noticed again the vivid bruise on her cheek. Perhaps she had struck her face as she fell from the gunshot wound. His eyes were drawn to the outline of her legs beneath the blanket. It was not an accidental shooting. Some monster had purposefully shot her, but not with deadly intent. The wound was too far removed from any vital organs for Matt to even consider that possibility. No, it had been strictly meant to incapacitate her. Why had someone wanted to stop this woman? How had she escaped?

He was aware of Doc Roberts quietly instructing Katie. His sister was perhaps the most nurturing person he had ever known. Katie would care for this stranger as if she were a good friend. A good friend just might be what this woman was going to need. Matt gazed at her bruised face. Yes, a good friend to nurture her back to health and maybe someone to look out for her too. His eyes narrowed with growing anger. No one should be allowed to get away with assaulting a woman.

Paul cleared his throat and looked quizzically at Matt. *Where to boss?*, his expression said, though the words were not spoken. There was only one empty bed in the house.

"Mother's room."

Katie's head turned sharply. Matt hadn't stepped foot in that room since their mother died last year. And it was upstairs. One of the men would have to carry her. Paul also hesitated.

Then Matt slid his arm beneath the woman's shoulders and under her legs. He gently lifted her, blanket and all, cradling her limp body easily as he strode to the back stairs. Paul recovered his composure, dashing ahead to open the bedroom door.

Matt had been in the room recently. He deeply missed Mother. At first it pained him to see reminders of her around the house. Lately he found himself wanting to be reminded; they were warm happy memories. He realized he needed to let go of his anger. She had been a strong, vivacious woman. It was her teachings that kept Matt's faith in the Lord, though seeing her wither away until at last she died shook that faith.

Katie kept the room much as it was when Mother lived. And so the bed was made and ready, perhaps for just this moment. Matt gently lowered the lady to the bed, using great care regarding her wounds. Then the stranger moaned, shifted out of his arms, and he glimpsed the bruises on her throat. The purpling marks looked distinctly like long fingers. Matt's mind numbed at this new information. He was beginning to suspect the reason she had been shot. The vileness of the thought was almost more than he could consider.

A small bright flash broke his train of thoughts. Light reflecting off a silver pendant that slid out from beneath the nightdress. It was on a delicate silver chain. Matt lifted the pendant to see that it was a Celtic cross. Well, that might explain what strength kept her alive. If she believed what the cross stood for. He let it fall into the hollow of her neck, gently pulling the quilt over her.

When Katie arrived in the room she took over. She had Paul drag the wing-backed chair from the window to the bedside and sent Matt to fill the water pitcher for the washbasin and also fetch fresh washcloths. Ty appeared; Katie sent him back to the barn to get any personal items that might be with the woman's saddle.

"Who is she?" Paul finally spoke the question that was on everyone's mind.

"Let's see if her saddle bags hold any clues."

Katie opened the first leather bag. It was practically empty, holding only a box of cartridges, a small cooking pot, and a coffee pot with a packet of matches wrapped in oilcloth tucked inside. The necessities for living on the trail. The second bag held more items but still no identification. There was a change of clothing, a pair of moccasins, a hairbrush, and a leather bound edition of Charles Dickens' *Oliver Twist*.

"She's a complete mystery." Katie said.

Matt looked down again at the cross. Was it a clue? He pointed it out and Katie quickly moved to examine the piece of jewelry.

"It's a cross."

"Aye," Ty agreed. "A Celtic cross. This colleen's Irish."

"Anyone could have a Celtic cross, Ty." Paul pointed out.

"Nonetheless, she's got Irish blood in her. Look at that red hair. And the backbone to keep on against all odds."

"Ty you are decidedly biased!" Katie laughed. "Many peoples are tough and persevering."

Now it was Ty's turn to smile, a dazzling and charming smile. True, he was from Ireland, still loved her more than any woman he'd ever known. "Ah, but none so stubborn as the Irish people." His smile deepened before he turned serious.

"And only stubbornness would prompt someone to tie themselves to the saddle so as to keep from falling."

Katie sighed. Perhaps he was right about the stubborn- . ness. "In any case, we can't just keep calling her, her. She needs a name, even if it's not the right one."

"Her name is Cristeen." Matt's declaration earned him bewildered stares. He passed the book, cover open, to Katie. Inside was an inscription. Katie read the words aloud.

To my dear Cristeen, May you always thirst for knowledge,

Father

THREE

D inner that evening was disquieting. As was their custom, Ty and Paul supped with Matt and Katie. The meal consisted of beef stew and freshly baked bread. Kneading the bread dough had been therapeutic for Katie. It troubled her to think what probably happened to Cristeen. Although the young woman was a complete stranger, Katie already found herself caring deeply for her welfare.

Remembering all the times she had ridden alone, Katie realized that she herself had been vulnerable. She grew up in the West, and here there was little law enforcement. Even now that Colorado was a state, sheriffs and marshals were few and far between. Oh, to be sure, Glenpark had a sheriff. And a fine, upstanding citizen he was. But this was a big country with great distances between houses and even greater distances between towns.

There was an unspoken code of rules amongst the people of the West. Here a man, or woman, was judged by his deeds not by who he was or had been. The past was just that, passed. Two men might settle their differences with guns, often resulting in the death of one or both. That was acceptable, if somewhat crude.

It was not acceptable to assault a woman. Bothering a lady was a sure way to get yourself hung. That's not saying women were treated like goddesses and were never in harm's way. Oh contraire! Mostly men faced each other in a fight, albeit with guns. Often times a man needed to watch his back, lest he find a bullet in it. A woman neither faced down a man nor watched out for bullets coming from behind. A woman needed to take care from dark, lonely places, safe havens for the depraved and vicious away from watching eyes.

Katie saw every bruise and mark on Cristeen's body. The welt across her cheek, the finger marks of a chokehold, the toe imprints from kicking. She noted the swollen lip that was companion to the black eye. The shirt torn to tatters, the smudged handprints on the camisole. And she knew all those years riding alone she had been lucky. Only the grace of God kept her from being that woman upstairs.

This thought planted a seed in Katie's mind. She began to wonder how would she react. A picture of Cristeen's personality developed. Seemingly, Cristeen had fought against her attacker, somehow winning her freedom. Fear drove her, riding who knew how long until at last reaching help. Katie saw in Cristeen a woman whose strength of character was to be admired. Someone she would like to get to know, to be friends with.

The problem was, that potential friend was now fighting for her life. It would be on Katie's shoulders to nurse her, and nurture her, back to health. When the men took their places around the table the weight of that responsibility showed in Katie's eyes. Ty saw it with the concern of an uncle, Paul with the love in his heart. Only Matt was willing to speak of it.

"It is not up to you, Katherine Maria Donovan, whether or not Cristeen is to live."

"I know," she said with a sigh. "It is God's will, one way or the other. But it's my hands He's using. What if I mess up?"

Tears welled in her eyes. Matt reached across to ruffle her hair, a move that was always irritating to Katie. She ducked her head but could not avoid his hand. She retaliated with an ineffectual slap; Matt chuckled.

"Don't you think the Lord knows if you are up to this task?" She bowed her head, humbled by her doubt. Matt continued, "Pray, Katie. It's the only thing you really can do. The rest is up to Him."

Paul grasped Katie's hand, giving it a reassuring squeeze. And with that small gesture, the matter was laid to rest. Paul quietly prayed, speaking words of thanks for the meal and adding a request for the guidance they would all need to care for the stranger in their midst.

* * *

Moonlight streamed into the room, glinting off the porcelain pitcher and washbasin on the dresser. A silver river of light flowed from the window to the bed and curved upwards to cross the quilt. Matt sat up, glancing around at the shadows. What was the noise that woke him? His ears strained to hear the sound again. There...a muffled moan.

He leaned forward in the wingback chair. Cristeen's breathing was much faster. Beneath the closed lids her eyes were moving rapidly. She was dreaming. About what, Matt wondered. He stroked her temple with the back of his hand. Her breathing slowed. The rapid eye movement ceased. He continued tracing a line from her temple along her hairline down to her ear.

Her breathing became slow and steady. She was pallid from the loss of blood; the silvery light made her look paler. Matt sat back again. The minutes ticked by slowly. Then she blinked. He sat up straight. Was that his imagination?

Cristeen's eyelids fluttered, then stayed open. At first she stared up at the ceiling. Slowly she turned to look at him, her eyes searching his. The tortured pain was gone, replaced by an almost desperate questioning. She blinked again; still the questions went unasked. In the end Matt spoke, unable to keep silent under the weight of her gaze.

"You're okay now," the half-truth sounded hollow to his ears. "You are safe here." At least that was honest.

The corners of her mouth twitched, almost smiled. "Where is here?"

She whispered the question, yet in the stillness of the night Matt heard clearly. He chuckled. "That's a fair question." Now she really smiled. "This is my home, my ranch. My name is Matt Donovan."

She continued gazing at him, a question still in her eyes. At last she asked, "Do you know who I am?"

The question was completely unpretentious. She truly wanted to know if he knew her. Which led Matt to believe she was unsure of her own identity. To avoid alarming her, he steered her attention elsewhere.

"Would you like a drink?"

The distraction worked. She accepted the offer and with his help drank a glassful of water. As he eased her back down onto the pillow her eyes began to close again. Matt brushed an errant strand of hair from her face. Then her eyes opened again and locked on his. "Thank you," she whispered and fell asleep.

He sat down but continued to gaze on Cristeen. She looked peaceful. He vividly recalled the pain in her expression yesterday as he carried her into the house. Now her eyes were closed, her face smooth. Nothing about her appearance the day before suggested femininity. She had been wearing men's clothing, boots meant for work not fashion. Her gun had five rounds in the chamber; one shot had been fired. Every bit of her gear was utilitarian, except the hairbrush with its ivory handle painted with a floral pattern. And the book.

Still, she was quite feminine. Her hands were callused, her nails cut short, but that could not disguise the slender gracefulness of her fingers. Katie had loosed the braided hair and brushed the red-gold strands so that now coppery tresses framed Cristeen's face. She turned her head slightly, hiding the ugly purple bruises covering her left cheek. Matt saw in her softly rounded face a vision of gentle kindness. Her quiet voice seemed to echo in his mind.

Strong, courageous, stubborn, tenacious, all these seemed good words to describe this woman. To that list Matt now added gentle, inquisitive, and vulnerable. An indignant ire grew inside him. The monster responsible for hurting this woman must be brought to justice.

Matt leaned back in the chair. He ran a hand through his hair and sighed. Could he possibly judge her character from their brief, very brief, interactions? The first time she had barely been aware of him. When she wakes and recovers, then he could learn about her. He let his eyes close even as he smiled. When, not if.

* * *

The following morning, Doc was obviously surprised to find his patient still alive. Matt saw and smiled; *so Doc hadn't really expected her to make the night.* Something about that amused Matt. Even unconscious Cristeen was stubborn.

After examining Cristeen carefully, Doc was ready to give a prognosis. "She'll live," he declared simply, a smile warming his tone. "She will need plenty of rest and good food. She's lost a lot of blood, her body will need to regenerate that supply."

He gave Katie a list of instructions. As he turned to leave the room his eye fell on the Dickens' novel. "Hers?" He picked it up and began thumbing through the pages. "It would seem to be a favorite. Look at the sheen on these pages," he held the open book for them to see. "Comes from being handled repeatedly."

He finished turning the pages and looked at the inside

cover. Matt could see the doctor's eyes moving across the words. Doc closed the book and returned it to the nightstand, beside the Bible. He did not comment on the inscription.

"Did she awaken during the night?"

The question momentarily confused Matt. He was sure Katie would have told Doc that tidbit first thing upon arrival. Apparently he was wrong. Then he remembered he only told Katie that Cristeen had stirred some. Not to hide anything, but because it seemed so trivial in the light of day.

"Yes, she woke." Matt pondered how to ask the question that gnawed at his brain. "She seemed disoriented."

"How so?"

"Well, of course she had no idea where she was."

"Naturally. What else?"

"She seemed to not know who she was."

"Ah, amnesia." Doc nodded. "Not uncommon in cases of acute trauma, be it physical or emotional. Typically it is retrograde, and although the duration varies the mind almost always recovers."

"I studied law, Doc. Can you say that again in plain English?"

Doc's laugh put Matt at ease. "What I said is just this; amnesia, loss of memory, sometimes happens when a person goes through an event too shocking for the mind to deal with all at once. Usually it is retrograde, meaning she has only forgotten what occurred before. She will be able to remem- ' ber going forward."

Matt nodded his understanding. Doc continued, "As time passes the shock begins to fade and memory returns. Sometimes all at once, sometimes bits and pieces at a time."

"Do the memories all return?"

"Eventually. They aren't actually lost. It's more like when you misplace something in the house. Sooner or later you find it, because it was never really missing. You just didn't remember where you had left it."

Katie had been quietly absorbing the conversation. Now she voiced a concern. "Sometimes what I think is just misplaced really is lost." Doc smiled, encouraging her to continue the thought. "What if her memories never come back?"

"It's a valid concern." Doc thought for a few moments. He looked intently at Cristeen and then glanced again at the book on the nightstand. "Hysterical amnesia, that's what it is called. Whatever traumatic or shocking event occurred the patient's mind can never fully accept it. So she forgets the objectionable memories."

"Events and people in our lives are woven together, much like a cloth or blanket. It is difficult to single out one event or one individual to be erased from one's memory. Other memories must suffer for it, as well."

Seeing Katie's puzzlement, Matt jumped in. "I see what you mean, Doc. Say I wanted to forget that Mother died last year. I would naturally avoid things that reminded me of her."

Katie stared at her brother, listening closely to his explanation.

"But just avoiding reminders would not be enough. Next I would have to forget Katie, who looks like Mother." He smiled. "Then I would block out this ranch, because all of my life to this point she was always here. And so on."

"Exactly. Cristeen might wish to erase from her memory the events leading to her injuries. But then she would need to forget anyone she interacted with on that day, perhaps family members. It's like a domino effect."

An uncomfortable silence fell on them. Doc broke it, giving himself a shake as he did. "I do not believe that will happen in this case."

"Why?"

"Well, Matt, remember when I said it is called hysterical amnesia?" Matt nodded. "Would a woman prone to hysteria ride a great distance, probably all night, in search of assistance? Would she have the presence of mind to tie herself to the saddle?"

"I reckon not."

"For another thing, hysteria and therefore hysterical amnesia are more common amongst the poor and uneducated."

Katie was again bewildered. "What's that got to do with anything?"

Matt tapped the novel. "She's read Dickens, often. Also, it would seem by the inscription that she has a passion for learning. For education."

Later Matt thought about that conversation, contemplating again the bruises on Cristeen's face and neck. Perhaps she had good reason to repress her memories. She might not want to remember, at least not everything. Recovery for Cristeen would be more than merely regenerating blood cells and mending of flesh. That she might be able to do on her own. Emotional healing would take a great deal of compassion. She would need support, a friend to talk to, to hold on to. Someone to watch over her.

That last thought startled Matt. He had never felt so protective of anyone, not even his sister. Was it just that she seemed so vulnerable due to her wounds? Yes, must be. She was, after all, just another person. When she had recovered Matt would feel towards Cristeen the same level of compassion he felt for anyone. Well, maybe slightly more. About the same level as his sister.

Before turning in that night, Matt looked in on Cristeen. She looked comfortable, half turned to her left with her hands tucked under her head and pillow. The chill night air was invading the room; Matt stoked the logs in the fireplace. He gave one last glance at Cristeen. Maybe it was just the firelight that made her seem less pale.

FOUR

Fever is part of the body's natural defense system. In ancient times, fever was welcomed, as people believed it would burn out the bad spirits that caused illness. As absurd as that sounds, it is essentially true. The increase in body temperature does in fact kill invading germs. Moreover, the heat produces reactions within the immune system that help to fight infection.

Katie knew nothing of the actual mechanisms involved in a fever. What she did know was that a fever was not a symptom to be feared. Managed, yes, even controlled when necessary.

Matt noticed the first sign of Cristeen's fever. He commented one morning to Katie, "She's not so pale anymore."

Chills set in later that day. Whenever Cristeen was alert enough to drink, Katie had hot tea at the ready. Mostly, though, Cristeen continued to sleep. She would shiver uncontrollably until Katie placed yet another blanket over her.

Late in the afternoon the opposite effect occurred. Returning from a trip downstairs, Katie found Cristeen completely uncovered. She gently pulled the blankets back over the young woman, careful of her injuries. Then she turned to locate the wingback chair and sat. Cristeen was uncovered again.

Three times Katie repeated the ritual. Exasperated, the fourth time she just pulled the sheet over Cristeen. Perhaps

Cristeen was also tired of throwing off the blankets, for this time she let the sheet remain. Katie sank into the chair, exhausted. *This is what it's like to be a mother!* The thought brought a smile to her lips.

Matt wanted to sit with Cristeen that night, allowing for Katie to get some much needed rest. He was vetoed.

"It would be inappropriate."

Katie's response puzzled Matt. He had sat with Cristeen for a few hours each night, not wanting her to awaken alone in a strange place. Why was it suddenly inappropriate? He asked as much. In answer, Katie led him down the hall and into the bedroom where Cristeen slept. The sheet, which until now had at least been tolerated, lay in a twisted heap at Cristeen's feet. Katie quickly pulled it up again.

"Watch." As Katie stepped back, Cristeen began to thrash. Not violently, just enough to remove the offensive covering sheet. "Her fever is spiking. She won't keep covered."

Matt understood now. The nightdress was damp with the perspiration of the rising fever. It would be improper for him to see her that way. Especially since she had no control over her own actions.

"When this is over," Matt waved a hand to indicate Cristeen's fever, "I want you to take a day for yourself."

Katie laughed. "How? There's still a house to care for, and you three to feed."

"We can survive. Do us some good to bach it."

"Bach? Oh, play bachelor." Katie laughed. "Well, Ty might remember how, and Paul would eventually adjust. But you..."

"What about me?"

"You have never bached it in your life. You would be lost."

"Do you think I had servants at college?"

Katie cocked her head to one side, momentarily checked by that statement. Then she saw an opening. "Yes, in a manner of speaking. You lived in a rooming house. Your meals were always prepared for you. You never even had to make your own bed."

Her smug expression amused Matt. "I did make my own bed. And I still do." After a moment he continued, "And who do you think does all the cooking when we trail the herd?"

The smugness turned to a victorious laughter. "Ty!"

She was right. Although Matt and Paul each took a hand at evening meals, Ty was by far the best cook of the three men. That wasn't saying much. All of them had been spoiled by Katie's skills in the kitchen. The thought put a damper on Matt's humor.

"I'll need the practice, anyway."

It was Katie's turn to be puzzled. "For what?"

"For living alone. After Paul sweeps you off your feet, and out of my house." He tried to inject amusement into his tone.

"Nothing will change. You and Ty will still eat with Paul and I, we'll just do it at *my* house."

"You're right, Shortcake." Matt ruffled her hair. Katie was so in love that she could not see that Matt's life would change drastically when she got married. He would not stand in the way of her happiness. Particularly over something as trivial as housekeeping.

Katie suffered the ruffling, and the childhood nickname. But her brother's words got her thinking. She sent him off to get some firewood. When he returned she picked up the conversation, steering it along her new train of thoughts.

"Matt, you aren't getting any younger."

"Why thank you for noticing," he drawled slowly, wondering where exactly his sister was going with this conversation.

"You don't want to be alone all your life, do you?"

Matt laughed. "So that's what this is about. I'm happy just the way I am, dear sister of mine."

"But," she was indignant, "don't you ever want to marry? To share your home and your life with someone?"

Matt clenched his teeth. *She's just happily in love,* he told himself. *Don't spoil it for her.* Still, when he spoke his tone was terse, "Leave my life to me."

He strode out of the room, unwilling to continue the conversation. Katie trotted behind him, as unwilling to let it end. It was not an unfamiliar topic, although it had been quite some time since she last brought it up. You couldn't really even say they argued over it; Matt walked away whenever Katie questioned his stance on marriage. He was stalwart in his reticence. Katie was mildly irritated at her inability to pry loose her brother's reasons for remaining single.

This was not the right time to press the issue. Matt was walking stiffly towards his study, retreating rapidly. Katie quickened her pace, calling out to stop him.

"I'm your sister, it's my duty to worry about you."

Her words stopped him. With a deep sigh, he turned to face her. For just a moment Katie saw something in her brother's eyes she had never noticed before. Sorrow, a melancholy expression that vanished before she could be sure it had ever truly been there. It was replaced with a quirky smile.

"Just remember, you are my *little* sister."

Glad to have his good humor returned, Katie countered, "Yes, you are much *older* than I."

"Older and wiser. Don't you forget that." Matt, too, was grateful to be on happier footing.

For Katie the night dragged by slowly, yet in the same token time passed without her realizing. Cristeen's fever worsened as the evening wore on, until she was soon drenched with perspiration. Katie bathed her face and arms with a cool cloth. A number of times Cristeen seemed to be having delirious nightmares, crying out unintelligibly and sometimes lashing out.

For the most part, though, Cristeen's delirium was constrained. She did wake frequently, and on those occasions Katie was ready with water for her to drink. Sometime after midnight the fever seemed to reach its peak. Katie was alarmed at the heat emanating from the young woman. She seemed ready to burn up, literally.

And then suddenly, it passed. For as long as it had taken her internal furnace to heat up, Cristeen seemed to cool twice as rapidly. Before sunrise, Katie draped a second quilt over the now soundly sleeping figure, added a fresh log to the fire, and shuffled off to her own bed. When Matt rose, he found his sister as deeply unconscious as her patient.

Paul and Ty wandered into the kitchen as Matt was preparing a pot of coffee. Without a word or question, Ty began whipping up a batch of biscuits. It often seemed to Matt that Ty could read his mind, although the reality was that Ty recognized any change in routine. The old man had lived with the Donovans since Matt was a small boy. He was kin by heart, as he was wont to say. If Katie wasn't making the coffee, neither would she be fixing breakfast.

"Where's Katie?" Paul had yet to develop the silent kinship Ty possessed. That and he was genuinely concerned about the woman he loved.

"Sleeping," Matt jumped as he burned a finger on the stove. "Us men folk gonna have to fend for ourselves today."

Paul laughed. Not at Matt's words nor his injury, but at how foolish they sounded spoken around the finger he jammed into his mouth. "Better dunk that in the wash basin to cool."

With more lightheartedness than effort, the three men put together a modest meal. Voices were hushed, as none wanted to risk waking Katie. There was an unspoken agreement that she needed the rest. A quiet conversation did flow amongst them.

"An' how is our colleen this fine morning?"

"She has a name ya' know, Ty."

"Let him call her whatever he wants, Paul." Matt smiled at his friend. "To answer your question, she seems to be doing better."

"Fever broke? Good. All the bad'll be gone now, an' she can start mendin'."

"Spoken like the true medicine man you are."

"Aye, I'll tell ye a thing or two aboot medicine..."

"Now you've done it. Won't be no stopping him now."

Ty did stop, feigning indignation. Actually, he knew very little about medicine. It was just fun to see Paul roll his eyes and hear Matt groan at the thought of another of his stories.

"Seriously, though," Paul steered the subject away from Ty. "Where do you suppose she came from?"

Matt shrugged. "Doesn't matter."

Paul raised an eyebrow. "No, then why'd you backtrack her."

"You know as well as I do that her trail petered out at the creek. Might have been nice to figure out where she belongs. Maybe someone is worried about her being missing."

Paul stared into his coffee. He sure would be worried if it was Katie missing.

"If you ask me," Ty watched out the window as he spoke. "She was decked out to be on the trail. Nice set up, too, although mighty meager."

"What do you mean?" Matt asked.

"Well, she got the right outfit. An' a good groundsheet, bedroll, cookin' stuff. Even gun and cartridges. But no food. Not even coffee." He grimaced. "That gun, only been fired once. Box of cartridges is full, like someone gave them to her with the gun already loaded."

After a brief pause, he continued. "Not much of a huntin' gun, anyhow. Needs her a rifle."

"What are you getting at?"

"Just this, if she's from here abouts, why is she on the

trail? If she's from far off, how's she been eatin'? I think she was with someone. Question is, where's that someone now and did he do that to her?"

It was an angle Matt had not considered. The ramifications, had she been traveling with the man that beat her? He thought on it, as disturbing as it was. Something just didn't seem right with the logic.

"I'll agree she was traveling, and from far off. If her companion did this to her, why now?"

Ty shook his head. "Who can say what makes a man snap?"

Paul had been staring into his coffee all the while. Now he looked up and suggested a more disquieting alternative. "Maybe she was traveling with another person, and they was attacked. What if she's the only one that got away?"

He had been so concerned about Cristeen surviving her physical injuries; Matt had given little thought to all the possibilities of what might have happened. He had briefly considered the probability that she had been sexually assaulted. And had given only slight thought to what it would take to help her recover from that type of emotional trauma.

What if Cristeen had been traveling with a companion, they had been attacked, and only Cristeen survived? When she realized that would she be able to accept the loss? The guilt of being the one to survive could be very hard to live with.

The silence deepened. Ty crossed the room to refill his coffee cup. He glanced at Paul and received an almost imperceptible nod of encouragement. Matt noted the gesture; obviously this was a subject the two men had discussed at length.

"There's something else we oughtta consider." Ty stopped, then interpreted Matt's quizzical expression as a signal to continue. "It's still all about her outfit. Dressed as she was, makes a body wonder. Wouldn't be the first woman runnin' on the wrong side 'o the law."

"Now you take that into consideration along with her gun. That forty-four mightn't be much for huntin' game, but sure be handy in a fight. An' it's bin fired."

Paul spoke up now. "Then there's that horse."

"What about her horse?" Matt was puzzled. "She's a beautiful animal."

"Exactly," the furrows deepened across Matt's brow. Ty explained. "That horse would cost a small fortune. If she's got the money for such a fine mount, what she doing dressed like a man and riding out here in the mountains?"

"What Ty's getting at, in his round about way," Paul couldn't resist the dig, "is that an honest person forced to travel on horseback would be riding, well, something more run 'o the mill than that palomino mare."

"Are you suggesting she stole the horse?"

"Nothin' like that, boy. But say she got in with the wrong crowd. Could be a posse shot her up. Maybe she got money from a saloon, and the boss don't like her leavin'." Ty sighed in exasperation. "I cain't figure it. Got a gut feeling she's all right, an' I trust my gut more 'n my brains."

Paul stood. "We just think you should be careful, that's all. No tellin' what she's really like, or what might come down the trail after her."

Matt walked with them to the door. "You're right, of course. But a body is innocent until proven otherwise. I'll give her the chance to show her true colors. And," he laid a reassuring hand on Paul's shoulder, "I will keep an eye out for anything else comin' down the trail."

He stood on the porch, watching the two cross the yard. A hollow *clop-clop* brought his head around sharply, but it was just Henry riding his mule across the bridge and into the yard. The boy waved to Matt then continued on to the barns. Matt glanced at the mountains looming above the park before going back inside.

The conversation had an unsettling effect on him. Try as he might, he could not discount the suggestion that Cristeen might have a shady history just waiting to step in and disrupt their quiet lives. Ty had a gut feeling, and Matt trusted Ty's gut even more than the old man did.

After cleaning up the kitchen, Matt climbed the stairs and checked on Katie. She was still sleeping soundly. He left her room, still thinking about the conversation of earlier. He walked without thinking, and was standing beside Cristeen before realizing where he had been headed.

She looked so peaceful and innocent. Not the criminal type. But then, what did the criminal type look like? The stories of famous outlaws spoke of men who were average in appearance, and some were even considered to be good looking. What of Ty's saloon-girl insinuation? Some of those women were quite pretty. And it wasn't unusual to see those girls at church.

Wholesome, that was the word that best described Cristeen's appearance. *Hole-some,* he chuckled to himself. With a deep sigh he left the room. He was going to have to resolve himself to let the issue go until she awoke. He would drive himself crazy contemplating all the possibilities, and still he would not know.

The sun was nearing its noontime high when Matt finished plowing the garden. Ordinarily it was a task he might have delegated to Henry. Today he wanted to feel the pull of muscles not accustomed to walking behind a plow. A little self-torture to keep his mind on work. Riding allowed for too much thinking.

Katie was sitting in the parlor reading, her legs curled up on the sofa. A steaming cup of tea rested on the table beside her. She smiled at Matt as he sat in the chair across from her.

"I'm glad to see you are taking me at my word."

"I realized I haven't let myself just relax in sometime."

"What would you like for lunch?" She looked surprised.

"I really meant what I said about you taking a day off. So, what will it be?"

Luckily there was bread and some cold meat. Matt fixed a sandwich and brought it in on a tray. Katie giggled at the service. Matt, too, had a sandwich that he washed down with a glass of milk. Katie teased him about the thin white mustache left by the milk.

"Maybe I should grow a real mustache, and maybe a beard." He stroked his chin and gazed at a corner of the ceiling as if trying to imagine himself.

"Not again! Every spring, you go off with the herd and come back looking like a scruffy black bear." Katie laughed.

"And every year you convince me to shave it all off. If I am to be a bachelor here in my own house, perhaps I won't shave it this year."

Katie was momentarily fearful of reviving the unpleasant conversation of the day before. Seeing the light dancing in Matt's eyes told her not to worry. He was all playfulness today.

"Come to think of it," Matt continued. "Paul was just saying how he envies my beard. I think we men should all swear off of shavin' while out on the trail."

"Oh, no, he better not." She stammered. Matt laughed.

The day passed quietly. Cristeen slept until late in the afternoon, at which time she woke only long enough drink a cup of broth. Matt was grateful Katie had prepared the broth the day before, so he had only to keep it simmering warm. Despite his proclamation of being able to care for himself, he was not as certain of his ability to care for an invalid. Katie declared he was successful, but vowed to return to her routine tomorrow.

FIVE

The trail stretched on ahead of him, but Mike Reardon had spotted something. A bright flash just off to his left, the glint of sunlight on metal. An old familiar wariness flared up inside him; this was once Indian country. For a brief moment he tasted fear - the fear that someone waited to ambush him.

Late morning sun chased away those demons. Mike chuckled at his own foolishness. Sure, there were plenty of bad men around, but this part of Colorado had seen its last Indian raiding party years ago. Still, he had been carelessly skylining himself, topping out on ridges without care. And for the past few miles he'd been so deep in thought he hadn't even noticed the landscape.

The shiny metal object turned out to be a canteen. Mike dismounted, curious about such a necessity abandoned a few feet off the trail. Had a passing rider dropped it, it could not have rolled here, for the ground sloped upwards from the worn path. Whoever lost the canteen must have been up in the aspens.

There was a bit of hound dog in Mike Reardon. It was what made him a good sheriff. He could sniff out a wrongdoing, then track down the culprit, with the same ease other men roped cattle. Right now the hound dog was telling Mike there had been trouble here.

He rode half-circle sweeps, working away from the trail.

It didn't take long to confirm his suspicions. He spotted the body, actually spying just a boot at first. He stopped his horse on the edge of a small clearing, using care to disturb no evidence.

The aspens along the trail gave way to a grove of spruce trees. The conifers had formed a natural circular clearing, a good place to camp. Near the center a small circle of stones showed the remains of numerous campfires. The body lay off to the side near the trees, although Mike could see wild animals had probably dragged it there.

The cadaver was a horrendous sight. An arm was mostly missing and there were signs it had been chewed away. A blackened hole bored through the forehead, between the eyes even with the brow line. Mike didn't need to look to know most of the back of the man's skull was gone. He could tell by the amount of darkened blood staining the ground. Plus he knew what a slug fired at close range would do to a man's cranium.

Despite the damage by gunshot and nature, Mike recognized the dead man. Hank Crespin, a notorious local outlaw. Crespin had wanted posters in several towns along the Front Range. Mike had been hoping to catch the man himself. Looked like he got his wish.

Cautiously, Mike moved about the clearing, noting the bits of evidence he found. There were signs of at least one struggle. The rusty pine needles lay thick on the ground, especially along the outer edges of the clearing. He found a scuffed area that gave him the impression of two people wrestling, their feet kicking up little piles of needles. Across from that area, he found more displaced pine needles. It appeared that something had dragged across the ground; a trail of blood lay in the trough of needles. The drag marks began near the fire ring; here was more blood. A lot of blood, yet seemingly not from Crespin. Mike crouched on his heels to get a closer look at the ground.

About ten feet away he could clearly make out the place where Crespin had fallen when shot. There, too, blood pooled on the ground. From that spot to where the body now lay there was a line of the blackened vital fluid showing that the body had been dragged shortly after death.

So, two persons had been wounded. Mike followed the drag marks that stretched to a nearby tree. Peering closely at the bark, he could make out some scrapes as if someone had clawed their way up from the ground. Higher up he saw an old scar where a bear had marked his territory. There was another pool of blood at the base of the tree; the wounded party had stood here for a space of time. In his mind's eye, Mike began to form a picture. Yes, having struggled to get upright he would have to catch his breath.

He crouched again, carefully examining the forest floor. Back at the start of the drag trail he found a button. Between there and the trees he found a shell casing. Circling the open ground, he made out several different footprints. Along the tree line he found where two horses had been tethered; opposite to that two more horses had approached from the uphill side. Hoof prints showed that three of the horses had taken out of there mighty fast. One horse had meandered away.

Moving back to Crespin's body, Mike Reardon frowned. This man's death should be cause for joy. Instead it raised questions and concerns. Hank Crespin was dead - where was his partner, Evan Marks. The two always operated together. Surely it was Crespin's horse that had simply wandered away. Marks must have been riding one of the horses that rushed away.

Irritating, to think he would have to investigate the murder of this man who so deserved to be dead. It worried him that someone capable of killing Hank Crespin could be on the loose in this area. Crespin was considered to be quick on the draw. How fast would his killer need to be?

He had a murder investigation on his hands. Ordinarily

this was the type of man he would be glad to bury and forget. It wasn't so easy this time; it never was really. He could not rest knowing a killer moved amongst the people he was sworn to protect. Someone capable of killing as dangerous a man as Hank Crespin.

He did bury the body, however, in a shallow grave removed some distance from the clearing. To discourage animals from digging up the remains, he piled stones on top of the gravesite. Then Mike began the tedious task of following leads, starting with trailing the three horses that had galloped away.

* * *

There was no end to the work to be done at the ranch. Some of the tasks were quite tedious, like oiling the door hinge. To procrastinate would only make matters worse. Matt knew from experience it was better to do it and get it over. No matter what it was. He was thankful, though, to have Henry performing some of the more repetitively menial chores like cleaning the barn.

It was mid April and spring was here to stay. Well, at least until the hot summer sun chased her away. Wildflowers were popping their colorful heads up all over the mountain slopes. The bright yellow-green of unfurling aspen leaves accentuated the deep reds of maple blooms. There was a sweetness in the air, the scents of hundreds of flowers and trees, grasses and soils, all mingling together.

Calves seemed to be arriving daily. So far all the first calf heifers were doing well. Ty had gone out to check on the herd at the north end of the park. The small valley narrowed at that end, the slopes both west and east quite steep. Only a slight amount of fencing was needed to hold in the cattle. Calving and newborns would attract predators though, and a human presence was a good way to discourage attacks.

Ty brought along a tally book. In it he would record how many head of cattle had survived the winter. The number of calves born, calving dates, the general condition of each animal, all would also be noted in the book. Range conditions and fence repairs to be done would be recorded. Later Ty would go back with the supplies he had determined necessary to perform such repairs.

Mostly the repairs would consist of tightening or restringing the barbed wire. In some places, natural fencing was employed, felled trees woven amongst the trunks of the slender aspens that dotted the hillsides. As the wood decayed it became necessary to add new logs.

Matt also kept a tally book, recording the same information about the cattle and the horses on the home pastures. He noted fencing repairs, but being as supplies were close at hand he was able to make the repairs right away. He spent a day clearing and re-digging irrigation ditches. The barns each required some minor attention, and a portion of the porch railing needed to be replaced.

Paul continued working on his house. Katie had been right when she said work was nearly complete. Soon the only things left to do would be wallpapering and moving in the furniture. Understandably, Paul was glad his new home was nearing completion. Katie had been reluctant to set a date for their wedding until now, not wanting to put pressure on Paul. Plus he was looking forward to riding out with Ty.

Ten days had passed since Cristeen first arrived at the Donovan ranch. In the days following her fever she had continued to sleep more hours than she was awake. Katie found she was able to keep up with her daily tasks and still find time to care for her patient. When Cristeen was awake she spoke very little. Alert was not the word Katie would have chosen to describe those moments of consciousness. Yet the woman was aware of what was going on around her. She thanked Katie so frequently that Katie finally insisted she stop, a request that brought a fleeting smile as response.

This morning Matt stepped in to check on Cristeen before heading out to start the day. The windows in the bedroom faced east; the early morning sun streaked across the room, bringing with it living color. Cristeen lay snuggled under the quilt, a contented expression on her face. Matt's gaze lingered there, noting the healthy pink flush in her skin tone. Now that her body had begun healing the ashen coloring had been replaced by a light tan.

He thought again of the conversation with Ty and Paul. Was it possible that this quiet, polite young woman could be a fugitive from the law? Matt found the idea absurd, yet she was still a mystery. Even if she had broken no laws it would be foolish not to watch her back trail. Whatever had happened to her could one day come riding down that trail.

The fire was low and although the morning sun would quickly warm the room Matt decided to add some wood. He stoked the embers, momentarily mesmerized by a shower of sparks. The log he chose was small, it would burn just long enough. He watched as tiny flames licked at the paper-thin bark, searching for a place to take hold.

"Staring into the flames will blind you."

Cristeen's soft voice startled Matt. He stood and turned to face her in the same motion. She was half sitting, propping herself up on an elbow. Seeing his surprise she quickly added, "Sorry, I didn't mean to startle you."

Matt regained his composure. "Quite all right." He flashed a smile at her. "But in response to what you said, no it won't blind me. It's only at night that staring at the flames makes it hard to see into the darkness."

"Oh," she nodded slightly. "I knew there was something about it."

He crossed the room and after propping some pillows behind her, dropped into the wingback chair. He leaned forward, resting his elbows on his knees. She lay back against the pillows, catching her breath after struggling to sit up. Her eyes were closed; for the first time Matt noticed fine lines radiating out from the corners of her eyes. She squinted a lot while out in the sun.

"Where is," Cristeen hesitated, her brow creasing. "I don't know her name." She opened her eyes, looking at him with a mixture of concern and curiosity.

"I'm not surprised. You've been asleep more often than not."

"I know your name," she grinned, "Matt Donovan."

It pleased him that she had remembered. He pushed that aside, focusing instead on alleviating her curiosity. "Well, then, her name is Katie, Katie Donovan. She lives here too."

An emotion crossed her face like a swiftly moving cloud. Matt couldn't be sure what it was; anxiety, frustration, or disappointment. Before he could ponder that more deeply, she sprung more questions on him.

"Are there others? Sometimes I hear voices but I'm not sure if they're real or just in my head." Concern wrinkled her brow.

"They are real," Matt quickly reassured her. "Paul and Ty."

"Your brothers?"

"No, well not yet. Soon Paul will be my brother-in-law."

"You have a sister, then?"

So that explained the little dark cloud expression. She had jumped to the wrong conclusion upon hearing Katie's full name. He chuckled, "Katie is my sister, not my wife."

Cristeen blushed, turning her head to hide her embarrassment. Immediately he regretted the chuckle. The remorse deepened as her silence continued. Nothing he could think of seemed right to lighten the mood. At last she spoke. She did not look at him and her voice was hushed. Yet the question implied if not trust at least respect.

"She, I mean Katie, calls me Cristeen. Is that my name?"

Caught off guard, Matt answered without thinking. "You still don't remember?"

Mutely she shook her head. When she looked at him the pain in her eyes was almost as sharp as that first time he had looked into them. She was fighting hard against the tears. He could only imagine what it would be like to remember none of his entire life, not even his own name. It was unfathomable.

"Doc says memory loss is very common after a traumatic event." He placed a hand on hers in a gesture of reassurance. She tensed, pulling her arm back slightly. It was a quick, instinctive reaction that dissipated at once.

"Have I had a traumatic event?"

Her soft voice was so sincere that Matt forced himself not to laugh. It wasn't easy; Cristeen saw the way his eyes crinkled and recognized the amusement. She glanced at her legs, hidden beneath the blanket, and giggled. It was a girlish, self-mocking kind of laugh.

"I guess that was a silly question." She rubbed her forehead.

"Headache?" She nodded. "I should let you rest then."

Her quick "No, no, I'll be fine. I am enjoying the company," spoke volumes about her. She didn't want to be alone. She was courteous even in the face of discomfort. She gracefully hid her stoicism. Matt cocked his head to one side, contemplating making her rest. Then her stomach rumbled.

"You're hungry!" Why hadn't he thought of that sooner? Of course she was hungry. She hadn't eaten more than broth and small amounts of bread in over a week. With hasty apologies, and a promise to be right back, he dashed downstairs on a quest for food.

Katie was delighted when she learned Cristeen was awake and hungry. She fixed a small meal that Matt carried back upstairs. Everyone accompanied him; much to Cristeen's discomfort. Seeing her unease at the attention, Matt sent them away. As she left the room, Katie raised an inquisitive eyebrow at him. He pretended not to notice.

"Thank you," Cristeen smiled tenuously.

"No one likes to be gawked at, 'specially when they're eating."

She ate slowly. "Tell me about this place," a sweep of her hand indicated the ranch in general. Matt gave her a quick run down.

"The house is situated at the southern end of a small park."

She frowned her puzzlement. "It's a term used to describe valleys up here in the mountains."

"So this ranch is in the mountains?"

He smiled and nodded. "We're up high, but still in the foothills, you might say. Higher up there's more parks; we pasture the cattle up there in the summer."

Matt described the lay of the land, told her about the flowers just now blooming, he even mentioned how swollen the creek was with melting snow. Cristeen seemed enraptured by it all. He wondered if she really enjoyed what he had to say or if she was just happy to be conversing. Occasionally she would ask a question that seemed to indicate a knowledge of cattle ranching. He filed that idea away for later consideration.

When she had finished eating he picked up the tray, planning to take it downstairs. She stopped him.

"Please don't go yet." It was almost a plea.

"You really do need to get more rest." But he sat back down, setting the tray on the nightstand.

Cristeen studied her hands. She seemed to be working up the courage to ask something. Matt waited patiently, not knowing her well enough to push.

"How long have I been here?"

"Ten days." Where was this going?

"And you've been taking care of me all that time? I mean you, Katie, all of you."

"Yes." His curiosity grew. She was becoming pensive, and even more quiet.

At last she got around to her point. "Why? I mean, you don't know me, right. So why are you doing all this?"

The question pushed him back in the chair. She might just as well have asked why the sun came up each day, or what made the flowers bloom in the spring and the leaves fall in the autumn. He took a deep breath and pushed a hand through his hair. What answer could he give?

As if concerned she had said something wrong, Cristeen began twirling the pendant on her necklace in nervous tension. A pattern of light danced on the wall where it was reflected from the cross. Matt said a silent prayer for the right words.

"I haven't done anything for you," he began. She started to say something but he continued. "Neither has Katie."

Her mouth snapped shut. Her eyes searched his face, looking for some sign that he was joking. What she found was a serious and interested expression. "But I thought, that is Katie, I mean," she stammered, unable to collect her thoughts. She sighed and looked down dejectedly. "I don't know what to think."

Matt smiled as he reached to still her hands. She stared at his hands clamped gently around hers. He noted that this time she did not tense or try to pull away.

"I did not mean to confuse you, Cristeen. What I meant was that it is not I, nor Katie, to whom you should be grateful. We did not bring you here. Neither did we provide you with a warm coat, a trustworthy mount, nor your iron will."

When she did not respond, he continued. "It is to the Lord you should be giving your thanks."

Cristeen looked at him then. Her eyes were a maelstrom of emotion, yet she smiled tremulously. "I suppose you are right."

Matt stayed a few minutes more, though he let go the

subject of God. It was apparent that she did not believe, or at least her faith was not strong. The Celtic cross then was not a symbol of her own belief. Perhaps it was merely a family heirloom. Another time he would try to delve into that subject. Later, when her memory was recovered.

Cristeen stubbornly fought against the sleepiness that came too soon. She really was enjoying the conversation, and the company. Though the subject of God had stirred something she had a feeling would be better left alone. Matt smoothly changed the subject, lounging back against the chair as he did. She appreciated his tact.

The subject of cattle and ranching had a familiar and comfortable feel to Cristeen. She could not grasp any real memory, yet Matt's words conjured pictures in her mind. She could almost see the cattle grazing, watch the calves cavorting in the frosty morning air, and even it seemed she could smell the musty sweetness of aged manure. That last sensation was finally explained when Matt stretched his long legs and Cristeen caught a glimpse of his boots. Of course, all the scents were ground into the leather, and the leather itself still held the aroma of cowhide.

She considered telling all this to Matt. If only she could keep her eyes open. He was easy to talk with and she really did not want the visit to end. She blinked quickly, trying to stay awake. To her consternation the action caused Matt to laugh.

"You really are stubborn!" He stood to move the pillows aside. "Don't be embarrassed, it's a compliment."

"Why am I stubborn?" She eased herself down onto the pillow. She thought she said the words in firm indignation.

Matt leaned close to hear, as she was actually whispering. He chuckled again and brushed an errant hair away from her face. "Go to sleep Cristeen," was his only answer.

* * *

"So, what did you two talk about?"

"Your cooking."

"I'm serious Matt."

They were standing on the porch, where Matt had found Katie when he returned downstairs. She was staring down the valley as if still seeing Paul's horse as he headed north with Ty.

"Did you enjoy breakfast with Paul?"

Katie glared at him. "Don't change the subject."

"I'm not." He smiled smugly. "I'm answering the question you want to ask; why did I send you away."

"And how do you know what I want to ask?"

"Indulge me," his smile deepened. "Did you enjoy Paul's company this morning?"

"Yes, of course."

"And knowing he'll be gone for a few days, you were looking forward to seeing him off?"

She sighed, starting to understand her brother's train of thought. "Yes," she studied him, gauging his sincerity. "I don't believe you. There's more to it than that."

In a conspiratal whisper Matt admitted, "I'm going to say this once, and never again. You make better coffee than I."

Katie laughed along with him. When she caught her breath she became serious again. "Okay, I'll buy that excuse for you kicking me out. But I really do want to know what you talked about."

"The ranch." Seeing her skepticism he added, "she still doesn't remember."

Katie was disheartened. She had hoped Cristeen would be able to answer their questions, resolve the mystery. Beyond that, she couldn't help but imagine what it must feel like to be in an unfamiliar place, surrounded by people she did not know, a stranger even to herself. Tears stung her eyes.

"C'm'ere," Matt engulfed her in a bear hug, tenderly rubbing her back. "It is not you up there. You are safe, and there is absolutely no way I would ever endanger you by letting you travel alone. And you wouldn't get beyond the gate without Paul."

That earned him a giggle. He stepped back, cupping her upturned face in his hands. "You talk with her."

"About what?"

"Anything, everything. Tell her about your house."

"The house? Why?"

"Just to get started."

"What good could I possibly do?"

"Are you kidding? I've never met anyone with your talent for getting people to tell you their deepest secrets."

She swatted at him. Matt had wisely stepped away from her before making the statement. Even so Katie connected, slugging his upper arm just hard enough to be felt without hurting.

"You are incorrigible!" Nevertheless she stood on tiptoes and kissed his cheek. "Thank you."

"Ever at your service, m'lady." He bowed low before jumping off the porch to head for work.

SIX

"In the morning, the sunrise bounces across the water like a skipping stone. But in the evening," there was a dreamy look on Katie's face. "The lake seems to absorb all the colors of the sunset, so that they melt and puddle together."

"It sounds so beautiful. And you built your house right next to the lake?" Cristeen inquired.

"Paul did, yes." She finished stitching the seam she was working on, tied a knot and cut the thread. "There, that should make it fit. Let's get you up and try this on."

It was Monday afternoon. Katie had followed Matt's suggestion to talk with Cristeen. The young woman was still amnesic, however that didn't seem to matter anymore. To Katie nor to Cristeen. To each of their delight a friendship was developing between them.

With a bit of effort Cristeen stood up, using the bedpost for support. Katie had altered one of her dresses; the two women were close in size, though Cristeen was a bit slimmer. A well-placed tuck here, some gathering there, and the dress fit as if made for Cristeen. She smiled shyly at Katie.

"Thank you."

"You're welcome, but I confess to purely selfish reasons for giving you this dress."

"Really?" Cristeen scowled. "What could I possibly offer you?"

"Company."

"I'm not going anywhere," they both laughed. "You certainly didn't need to give me a dress for that."

"You should sit back down." Katie eased her onto the bed. "I'm going somewhere. I need to work outside tomorrow morning and I thought you might like to sit outside for awhile"

"And keep you company." Cristeen smiled broadly. "I would like that. Will I be able to see the mountains? And the lake?"

"Whoa, slow down! And Matt says I get carried away."

"I'm sorry. Two weeks is a long time to be cooped up inside." Then hastily she added, "Not that I don't appreciate all you have done for me."

"You're bored." Katie's smile said she understood. "The best thing about springtime is finally being able to go outside and not freeze. I think you are very much the outdoor type."

Cristeen grew pensive. "I don't remember." It was the first time the subject of her memory had come up in over three days.

Katie sat beside her new friend, draping an arm around her shoulders. "You will remember."

They sat quietly for a few moments. Cristeen fidgeted with the Celtic cross on her necklace. Katie watched her expression become more contemplative, almost despondent. Then Cristeen sighed deeply, cleansing away the gloom. Her inquisitive side was back again.

"There's an owl living in one of the barns."

The topic change startled Katie; it took her a moment longer to gather her thoughts. "Yes, in the haymow."

"I heard it last night. Such a haunting sound."

"I guess I've gotten used to it; I didn't hear a thing last night."

"It was late."

"Are you having trouble sleeping?"

Cristeen shrugged, taking a moment before turning back to look at Katie. "I slept for ten days, seems only natural I'd be weary of it."

Katie searched Cristeen's expression. She suspected there was more to it than mere wakefulness but was willing to let it go for now. "Well, tonight you should sleep well. With all the standing up and sitting down you've been doing you ought to be exhausted."

* * *

"You cannot walk downstairs on your own, Cristeen." Katie was adamant.

"I can hop to the stairs, then..."

"Then what?" Matt cut her off.

He stepped into the room, noticing Cristeen start as he spoke. She was jumpy today. Maybe it was excitement at going outdoors. Perhaps it was the lack of sleep that was evidenced by the dark circles under her eyes. Ironic, only days earlier they had been worried that she might never awaken and now the worry was that she was not sleeping.

"Why walk, when you can ride?" He held out his arms in a gesture to indicate he would carry her.

"Spoken like a true cowboy," Cristeen responded dryly.

"Your carriage awaits, m'lady." He bowed low.

"You are to be my conveyance then?"

"Verily. First, let us get thy royal robe." He wrapped the bed quilt around Cristeen's shoulders. She was only a few inches shorter than he, so that she was able to look him in the eye barely tilting her head up.

Her eyes narrowed and her lips twitched in a smile. "Pray, art thou a worthy coachman? Doth thou knowest well the way?"

Matt smiled broadly. "Thy concern is befitting a Queen."

"Nay, not Queen."

"Thou wishest not to be Queen?"

"Nay," she thought a moment, "thou mayest call me Princess."

"Come, then, Princess Cristeen." He scooped her up before she could protest again.

Katie watched their performance and rolled her eyes. "You two deserve each other. I need to finish some wash to take advantage of the good weather. Cristeen, I'll meet you out on the porch." She went downstairs ahead of them.

Matt held Cristeen close against his chest, smiling at her flustered expression. She pulled the quilt tight around herself as if to hide. He bent his head to whisper in her ear, "You need to eat something more than soup, Princess Feather." She giggled and relaxed enough to rest her head on his shoulder.

As they descended the stairs, Cristeen asked, "Will I be able to see the mountains?"

"Is that what you would like?"

"Yes," she answered wistfully.

He considered her for a moment. Perhaps this was a clue to her identity. This desire to see the mountains could mean she was mountain born. Or maybe it revealed something deeper about her, more about her personality than her identity.

"You are in luck," she looked up at him. "There is almost no where on this ranch where the mountains cannot be seen."

"Except from inside the house."

Matt smiled. "Ya', inside it's kinda hard to see them."

They crossed the kitchen and were at the porch door. "Close your eyes."

"What? Why?"

"Trust me. Close your eyes until I tell you to open them."

Cristeen hesitated, an inexplicable fear gripping her. She looked deeply into his brown eyes and found nothing there of which to be frightened. She closed her eyes. She could feel him moving, heard the door open and close, the sound of his footsteps on the porch floor. Then her legs were being lowered so that she could stand. The sensation was scary; she grasped his arm and opened her eyes.

Matt steadied Cristeen as he placed her feet on the floor. When her eyes opened they were wide with fear. "It's okay, I won't let you fall." Her smile trembled; he slowly turned her to face away from him. "Look out there."

Cristeen looked across the meadow, up over the aspens that edged the valley. Up, up, up, the mountains rose to the heavens. She inhaled sharply, the beauty breathtaking. In the morning light, the slopes were a blue-green topped with steel gray and streaks of white.

"They're majestic," she whispered.

"Truly." Matt, too, spoke softly.

"What's up there?"

Matt turned his eyes away from the mountains to look at Cristeen. She was enthralled. Her eyes, moments before wide with fear were now full with awe. His arm across her back registered her breaths as deep and slow. Cristeen was in love. The realization made Matt smile more deeply, for he also loved these mountains.

"Matt?" Cristeen glanced at him, though to his relief she did not notice he was staring at her now and not the scenery. "What's up there?"

"Everything beautiful that God has ever created." He said it without thinking, and was rewarded by her shining smile. "See where that slope seems to fold over into the one above?"

Cristeen sighted down his outstretched arm and located the spot indicated, about half way down the horizon. She nodded, still spellbound.

"That's about where the summer pasture is. We'll be taking the herd up there soon."

A change came over Cristeen. She sighed, and Matt watched her expression change from awe to resignation. Her eyes dropped, her head lowered, her shoulders sagged.

Almost she seemed ready to cry. She moved away from the porch rail, pushing aside Matt's attempt to assist her as she moved to the bench along the wall.

Matt looked back at the mountains and again at Cristeen. She had pulled the quilt tight around her shoulders and was staring out at the garden. Her body language fairly screamed *leave me alone!* It was the reaction of a wounded animal, retreating to lick its wounds. And he had an idea where the wound had been struck.

When Matt sat beside her on the bench, Cristeen pretended not to notice. She was, in fact, sneaking glances in his direction, covertly and without turning her head. She did not want to be rude and actually tell him to go away, but go away was exactly what she wished for him to do at this moment. So that she could be alone with her thoughts, her self pity. Looking at the mountains had filled her with a longing; Matt's comment about trailing the herd drove home to her that she did not belong here. She was an outsider.

He wasn't going to leave her alone. She clenched her jaw, felt her teeth grind. She fixed her stare on a small shrub growing on the far side of the garden, determined not to look in his direction. *Ignore him and he'll go away,* the voice inside her said. It seemed to be an experienced voice. So focused on it was she that Matt's voice made her jump.

"I'm sorry, Cristeen, I was thoughtless." He saw her jaw clench tight again. "When you are able to ride, it would be my pleasure to take you up to that valley."

The silence between them dragged on towards uncomfortable when she at last responded, continuing to look away as she spoke. "You don't have to. If I want to see it, I can go myself."

Matt bit back his first instinctive comeback of, *I don't think so.* It would hardly be the tactful response. Cristeen was living up to his initial impression of her—stubborn, strong willed, and independent. Seemed like a good impression back when she was unconscious. Now that those traits were being put into action, he began to reconsider. Still, he admired her gumption.

"I did not offer out of pity," he carefully worded the explanation. "I grew up here, I know the trails up there. Moreover, I understand the attraction, the draw that you feel."

Her attitude softened. She glanced at him briefly before turning her gaze back to the mountains. An ember of awe still glowed in her eyes. "What's to understand?"

"More often than I would like, business takes me away from this ranch, down to Fort Rossiter and sometimes Denver." He paused, considering how much to say. "There have been times when I have had to be even farther away."

Cristeen looked at him now, curious. He continued, "Whenever I am away, my only thought is to return. It's as if the mountains pull me back. In Denver I can see this same mountain range, yet is not the same. My mountains call to me, and I am filled with a longing to be once again here."

Cristeen spoke after a moment's quiet, "I don't know where I grew up, yet from the very first time I saw these mountains I felt that pull. My very soul seemed to resonate so long as I rode for the mountains."

"When I woke, I felt something missing. Oh, not my memories," she smiled. "Then you mentioned the mountains, and again I felt it. They call to me; *Cristeen, here there is peace, here you can belong.*"

She stopped, a pink blush tinting her cheeks. "I'm babbling, aren't I?"

"Does the babbling water make the stream less beautiful? Babble more, I like the way your mind works."

Her blush turned crimson. "I will accept the offer to visit the valley. I cannot promise to babble more."

"Then I will have to encourage you," she scowled, causing him to laugh. "Alright, I'll leave it alone. Truce?"

She accepted his outstretched hand, giving it a firm

shake before releasing her grip. Matt went on, now with a tone of conspiracy.

"If all goes well, maybe we can get Nurse Katie to let you out for a drive around the ranch."

"How will we ever get her to agree to that?"

Matt cocked his head to one side, as if contemplating the possible solutions. "Let's see, whenever I want to do something she objects to, I first agree to help out with some household chore. Then I tease her, and generally make myself unpleasant company until she finally gives in and sends me off to do whatever it was I really wanted."

Cristeen gawked at him, "That's awful!"

He laughed. "No, not at all. It's exactly what she deserves after the way she'll nag at me to get her way."

"Wouldn't it be much better if I just asked her?"

"That just might work, coming from you of course. You women have a way of communicating with each other."

"Oh, and you men don't? Without any words spoken, two men somehow have an entire conversation." She made the accusation with a sweep of her arm.

He feigned confusion. "Whatever do you mean?"

She pointed a finger at him, "You know precisely what I am talking about. A nod, a tipped hat, a shrug. It's like some kind of sign language," she stopped abruptly. "Why are you shaking your head?"

"For someone with amnesia, you seem to remember a lot about human nature."

He regretted the statement immediately. Her eyes dropped, only for a moment. When she again looked at him a wall had gone up; her eyes narrowed and her lips pursed, giving her a jaded appearance. *Matt, you insensitive fool!*

"I've done it again, haven't I?"

Cristeen looked away. As her head turned, Matt saw her bite her lip. Her shoulders rose and fell rapidly as she took several quick, deep breaths. She did not look at him again as she spoke, "You did nothing. I am the one who should apologize. I know nothing and yet presume to know all."

It was a self-incriminating statement. At once a profoundly humble recognition of the need for knowledge and a condemnation of arrogant confidence. An intriguing revelation. To realize that life is a journey of learning paradoxically put her in the category of well educated. Assuming her opinions to be unworthy of consideration showed a low self-esteem heretofore hidden.

"You are an intriguing conundrum, Cristeen." He could see her brow crease in bewilderment. "A bit of a riddle, that's what you are. Nonetheless, I am in the wrong this time. I assumed you knew your opinion is valued. Please be assured of that. It is the basic rule here, everyone matters."

She was obviously uncomfortable, with him or with herself it was hard to say. In either case, he preferred her smile over this glowering. A simple apology seemed inadequate; therefore he got down on one knee, his hands clasped as in prayer.

"I beseech thee, fair maiden, willst thou forgiveth me?"

Cristeen giggled. "Wherefore, dear knave?" Before Matt could respond she added, "I thank thee for thy kindness. No illumination canst I shed upon my actions."

He sat down, leaning his shoulders against the porch rail. He kept one leg bent, to give his arm a place to rest, the other he stretched out. "For whatever reason, you have cause to believe your opinions are of little value. I can't change a lifetime of experience, and you certainly have no cause to believe me. That said, I repeat, what you think matters here."

"I want to believe you." Her soft words were matched with a timid smile.

"Please do. I listen to everyone, even Fen and Coop when they bark, for I know that means they see something." Both dogs had begun yipping. "Of course, at the moment I know what it is they're seeing."

"How can you know, you haven't looked?"

"As much as I would love to mystify you," he smiled mischievously, "I know what time it is, and I also saw Henry go to the feed room a few moments ago. So I know the dogs are yapping with impatience."

Cristeen glanced at the complex of barns. Sure enough, she saw a boy crossing the space between buildings carrying two bowls. She smiled, and when her eyes turned back to Matt he saw an elfish humor dancing in them.

"See, no words spoken yet you men communicated."

He laughed and the tension between them was gone. An easy, comfortable quiet filled the next minutes. Cristeen was looking across the yard at the barns. Matt tilted his head back and watched her through half-closed eyes. She was indeed a conundrum, with her educated language and slightly Eastern accent mixed with an understanding of cattle and Western life. In addition to her clothing, and that horse, it was obvious she was familiar with ranching.

"Why Fen and Coop?" Matt opened his eyes to see she was looking at the barns. "I mean, how'd you come by those name?"

"Do you always shift subjects without warning?" She looked down at him and smiled. "I named them Fenimore and Cooper in a moment of weakness."

"You were drunk."

"Hardly," he frowned. "I had recently returned from college and was going through a phase of giving everything literary names."

"What's so weak about that?" He shrugged and she chose to let it go. "Who else is lurking around here? Must be a Natty or a Bumppo, at the very least."

"There's a veritable library out there," he nodded his head to indicate the barns and pastures. "Katie got into the act, so now we have a barn full of cats with names like Emma, Esmerelda, Camille."

"Surely there's also a Quasimodo, perhaps hiding in the loft?"

"Could be," he replied somewhat distracted. His mind had become sidetracked again by the enigma that was Cristeen. She was certainly well read. The references to the works of James Fenimore Cooper and Victor Hugo came effortlessly. What other writings was she familiar with, he wondered.

It had been many years since he had discussed academia with anyone. To debate the meaning of some work of literature. Or simply express a liking or disliking of a particular writing. He was a bit surprised to find he missed those conversations. The possibility of conversing with Cristeen was appealing. Later, though, as it was high time he got to work. For Katie was coming out the kitchen door, a wicker basket full of wet clothing balanced on her hip.

"You'll have to ask Katie about Quasimodo," Matt said as he leaped to his feet. He flashed a smile at Cristeen. "Don't say anything about the drive, though. We still have to plan our strategy for that. Okay?"

She grinned in answer. "I can keep a secret."

Katie set the basket on the bench. She saw the look passing between her brother and Cristeen. She did not know the young woman well enough to be suspicious; in Matt's eyes she recognized the gleam of conspiracy.

"What are you up to?" The accusation was made against Matt.

"I have no idea what you are talking about." He managed to look hurt. Cristeen suppressed a giggle.

"You are a lousy liar, Matthew Donovan."

"Ouch! I better leave before she uses my middle name, too."

Katie glared at him. "Don't you have work to do?"

Both women watched him bound off the porch and stroll across to the barn. Katie was smiling when she turned back to Cristeen.

"I know that look in his eyes can only mean trouble for me." She considered Cristeen and added, "But I don't suppose you're going to tell me anything, are you?"

Cristeen laughed heartily. She shook her head in answer then steered the subject away from Matt. "Tell me what you are growing in the garden."

* * *

"I have a surprise for you."

Cristeen looked up sharply at the sound of Matt's voice. The evening twilight had deepened to complete darkness. She was once again in her room. Katie had consented to moving the secretary desk closer to the bed. By placing the wingback chair half way between the secretary and the bed, Cristeen could maneuver about the room on her own.

Matt stood in the doorway. He'd been watching Cristeen for a few minutes before speaking. She was sitting at the desk, completely absorbed in what she was reading. The lamp wick was up high, making reading easier and also throwing long shadows across the room. When she slowly turned a page he was able to see by the onionskin paper it was his mother's Bible that held her interest.

Her startled reaction amused him, as did her apparent annoyance at realizing his amusement. She closed the book and turned her full attention on him.

"Are you going to stop grinning and tell me about this surprise?" Despite her irritation there was a tinge of excitement in her voice.

Matt stepped into the room, carefully concealing his surprise behind his back. "Nope, I'm gonna drive you crazy trying to guess what it is."

Cristeen frowned. "I don't like guessing games."

He stepped closer. "You're cute when you get angry."

After a disoriented moment she rose to the challenge. He saw it in the narrowing of her eyes, the way her chin jutted out in defiance even while a smile tugged at her lips. She really was pretty, he realized. The thought caused him to hesitate, his grip loosening on the objects he held. He recovered quickly, but not soon enough.

"Ha!" She gloated. "I saw it."

"Then tell me what it is." She bowed her head, defeated. "You're not going to give up that easily, are you?"

"Katie is right, you are an impossible imp."

Matt laughed. "Now you're pouting." He stepped within arms reach of her. Her lower lip protruded in a classic pout.

He should have perceived the trap. She seemed so innocent, genuinely upset at not being able to guess the surprise. He was drawn in like a fly into the web. With one hand he maintained his concealment; with the other he reached out to Cristeen, intending to comfort her.

Cristeen watched Matt closely, her breathing nearly stilled as she chose the timing of her move. As his hand neared her arm she pounced, latching onto his arm with a viselike grip. She used his own forward motion against him, pulling his arm so that he was forced to take another step closer lest he should fall. At once she let go of his arm and reached around to grab at his other arm.

He was stunned by her stealth and speed. For a moment only she seemed about to overpower him, until he regained his composure. With little effort he was able to wrest free of her hold. As he stepped back she nearly toppled out of her seat, but caught herself.

"You, you, you tricked me!" he stammered.

Cristeen giggled; the giggle evolved into a full-blown laugh. She clutched her sides and doubled over with glee. When at last she stopped there were tears wetting her cheeks.

"Oh, the look on your face. Precious."

Her face was deep red with her joy. Blue eyes sparkled,

like the morning sun glinting off the lake. Copper-gold strands of hair wisped loose from the braid meant to control it. Matt's vexation died ignominiously. She wasn't pretty; she was beautiful. And she had just pulled a prank on him the likes of which he had never experienced. He was unaccustomed to being the subject of a practical joke; he was usually the prankster.

Cristeen became alarmed as Matt remained silent. He was studying her; the intensity of his gaze became uncomfortable. She squirmed. He smiled. She grew flustered.

"Say something," it was a plea.

"You better watch your back, girl." The threat was tempered by jocularity. Nevertheless, the gauntlet had been thrown down.

"Why do I get the feeling I just poked a Grizzly Bear?"

He liked that analogy. "Just remember that," then he recalled what had begun this whole game. "My surprise for you seems paled by your surprising me."

"Don't you dare leave without showing me!"

He had begun backing towards the door. "What are you going to do about it?" She started to stand, using the chair for support. "No! Sit, stay!" He barked.

"Do you think I am one of your dogs?"

"I think you are far more complex than any animal I have ever encountered, and possibly more than any person."

"I'll take that as a compliment."

"It was meant as one. I am almost certain that you will enjoy this gift." With that, he held out the concealed item.

"Crutches!" She took the offering, immediately putting them to use. The smooth wood spoke of skilled work with a lathe. The top part that rested under her arm was thickly padded for comfort. She leaned her weight onto the supports, and discovered handgrips at exactly the right spot.

"I don't know what to say." Emotion choked her voice.

"Say thank you."

"That hardly seems sufficient." She examined the apparatus again. "The work involved. Where did you get these?"

"Henry's father works for the local mill. He's quite a skilled woodworker, though he doesn't usually get the chance to use the talent."

Matt moved to the wingback chair, grateful that Cristeen was busy trying out the crutches. She was mastering the technique rather quickly; putting her weight on the crutches she could then swing her good leg forward, take her own weight to move the crutches, then repeat the process. The critical part was how far forward to swing; too far skewed her center of balance. A few shaky landings set her to giggling. Absorbed as she was, she did not look at him as he explained the creation of the crutches.

"Once it became apparent that you would live, the question was raised about walking. Katie first suggested the crutches, actually. The trick was figuring out the right length and the proper placement of the hand holds."

"How'd you work that out? Perfectly, I might add."

Matt leaned his elbows on his knees and rested his mouth against his clasped hands. He could not quite bring himself to tell her the truth. Katie didn't even know the exact technique he had employed. It would be utter folly to tell a woman she had been measured like a horse. The height of a horse is given in hands, the span of the human hand being four inches. As Cristeen slept, Matt had counted the hand spans from her heel to her shoulder, and from there to her palms. No, not a flattering image.

Cristeen had managed to turn around and was headed back across the room to him. "Matt, are you going to answer me?"

"No, I prefer you think of me as a magician."

She frowned. "Some magician. Why couldn't you conjure me up a flying carpet?" Exhausted by the short workout, she let herself fall backwards onto the bed. "I'm wiped out."

"Not surprising. You've been more active today than all the past fourteen days combined." He glanced at the mantle clock. "And it's getting late. You should get some rest."

He rose to leave. "Thank you, Matt." Her voice was soft. "Sweet dreams Cristeen."

SEVEN

When Peter Donovan picked this valley as the sight for his home, he chose well. There was good grazing along the bottom, with scattered stands of trees to provide shade and shelter. Riding out at the north end he found a series of mountain meadows, each one a bit higher up and all of them closed-in enough so that he needed few cowhands.

The ranch had prospered under Peter Donovan. And it continued to prosper now that Matt was running the show. The work involved, sun-up to sundown, had its rewards. Plump, healthy cattle were but one of those rewards. Spending his days in the saddle, out in the sun or under the stars, was perhaps the greatest reward.

Then there were the adrenaline pumping duties; rounding up strays, chasing down mavericks, cutting the yearlings from the main herd. Trailing the yearlings to spring pasture and driving the entire herd to summer pasture had their thrills as well. There were always one or two steers determined to go their own way. The leaders often needed to be coaxed across streams and away from lush grazing on tiny meadow oasis.

Horses that had languished in near wild freedom over the winter months needed to be topped off. It became something of a sport with the three men, to see who could stay the longest on the most horses. For the most part each horse bucked for a few moments then settled down; they just needed to let out some pent up energy, and perhaps express disappointment that the carefree riderless days had come to an end.

Last spring, Henry had watched the proceedings intently. It was clear that the boy dearly wanted to join in. After discussing the matter with Ty, Matt had decided Henry was not ready for such rough riding. Up to that time a bad ride had been when Ajax, the family mule, decided to simply sit down and go no further.

Over the course of last summer Matt had gradually honed Henry's riding skills. Nothing could prepare him for this first bronc riding. His charge, Monk, not the wildest horse in the bunch, yet the gelding's heavily muscled hindquarters had plenty of bounce. Monk lowered his head, arched his back and sprang upwards, landing stiff legged. The impact jolted up Henry's spine, made all the worse by his own stiff posture. He went airborne on the next hop, wisely letting his body go limp as he hit the dusty ground and rolled away from the still bucking horse.

You alright?" Matt was concerned, remembering the first time he had been thrown from a horse.

Henry stood slowly, pain evident in his grimace. Once on his feet, though, he was grinning ear to ear. "That was fun!"

"He'll do," Ty declared. "Let 'im take The Count."

"Very funny, old man." The joke was lost on Henry. The Count had quite a reputation with the three older men. The stallion had the unique ability to neatly dislodge a rider within seconds of mounting. And he did it almost every time he was saddled. Matt had grown accustomed to mounting the stallion three times before being able to stay. Once his rider remained seated for more than five or six bucks, The Count settled into one of the savviest horses on the ranch.

They spent the majority of that day working the horses. Late in the day, Matt began to consider Cristeen's horse. The mare had not been ridden in two weeks; it would be a good idea to exercise her and keep her conditioned. Plus, he was more than a little curious about her abilities.

The palomino mare was built for cutting cattle. Heavily muscled hindquarters gave her the ability to accelerate explosively from a standstill. A long shoulder gave her a comfortable gait; coupled with the flexible neck she was able to pivot quickly. Her wide forehead and large, alert eyes showed intelligence.

Matt gave in to the temptation and saddled the mare. She came to him willingly when he whistled. As he slipped on the hackamore, she lowered her head and nuzzled his hand.

"So you want a treat, do you?" Her ears perked forward. "Show me what you can do, then we'll talk treats."

The mare's ears moved backward and forward as he spoke. She snorted at him, accepting his challenge. When he mounted, she tossed her head in eagerness. Matt jogged her across the meadow towards a bunch of cattle. He cut an older calf away from the group, moved it down the valley then let it go back. The calf was very unhappy, and did its best to return to its mother. The mare countered every move; she whirled and pivoted, bounced right, then left. Matt was simply along for the ride, never once directing the horse's actions.

Next he tried her out roping. As the lasso settled around the neck of another calf, the mare set her feet. She backed up when necessary, keeping the rope taut as Matt vaulted off her back. Under ordinary circumstances this would be when the calf was branded. Today he was practicing and immediately released the critter. A gentle tap on the taut rope brought the mare a few steps closer, loosening the lasso and freeing the calf. As Matt looped the rope, the horse returned to him. She was a perfect working horse.

The mare ambled slowly back towards the barn. Matt recalled the conversation with Ty and Paul a week earlier. Of all the mysterious things about Cristeen, this horse was far and above the most puzzling. She wasn't the average cowpony, yet she certainly was meant for working cattle. If someone wanted to buy a horse of her age and training, why he could expect to pay a good deal of money. On the other hand, a man could get a filly cheap and invest time and effort for the same result.

Had Cristeen done that, raised this horse? It would explain the whole money issue. However it brought up another point. Whose time and effort had been invested? Was there someone in Cristeen's life, past or present, to whom this horse had belonged, or who had trained her? That training had to have been done on a ranch, there was no other way to account for the mare's skill. Whose ranch? Where?

Matt let out a breath of exasperation. Too many questions. He tugged his hat, adjusting the brim to block the sun. There was still the concern that one day Cristeen's past would come riding down her back trail. At least the past week had unraveled one puzzle, what Cristeen was really like. She was too considerate of those around her to be a thief. She was too intelligent and independent to blindly follow the lead of say a father or brother if that meant harming another. She was polite and quiet, uncomfortable when attention was focused on her; he could not picture her as a saloon girl, where loud, gaudy self-selling was pivotal.

She was capable of deception, he thought, recalling the incident with the crutches. But that had been strictly in jest, not a serious fraud. Her sense of humor ranged widely from dry to razor sharp wit. His smile faltered; if she turned that wit on the wrong man the result could be disastrous. More than a few gunfights had been started over something as trivial as an implied insult.

"Sure wish you could talk to me, girl," Matt stroked the mare's neck, getting a soft whicker in response.

Ty was waiting at the gate. "Nice critter." It was a statement, not a question. "A horse says something about the man, or in this case the woman, what rides it.

Matt dismounted and led the palomino into the barn to be untacked. Ty followed. Neither man spoke for a few moments; Matt waited for Ty to spit out what he had to say. As was his way, Ty took the long way around, as if sneaking up on his own opinion. In the meantime, the mare relished the feel of the sackcloth rubbing over tired muscles.

"Cristeen come over here this morning," Ty began at last. "Said she liked the smell o' the horses."

Matt kept silent as he worked. Ty went on, "Fen an' Coop took to her straight away. Never seen Coop fawn all over nobody like that." He chuckled.

"I was dolin' out some corn to the mares," Ty nodded his head to indicate the broodmares in their box stalls. "Cristeen hobbled along behind; she's gettin' quick on them sticks you give her."

"Quick?" Matt smiled. "I think she could outrun either one of us, 'cept she hasn't quite figured out how to keep her skirts from getting wrapped around the crutches." Both men laughed.

Another long quiet ate the minutes. Ty shook his head as he recalled the morning visit. "Yup, she stopped to say something to each horse. O' course, she was all ga-ga over Fanny's filly. Fanny was right proud to show off her little one."

This time when Ty paused, Matt could see he was getting around to making his point. "You know, all the animals seem to like her. Horses are good judge o' character. They can see past all the facade right into yer heart. Why even Grizzy seemed taken with her."

Matt gave the palomino mare a handful of corn before turning her out into the corral. He knew what Ty was trying to tell him; whatever the circumstances of Cristeen's past, she was a good person. Trustworthy. It meant a great deal to hear it from Ty, even if it was an echo of his own conclusions.

They passed back through the barn. "Grizzy liked Cristeen?" Ty's comment finally hit home. Grizzy tended to be aloof.

"Well, now, I'd not say that exactly," Ty grimaced. "Tolerated a pat on the neck, she did. She's in foal heat, by the way."

Grizzy was a good working horse, and had proven a good dam as well. Except when she came into season. At those times she went from aloof to downright ornery. Any passerby, be they human or horse, was wise to swing wide or suffer a bite or kick. That went for her foal, as well. Mare and foal were turned out in a good-sized paddock to allow for safe distancing.

"That explains The Count's extraordinary ill-temper today." Matt absently rubbed his shoulder where it had slammed into the ground when the stallion unceremoniously unseated him.

"Aye," was the only answer needed. The Count had been stud horse for a number of years. He knew when any of the mares came into season, for they were his brood. Grizzy had other ideas about his leadership in general; in season, she was particularly brutal in her treatment of the stallion.

"She throws good foals with him," Matt mumbled more to himself than Ty. "Sometimes I'd like to just sell her, but that would not be fair to whomever bought her."

Ty laughed. As if she knew they discussed her, Grizzy chose that moment to put in her two cents. A shrill squeal split the air, punctuated by a *thwap* as her hoof struck the fence rail.

"If she gets too rough, we'll have to wean the colt early." Matt and Ty headed for the paddock to check on the situation.

* * *

The first morning with her new crutches, Cristeen set about exploring the house. To her consternation, Matt still insisted on carrying her down the wide front staircase. She silently vowed to prove she could maneuver on her own up and down those steps. That could wait.

Her journey began in the kitchen. As Katie cleared the table, Cristeen moved up the hallway that stretched the length of the house. She had notice the dining room, now off to her left, as Matt carried her past. Directly across from that was another room, the entryway a large arched opening.

Here she discovered a parlor, formal decor mixed with casual, lived-in furniture. There was an upright piano in one corner, a glass lamp on the side table, a sofa with a neatly folded afghan across the back, and two plush armchairs. The windows, which faced west and afforded a view of the mountains, were framed with lace curtains. A fireplace dominated the north wall; a clock anchored the center of the mantel, flanked by a photograph on each side.

Cristeen examined each elaborately framed daguerreotype. The first was of a woman, possibly in her early twenties, standing in an austere pose yet smiling broadly. Cristeen recognized in her Katie's hair and Matt's eyes. Surely this was their mother.

The second photograph was of the same young woman, this time accompanied by a slightly older man. There was no mistaking that this man was Matt's father. He was gazing with a mixture of love and protectiveness at his wife and the infant in her arms. A sense of family happiness emanated from the images despite their age.

The display held Cristeen's attention for several minutes. When she turned around she spotted the other doorway. Thick wood pocket doors were pushed almost completely open, inviting her to investigate. She passed beyond the mahogany doorpost and stopped, overwhelmed by what she found. A library.

Two narrow, floor to ceiling length windows flanked a bookcase lined with volumes of literature. To her right another west facing window offered a view of the mountains.

This window bowed out and a padded seat was built into the space. Bright sunshine filled the air, illuminating the books. Every available wall space had built in shelving to hold the paper treasures. In the center of the room an arrangement of chairs encouraged one to sit a spell and read.

Cristeen had found her sanctuary.

EIGHT

S heriff Mike Reardon sank into the chair in his office. *Some office,* he snarled to himself. His desk was pushed into a corner, making room for desks for his deputies. The room was the smallest in a small building. The cramped quarters were necessary to provide for jail space and the courtroom.

Mike turned to gaze out the window. He could just make out the rooftop of the new city hall. The massive building also housed the recently formed fire department. The new courthouse wasn't slated to begin construction until next year.

"Face it, Reardon," he spoke to himself. "You're jealous."

Admittedly the city hall had been desperately needed. The first mayoral election was two years ago, but there had been no centralized municipal offices.

Fort Rossiter's population was growing at an almost alarming rate. Barely more than a decade ago there were maybe one thousand people in the entire county. Now there was nearly that many living within the city limits alone. Most of that growth had been the result of the Colorado Central Railroad laying tracks through town.

Prior to 1877, inadequate transportation had hindered the economics of the Fort Rossiter area. Wagon roads, including the Overland Trail, were passable only in good weather. That left out a large portion of each year; winter snows and spring mud ate up much of the calendar.

When the Colorado Central chugged through Fort Rossiter in June 1877, most townsfolk had cheered. A handful predicted the town would rue the day. Mike was one of those with mixed emotions. On the one hand, the economic growth and communication potentials would make Fort Rossiter a culturally and technologically modern city. On the other hand, more people meant more crimes.

The challenges were greater, but Mike loved a good challenge. The real problem was the saloons, thirteen all told. They seemed to attract riffraff, gamblers, and loose women from all over the state. An exaggeration, he knew. However those establishments were a haven for idle and vicious men, driftwood from the railroad and ditch camps. They were irresponsible at best, and most held no respect for the law.

Mike Reardon was the law in Fort Rossiter and the surrounding country. At times an indomitable task, it was a job he relished. As the town population grew so had his staff. Even so, the sheriff's office was stretched thin, barely able to keep up with the daily petty crimes let alone the felonies.

He really didn't need the hassles of this murder investigation. During the past week he had been sorely tempted a number of times to just let it drop. Hank Crespin deserved to be dead. That was justice. If only some of the questions could be answered. Like where was Crespin's partner, Evan Marks?

The trail was cold and getting colder. He had been able to track the three fleeing horses only a short distance. It had rained, washing away the hoof prints along the wagon trail. The only thing he could say with some certainty was that the three had headed away from Fort Rossiter. At least initially; no telling if one or more had doubled back. The rest of the evidence indicated Crespin and Marks had started that final journey from Fort Rossiter.

It had become a matter of pride for Mike Reardon. Fort Rossiter was his jurisdiction; in striking out from his city the perpetrators had struck a blow against him. There had never been an unsolved murder in the city's history. Mike wasn't about to go into town annals as the first sheriff to fail.

With a sigh he returned his attention to the notebook laying open on his desk. The law's version of a tally book, Mike chuckled. He should share that comparison with Matt Donovan the next time they got together. A glance at the calendar reminded him that Matt would not be back to Fort Rossiter until late June. Ah well, the observation could wait. By then this case would be long solved.

Reviewing his notes did not reveal the answer he so hoped was hiding there. He had been able to discover Crespin's last known location, a roadhouse just outside of town. Formerly a stage station, The Cherokee Inn had a reputation for setting a fine table. Its position made it possible to get in and out with little detection. That made it a favorite for the men of the outlaw trail. Mrs. Tabor's cooking was the icing on the cake.

As a man of the law, Mike was familiar with the outlaw trail. Really a maze of trails ranging from Mexico to Canada, its notoriety had reached mythical proportions. Stories were told of thieves stealing stock from emigrants along the Overland Trail and then selling the stock to travelers on the Oregon Trail. Still it was true that the homesteaders along the trails were friendly to any drifter, asking no questions. *And providing no answers*, Mike scowled.

Tight lipped as the people were, Mike long ago learned how to charm the answers from them. Mrs. Tabor always had soft spot in her heart for him; she dreamed of a law-abiding West even while she catered to men who broke the law. It was a dangerous dance, for the men who frequented The Cherokee Inn knew she would cooperate with the law. She never asked questions and most of her patrons kept their secrets to themselves. There was always someone who needed to brag, however. "Loose lips sink ships," Mrs. Tabor fondly quipped. And Mike was grateful for her ears.

Crespin and Marks had been at The Cherokee the evening of Monday, April 3rd. Mrs. Tabor stated that Marks bragged of a recent influx of income and Crespin was badgering other patrons, as was his habit when in a good humor. Mr. Tabor reported seeing Crespin interact with a pair of newcomers; he was in the barn and could not recognize the strangers.

Mrs. Tabor did not see the strangers. Penny, the serving girl, also saw the strangers speak to Crespin. They seemed to be having a disagreement of some sort. The newcomers left without eating; Crespin and Marks took off shortly after.

All circumstantial, yet Mike had a gut feeling the strangers were the key factor in this case. No one at The Cherokee knew them and he could find nothing to indicate they had stopped or even passed through the city itself. They seemed to have vanished, and Evan Marks with them.

Voices in the hallway alerted Mike to one of his deputies returning. Rory Johnston stepped into the office, hat in hand.

"Got something for ya', Boss."

Mike did not look up. "You handle it, Rory. I've got a dead thief, his partner missin', an' a trail that's as cold as it is old."

Rory scuffed his feet, signaling his discomfort. "You gonna want this one, Boss."

Mike pinched the bridge of his nose as he looked up. "I've also got a rip roarin' headache." The younger man uneasily rolled his hat brim and Mike regretted snapping. "Alright, Rory, what have you got for me?"

* * *

The house was quiet at this late hour. Cristeen sat up in bed. Her ribs and shoulder were still sore, more so after a day of clumping about on crutches. That wasn't what disturbed her.

The oil lamp on the bedside table was easy to relight.

She turned the wick up high to chase away the shadows. Now she could see the mantle clock, half past ten. Not so late after all. Still, Katie had likely gone to bed long ago; her days began at dawn.

Cristeen didn't really want to bother Katie anyway. The dream wasn't that bad, it just left an unpleasant impression. A feeling of being the only person left in all the world. Rationally she knew that wasn't the truth, still the sentiment lingered. And it wasn't like she could remember the names for the faces in her dream. Nevertheless she knew who they were; every person who had ever touched her life. Mother, father, family, and friends. One by one they slipped away until she was the only one remaining.

Was that reality, or just her subconscious perception of the current situation? She sighed. Katie tried to make her feel like she belonged, even let her help out around the house. She was still an outsider. Paul was always watching her, looking away whenever she glanced at him. He was sizing her up, deciding what kind of trouble she was hiding. Oh, he was always nice to her, but he was first and foremost protector.

Ty, too, seemed to examine her every move. He was just smoother about it so that she almost did not realize. *Must be that famous Irish charm*, she smiled to herself. His lilting speech felt familiar, like the talk of cattle and the horses.

Her gaze fell on the wingback chair. Matt. He wasn't waiting for her troubles to show up. If he felt threatened by her unknown past he was good at hiding it. Like Katie, he treated her as if she belonged on his ranch. He did not include her in his daily activities; he spent his days working on the range. But he made time each evening to sit and talk with her, mostly about literature.

After discovering the library, Cristeen made it her routine to spend a few hours each day reading. She could only help Katie so much; inability to stand for lengths at a time limited her. And just moving around was still very tiring.

The books she found on the shelves were like old friends. It bothered her that she so readily recalled characters from these stories yet could not conjure even the hint of a memory about her family.

The clock ticked loudly. The loneliness was clinging tonight. Cristeen wondered if Matt was still up, and would he be coming in to check the fire. No sooner thought than rejected. He hadn't worried about the fireplace all week; the nights were much warmer now and Cristeen could add a log herself if necessary. She'd have to think of an excuse for him to visit.

That thought surprised her. Yes, she admitted to herself, she did look forward to their talks. His unquestioning acceptance of her was only part of it. He was thoughtful, intelligent, and funny. When he smiled it showed in his eyes. Kind eyes they were, too. Went well with his handsome face. *Cristeen!* She could feel her cheeks getting hot with a blush though she was alone.

She swung her legs over the edge of the bed and reached for the robe hanging on the bedpost, another one of Katie's loans. Cristeen was going to owe Katie an entire wardrobe by the time she was fully healed. Not that Katie would accept it; she made it perfectly clear that she wanted nothing in return. Cristeen wasn't about to let that stop her from doing what was right.

Taking up the crutches, she swung herself over to the fireplace. Flames lazily lapped at two large logs in the hearth. Additional fuel would not be needed tonight. She stared at the glow, leaning her weight on the crutches. The flickering light was mesmerizing.

Time to face the demon she had been avoiding for sometime. What if her memory never returned? She would love to stay here on the ranch for the rest of her days. That, however, was a utopic dream. Katie had set a date for her wedding, the first Saturday in September. Then Katie would move into her new home, leaving this house to Matt. Cristeen could not stay here beyond that; it would be inappropriate for an unwed woman to live in the home of a man who was not a blood relative.

Who cares what people think, a little voice told her. She focused on the thought. Did it matter what the rest of the world thought? What mattered was her own sense of right and wrong.

She began to twirl the Celtic cross between her fingers. Firelight reflected off its surface, shining pinpoints of light on the wall. Ultimately it was up to God to decide right from wrong. That truth settled in her heart and set her wondering on a new track. Did she believe in God?

Before discovering the library downstairs, Cristeen had filled her hours reading the Bible. She had spotted it soon after waking. The leather cover was worn from frequent use. It didn't take long to realize the Bible had been Mary Donovan's; her delicate handwritten notes lined the edges of most pages. Initially Cristeen feared Katie and Matt would be angry at her for reading their mother's Bible. But neither made any comment one way or the other whenever they saw her with it.

Many of the passages she remembered, much as she did other works of literature. There were a few, however, that she not only remembered but that also seemed to have significance to her. As if someone had taught her the meaning behind the words. Apparently she believed those words; at least she had at one time. Did she now?

Matt and Katie believed. She knew that from little things each said, but also because one or the other said grace each night at dinner. Some people say the words; these people felt the words. Whenever Cristeen heard them say, "Lord watch over us and guide us," she felt a sense of comfort. Not unlike the sensation a child might feel knowing a parent is nearby, in case trouble should arise.

A sizzling sound startled her. It was the sound of the fire being stoked and sparks flying up from wood newly exposed to flames. Cristeen had not moved; it was some kind of a trick. As her mind spiraled into a fright, believing ghosts inhabited her room, she heard a scuffling footstep. Another moment and she understood. The room adjoining this one shared the chimney. The fire being stoked was on the other side of the wall.

Someone was still awake; Cristeen was fairly certain who.

* * *

"Are you going to stand there all night?" Matt asked the question without looking up. He heard Cristeen coming down the hall; the regularly spaced *thumps* had become her signature. His initial concern faded as soon as she stood in the doorframe. He had glanced up; she was looking down, gauging the placement of her step, clearly unharmed.

Cristeen's eyes narrowed as she studied him. She was mildly irritated that he knew she was there without even looking. Then she realized he had heard the crutches as she came down the hallway. *Playing it casual,* she thought, *we'll see about that.* An impish streak seemed to be part of her personality.

"So this is where you retreat," she really had no idea where she was going with this. She'd base it on his responses.

She had his attention, albeit divided. "Retreat? What are you talking about?"

Cristeen moved into the room. The rest of the house bore a woman's touch, Katie's and her mother's before her. This room was completely masculine. Mahogany furniture, bare wood floor, fieldstone hearth. A large framed map of Colorado hung on the wall. There was a bookcase with glass doors. The room was neat if somewhat spartan.

She kept her silence just long enough for Matt to put

down the pen he held. The lamplight had grown dim; he really shouldn't be reading or writing in such poor lighting. She was tempted to tell him that, but another thought arose.

"Katie says you retreat whenever she's winning an argument."

"She said what?"

So those brown eyes can get angry, Cristeen was pleased with his reaction.

Matt continued, "I don't back down from a fight, Cristeen. If she's talking about the last argument, she knew it was a closed subject." He took a deep breath, "But she didn't say anything at all, did she?"

"You looked so serious. I just thought you needed to lighten up." She leaned over the desk, eyeing the charts and tally books strewn across the surface. "You're gonna go blind working like this."

Matt smiled. "Perhaps, but the work needs to be done."

"Why not in the morning? Do you have something against sleeping?"

"I can't sleep with unfinished work."

"Now that's a lousy excuse," she carefully lowered herself into the padded armchair in front of the desk.

"You got a better one?"

"I just can't sleep."

Matt leaned back in his seat. He tilted his head and scrutinized her expression. Stoic, yes, but there was something more. She used humor to mask her real feelings.

"Bad dreams?" She lowered her eyes. "Wanna talk about it?"

"Not really," she shrugged.

I shouldn't have come here, Cristeen groaned inwardly. *I've disturbed his work and for what, a silly fear of being alone?*

After a long silence, Matt softly observed, "The house is quiet at night, almost eerie."

She held his gaze for just a moment. He went on, "Katie mentioned you heard our owl."

"Ya', couple of times. Not tonight though."

"I have always thought it was a haunting sound."

Matt watched her closely. Cristeen was fidgeting with the Celtic cross again. It was her tell, a trait that gave away what she was thinking. Not her actual thoughts, of course. For whatever reason, she had to work up her courage to say what she came to say. He got the impression she would face down the fiercest nature could throw at her but people terrorized her.

With a deep breath, Cristeen plunged in. "You believe in God, right? Why? I mean, how? Oh, I don't know what I mean."

Matt let out a long, slow breath and ran a hand through his hair. "Whew! I was afraid you'd ask me a hard question."

She giggled a little, some of her tension released just by asking and more when she saw he was not offended. She was grateful when he moved to the fireplace. Having bared her true feelings, she felt defenseless. Matt stared into the flames for a long time before turning to speak again.

"I would gladly try to explain my faith to you, Cristeen. I haven't given it much thought lately." He prayed for the right words. "I have always believed in a god; when I was old enough to understand I came to believe in the God."

Cristeen sat perfectly still. She turned in the chair to face him when he moved, but her eyes were focused on the fire. She no longer twirled the cross, her attention was on his words.

"I believe the promise the Lord has made. He loves me, and all I have to do is accept that love to receive all the Kingdom of Heaven has to offer."

He moved to her side, squatting on his heels to bring his face level with hers. As he blocked her view of the fire, Cristeen was forced to look at him.

"I think the more important question is, do you believe?"

The tears he saw welling in her eyes surprised Matt. He'd seen her reading his mother's Bible. And had assumed that she was a believer. She bowed her head respectfully when grace was said at meals. Any reference to her life being saved by the grace of God brought no objections.

She wore that Celtic cross, turning to it whenever she was in turmoil. Except now. Her hands lay still in her lap; she did not know where to turn in this situation.

"I don't know what I believe," she whispered.

Matt stood abruptly, before his legs went to sleep. Deep knee bends always had that effect on him. Glancing down it seemed like Cristeen was wilting, interpreting his movement negatively. He placed his hand on her shoulder and gently squeezed.

Cristeen took courage from the gesture. "I think I believe in God."

"That's always a good place to start."

She heard the tender smile in his voice. "I think I remember going to church, and being happy."

"I hear an however in your tone."

"I've been reading the Bible." She looked for a sign of disapproval, instead saw encouragement. "I can't reconcile this," she gestured at her leg, "with what the Bible says about the Lord providing for and protecting me."

"Have you read Romans, chapter eleven? *'O the depth of the riches both of the wisdom and knowledge of God! how unsearchable are his judgments, and his ways past finding out!'* "

"Is that the Biblical way of saying trust me?"

"In essence. No one knows what God is planning for us. It is fruitless to try to understand, just accept His wisdom."

"I can accept it, even believe in it." She took a deep breath, letting it out slowly as she used the crutches to help her stand. "I just don't know if I can trust it."

Matt stepped in front of her, putting a hand on each of her shoulders. "Cristeen, I know He can be trusted. I have a lifetime of experiences that have taught me that." She bowed her head; he caught her chin in his hand and gently upturned her face. "For now it's enough to just accept His wisdom."

Cristeen closed her eyes, taking comfort from Matt's words. Maybe, just maybe he was right. After all, here she was surrounded by care and compassion. This family had swallowed her up, made her part of their clan. For the present she would lean on Matt's faith just as she leaned on the crutches.

Matt caressed his thumb along her jaw line, pleased to see her smile returning. When she opened her eyes he saw a peacefulness that had not been there moments earlier. "Did I help?" he asked softly.

"Yes."

"Then let me walk you back to your room. You need to rest."

"So do you," the humor was back. "I won't budge an inch unless you promise to stop working and get some sleep."

"Is that a challenge?" His grin was equally impish.

"You betcha." She would have firmly planted her feet on the floor, if she could actually stand on both of them. Nonetheless, she did a good job of conveying her point.

Matt laughed. "How quickly you forget." With that he scooped her up. The crutches clattered to the floor.

"Put me down! Okay, I give, you win. Now let me walk on my own.

Carefully he lowered her feet to the floor, then supported her while retrieving her crutches. "Then I'll give in, too. You are right, I do need some sleep."

They stopped at the door to her room. Suddenly Cristeen felt awkward, unsure how to say thank you. And goodnight. Once again, Matt saved her. Jauntily he raised her hand to his lips and lightly kissed it, saying, "I had a lovely evening, Miss Cristeen. Do stop by again sometime."

"Go to bed, Mr. Donovan. You are getting punch drunk." His smile deepened, crinkling his eyes. She became serious just long enough to say, "And thank you for allowing me to interrupt your work."

"Feel free to interrupt me anytime you need to talk." He hesitated before adding, "Even if that means waking me up."

"I'll be fine, goodnight."

"Sweet dreams."

NINE

"**M**att!"

"Cristeeeen," he mimicked her whine.

"I am trying to hide behind you."

"I'm well aware of that."

"Then why do you keep moving to the side?" She tried again to position herself directly behind him, only to have him sidestep as he turned to face her.

"Why are you trying to hide?"

She groaned. "I should never have agreed to this."

The evening before, Matt invited Cristeen to attend church with the family. She hesitated. What finally won her assent was Matt's theory that once Cristeen rode to town in the buggy there would be no way to deny her a ride around the ranch. Now Cristeen saw that Matt played both herself and Katie, using her own desire to see the ranch along with Katie's eagerness to bring her new friend to church, to get what he wanted.

"You didn't answer my question." Matt crossed his arms on his chest and stood blocking the walkway out of church. "Why are you trying to hide?"

"Everyone is staring at me."

"Of course they are." Noting Cristeen was more agitated than embarrassed, he added, "It's natural to stare at the pretty new girl."

Cristeen felt her face getting hot. "Don't patronize me."

He dropped his arms and resumed walking beside her. "I'm not patronizing you, Cristeen. You look very nice."

Cristeen glanced quickly at him. He hadn't worn a suit, much to her surprise. Dark twill trousers topped with a white shirt, the overall effect was quite pleasing. He looked dignified and formal at the same time relaxed and friendly. "You clean up nicely, yourself."

His eyes smiled. Cristeen looked away, focused on walking. He was indeed very handsome. Tall, if she stood on her own two feet the top of her head would be at his eye level. His dark hair held just the hint of waviness where it met his shirt collar at the nape of his neck.

Beyond his appearance, he had a way of making a person feel at ease. He seemed to know everyone in the small congregation, and all greeted him with respect, as a friend. It was apparent this community held him in high regard. Yet he was one of them, down-to-earth, equally at home debating theology as he was discussing range conditions.

Matt was handsome, successful, and well liked. And what was she? *Nobody, that's what,* she told herself. *Don't foolishly misinterpret kindness and compassion for something more.* Without a past she was nothing. She should accept the friendship at face value, but understand it was only friendship.

"Penny for your thoughts."

"Huh?"

"You look deep in thought. Care to share?"

"Not this time." She smiled to soften the rejection.

Katie was at the door as they stepped into the bright sunshine. "Sarah's looking for you," she whispered to Matt before going back inside.

"Great," Matt grumbled. Suddenly he stepped behind Cristeen. "Hide me."

"You can't hide behind me! You're too tall."

"I'll duck down."

"Your shoulders are too wide."

"Stand still. There, if you stay just like this I'll be hidden." Cristeen tried to look over her shoulder at him. "And look, now you have extra hands."

As he made the last statement, he extended his arms so that she did appear to have an extra set of limbs. Cristeen laughed, her earlier pensive mood forgotten. At that moment the embodiment of Matt's fear swooped down on them.

"Matthew Donovan!" The woman seemed about his age, although Cristeen had no idea exactly what that was. She was dressed ostentatiously, a bit too overdone to be called classy. She continued to address Matt in a loud voice, ignoring Cristeen.

"I thought I saw you here. I said to Mother, *Mother, there's Matthew.* She did not believe it was you. Where have you been keeping yourself? We have missed you."

Matt stood straight, placing his hands on Cristeen's shoulders. As Sarah prattled on he leaned close and whispered, "Yackety, yackety. Tell me if she says anything."

Cristeen giggled; Sarah stopped in mid sentence.

"And what have we here? Oh my, you must be the waif that Katherine was telling me about."

Cristeen felt icy hot at being called waif. She stood rigid, willing herself not to react.

"Cristeen," Matt stepped around to stand beside her. "Allow me to introduce Sarah Hatcher, our town magpie."

Sarah was clearly offended. Her reaction so much resembled a bird ruffling its feathers that Cristeen snickered. She stopped herself from laughing outright, biting down on her lip. As Sarah sputtered indignities, Matt placed his hand on Cristeen's back to steer her away.

"Sorry about that," was his only comment.

Doctor Roberts hailed them loudly, his enthusiasm obliterating the sourness of Sarah. "Cristeen, my dear! You look wonderful." He shook Matt's hand, then turned back to

Cristeen. As he looked her up and down she had the sensation of being examined. But it was with a kind eye, as his next words showed.

"Your color has returned. You look rested." He leaned closer, carefully pointed to her eyes. "Although, I see some restless nights here."

"I slept a lifetime, Doc. Allow for some wakefulness, please." She spoke amiably.

Doc nodded. "I understand, Cristeen, I understand." She saw in his eyes a tender melancholy of understanding.

After a brief quiet, Doc turned the conversation light-hearted. "Heard about these crutches. Let's see how well you get on with them."

Cristeen took a few swinging steps away, then came back. Doc's approval gave her a warm sense of accomplishment. She returned his broad smile.

"Ah, Reverend," Doc greeted someone behind her. "Come, meet Cristeen. She has restored my faith in the grace and goodness of God."

Reverend Polchek stepped in front of Cristeen. "It is good to finally meet you." He gave her hand a gentle squeeze. "I have heard so much about you. Dr. Roberts cannot stop telling me how miraculous is your recovery."

Cristeen might have become uncomfortable with the attention had the Reverend not perceived her unease. He gracefully turned the spotlight to Matt, asking this and that about the ranch.

"I do hope you will join us regularly again," Reverend Polchek stated in closing.

"Perhaps Reverend. Has Katie invited you for dinner?"

"Yes she has. I do look forward to her meals." He smiled wistfully. With a final handshake and a nod to Cristeen he moved away.

"He's coming to dinner today?" Cristeen asked as Matt lifted her up onto the buckboard.

"Yup." He swung onto the seat beside her. "Wanna take a drive out to Katie's? She'll be heading straight back to cook, so you can get a look around without her knowing."

A few days earlier, Cristeen told Matt that she wanted to see Katie's new house surreptitiously. "Somehow, I want to give her something for her wedding," she admitted. Matt thoughtfully suggested he could help. Cristeen had no idea what kind of gift she might give; she hoped a look around the new house would be inspirational.

The drive home was quiet; neither spoke until the ranch house was in sight. It was a comfortable silence. Cristeen watched Matt handle the horse, admiring the affection he showed towards the animal. Watching the pony trotting before them, a new stirring began in her. Each stride caused muscles to ripple beneath the gleaming hide; alert ears flicked backwards and forwards, listening for instructions.

The beauty of the horses clutched at Cristeen's heart, as the mountains had the week before. Whereas the majesty of the high country filled her with a yearning, watching the horse gave her an ache. The emotion was akin to the heartache one would feel having lost someone cherished. She closed her eyes, trying to shut out the pain.

"Are you alright? Is your leg hurting?" Matt stopped the rig as he noticed Cristeen's eyes squeezing shut.

She looked at him and saw such tender concern it alarmed her. Looking away she answered, "I'm fine."

The carriage did not resume movement. Cristeen could feel his eyes on her still. She could not explain the feeling that had come over her, yet she had to tell him something. Otherwise he was liable to smother her with his anxiety. She chose her words carefully.

"My leg is okay, I am not in pain." She took a deep steadying breath then turned to look at him again. "I thought I remembered something, but it's gone now."

Matt searched her blank face. She was hiding whatever

emotion had threatened to overwhelm her. He felt sure he would be able to tell if she were fibbing about the physical pain. There would be some detectable sign - clenched teeth, white knuckles, something. He saw nothing.

This was a different Cristeen than the girl he had come to know. Her expression was impassive, not quite stony. Matt wasn't going to be able to read her emotions this time. She wasn't even twirling the cross. At least she seemed to be attempting to smile. He would have to be patient.

"You're starting to remember? That's great."

She forced a smile in response. *No, it is not great, it's awful,* she wanted to say. To be openly honest about how scared she was becoming. What she was remembering was not wonderful nor pleasant. Maybe if it were actual memories, not just impressions, she would understand what made her feel these emotions. Perhaps then they would not be so frightful.

She wanted to tell him all that. Instead she smiled briefly and nodded her head. This was another one of those impressions; wary distrust, a reluctance to share her thoughts or reveal her true feelings. It began a few days earlier, keeping her from telling Matt about the dream. It was snowballing. She could see that in a detached way, looking back at her actions and thoughts of this morning. She had been afraid the people stared out of pity, tried to hide the fear by literally hiding behind Matt. And she had begun telling herself not to get attached to the Donovans.

An awkward silence was developing. Cristeen brooded over her emotional turmoil. Something in her past made her feel this way, if only she could force herself to remember actual events. Surely she must be an orphan, why else could she not recall even the slightest detail about either of her parents. Had she ever gone to church with her own family?

Matt stopped the buggy in front of Katie's house. Cristeen was twirling the cross now. He felt relieved; at least she was letting some emotion show. He placed a hand over hers, stilling the motion.

"The memories will return when the time is right, Cristeen."

She turned to face him. The emotion was showing, all right. Frustration. It was pushing her to the brink of tears.

He felt lost. He had never been one to sit by and watch a friend hurt. It was his way to jump right in, lend a hand, do whatever was needed for friend and family alike. In this situation he just did not know what to do, how to react. He wanted to take away the hurt, somehow comfort her. What could he possibly say to make up for a forgotten lifetime? *Dear Lord, please help me!* It was a passionate plea; he had no idea how to deal with a woman crying.

That wasn't true. He had always been able to comfort Katie through her tears. No, it wasn't the prospect of a woman crying that unnerved him. It was the fact it was this woman. Cristeen had not cried even at the pain of her injuries. She was stoic, independent, reserved. She had an inner strength he admired. He worried what it would mean to her to be seen crying; what would it do to her sense of self-control.

"I'm afraid time will run out," Cristeen whispered.

Matt looked at the Celtic cross lying in the palm of his hand. "Trust in the Lord, Cristeen."

She bowed her head in defeat. "I don't think I can."

He dropped the necklace and clasped her hands. "Yes, you can. He is worthy of your trust."

He saw earnestness in her eyes. "I want to trust Him. I just, can't."

"Why?"

"I don't know."

Empathy wasn't helping her right now. She believed in God, she just felt incapable of trusting. Matt did not know how to counter that. There didn't seem to be anything he could say or do to make it all better. This was something Cristeen would have to work through on her own.

Stroking the back of her hand with his thumb gained him a weak smile in reward. He let the silence stretch on while he continued the calming caress. At last she took a deep, albeit shaky, breath and looked up with a real smile.

"Thanks for not pushing."

"You're welcome," he paused. "I meant what I said the other night. Anytime you need to talk I'm all ears."

She seemed to examine him a moment. "No you're not. You have a perfectly normal head."

When they stopped laughing, Matt hopped off the buckboard. As he lifted her down, he noted the laughter dancing once again in her eyes. "It's good to hear you laugh, Cristeen."

TEN

"So there I was, poised to git that varmit what bin killin' our chickens." Ty paused for effect.

Cristeen, already on the edge of her seat, leaned forward in anticipation. "What happened?" She asked breathlessly.

"The varmit struck first." He gave a quick thrust of his chin in emphasis.

Her eyes widened; she was spellbound. "What was it? Coyote, cougar, wolverine?"

Paul shook with laughter. "It was a polecat!"

"A polecat?" She was perplexed. "But skunks don't attack people."

"Aye, that they do lassie," Ty looked sheepish. "Not all attacks are with claws and teeth."

As comprehension set in, Cristeen laughed with Paul. "Oh, you must have stunk for a week!"

"It is a wise man that makes himself pleasant," Ty grinned. "No matter how many dunkings it takes."

"And that's when Fenimore and Cooper moved into the barn?"

"Seemed tactical; better the dogs get sprayed by a skunk than one o' us again."

Cristeen leaned back in the armchair. It was late Sunday afternoon and Ty was entertaining them while they waited on dinner. Matt and Reverend Polchek had withdrawn to the library, ostensibly to discuss the Reverend's pending purchase of a new horse. Ty maintained the two were actually debating theology.

"Lass," Ty cocked his head, looking like he was about to proclaim a most wise statement. "I believe deep blue is the right color for you."

Cristeen radiated. He continued, "Brings out the blue in yer eyes."

"Hey Matt," Paul shouted, turning his head towards the partially closed door. "Ty's flirting with Cristeen."

The door slid open and Matt stepped into the room. "What?"

"Ty is flirting with Cristeen," Paul repeated. Glancing at her, he added, "and she's enjoying it."

Cristeen blushed. Matt looked from her to Ty and back to Paul. His future brother-in-law had a puckish grin on his face. And Cristeen did seem to be enjoying Ty's attentions.

"Ty you old reprobate."

"Mattie-boy, even old eyes recognize beauty. T'would be impolite to withhold a compliment."

"Aw, leave him alone. He's just being nice."

"And you," Matt pointed a censuring finger at Cristeen. "Why, he's old enough to be your grandfather."

Before Ty could sputter out his indignant rebuttal, Cristeen calmly corrected Matt. "My father perhaps, not my grandfather. I appreciate the flattery, however I am much more than sixteen."

A silence fell over the group. Matt recovered first, taking the smug expression on her face as a challenge. After all, it was his eyes she held with her gaze. "How much older?"

"Matt!" she admonished. "Have you learned nothing from Ty? It's not good manners to ask a girl her age."

"I didn't ask your age, I asked how much more than sixteen you are."

"Well, I wouldn't want to be sinnin' by telling you an untruth." She was being very coquettish.

Matt was enjoying the game but proceeded cautiously. She'd tricked him before and he was determined not to fall into another trap. "So tell me the truth."

"I'll answer your question if you answer mine."

"Twenty-eight."

Cristeen blinked. He surprised her by volunteering his age so quickly. Her eyes darted to the photograph on the mantle, the one of an infant Matt. For a moment she had lost the game. The moment passed; she had her challenge.

"You didn't wait for my question."

Matt wasn't sure he liked her confident tone, and he was definitely uncomfortable with the speed at which she recovered.

"What's your question?" He gingerly asked.

"I'll tell you my true age if you'll tell me why you haven't been to church in a year." Matt blanched and Cristeen immediately regretted the challenge.

He regained his composure quick enough. "Did Katie put you up to this?"

Reverend Polchek chuckled. Cristeen mutely shook her head in denial. Matt searched her expression; she looked genuinely remorseful. The week's conversations finally clicked, and he saw the truth about her. She used words the way most people used tools and weapons. She liked to play with words, to joust wittily. Words were her first line of defense when threatened. They were her friends; in them she found joy and comfort.

"Dinner is ready," Katie interrupted. "Paul, could you help me with the roast please?"

The others left the room. Cristeen sat fidgeting with the Celtic cross. To be lost for words spoke volumes about her discomfort, Matt now realized. Earlier today, her frustration was not from the inability to remember. She was driven to the verge of tears because she was incapable of expressing her feelings in words. Here she sat silenced again. How long before the tears welled in her eyes? He would not wait to find out, not when it was in his power to prevent those tears this time.

He moved to her side and once more stilled the twirling cross. "Cristeen," he spoke gently, "I'm not angry at you. You called my bluff, touché." That last brought a brief smile. "That's better. I like your smile."

She blushed. Matt liked that, too, but chose not to add to her discomfort. "Come on, Katie will be angry at both of us if we're late for dinner."

He helped her out of the chair. "I'm sorry I asked such a personal question, especially with everyone around."

"Would it help if I said I'll get you back?"

Cristeen chuckled. "A little."

They crossed the hall. Matt stopped Cristeen before they entered the dining room. "I'll answer your question, later, but I'm raising the stakes." She raised an eyebrow in question. "I won't settle for just your age. I want to know what you were remembering on the ride home today."

Cristeen's groan was tempered with a grin. "Can I distract you, make you forget the question?"

"Nope," he mirrored her grin. "But you're welcome to try."

Dinner was enjoyable, a lively mixture of good food and wonderful company. Cristeen quietly absorbed the conversations and interactions taking place around the table. After the meal they retired to the parlor for dessert.

Cristeen accompanied Reverend Polchek to the parlor while the others cleared the table. The Reverend walked casually beside her, carefully allowing her space to move while still seeming to be by her side.

"How did you like our little congregation?"

"It was nice," she answered delicately. "The people are very friendly."

The Reverend chuckled. "Yes, I was afraid of that. You

see, we have all been very curious about you. Finally meeting you, well it was highly anticipated."

He helped her ease onto the sofa, pulling the ottoman close for her to rest her bandaged leg. Learning that she had been the object of curiosity was disquieting for Cristeen.

Reverend Polchek sat in the armchair across from her. "I did not mean to discomfort you, my dear. Glenpark is a small village, and the doctor has been rather pleased with your recovery."

Cristeen relaxed a little. "I wish he could fix my mind."

"I'm afraid that is out of his hands."

"I know," she sighed. "It's my mind, I'll have to heal on my own."

"That's not at all what I meant." He was dismayed.

She searched his face. "What do you mean?"

"My dear, there is only One who truly heals our wounds, and makes whole our souls and minds."

She frowned. What else did she expect from a minister but to be told she must trust in God? It just wasn't that easy. If God wanted to heal her, why did he let her get wounded to begin with? Reverend Polchek looked discouraged; she really didn't want to get into this subject tonight.

"Do you believe in God, Cristeen?"

She shrugged. "Yes, I suppose I do."

He shook his head sadly. "No conviction. Where do you put your faith? In whom do you trust to take you safely through this world?"

The minutes ticked by. Cristeen began to twirl the cross at her throat; this time she noticed herself doing it. A resigned smile stretched her lips.

"I understand why you feel as strongly as you do, Reverend."

"Look to the Lord for help, Cristeen. It is foolish pride that deceives us into believing we can handle our problems ourselves. Help cometh from the Lord only."

Her expression hardened. As reluctant as she was to delve into the subject, the pastor's words drew her to voice her doubt. Pointing to her leg, she asked, "And what of this?"

"The Bible tells us not the despise His corrections, for the Lord chastens those whom he loves." She rolled her eyes at him and he smiled indulgently. "Your memories will return. I don't want to push, my dear, so I'll finish this with one request. Think about what Proverbs 3:5-6 says; *'Trust in the Lord with all thine heart; and lean not unto thine own understanding. In all thy ways acknowledge him, and he shall direct thy path.'* "

"I think about that constantly, Reverend."

He smiled broadly, seeing the truth in her words. Her smile reflected her gratitude that he was letting the subject drop. Katie swished into the room, followed closely by Matt and Paul with Ty bringing up the rear of the cavalcade.

With plenty of laughter and just a bit of ceremony the apple pie was served. Matt sat on the sofa beside Cristeen, Ty on the other side of him. Paul stood by the fire until Katie sat down; then he perched himself on the arm of her chair. For a short time only the sound of forks scraping plates was heard.

"Delicious," Ty sighed when done his slice of pie.

"The best you've ever made." Matt agreed.

A look passed between Cristeen and Katie. Cristeen shook her head ever so slightly. Katie chose to ignore that signal.

"Cristeen made the pie."

"Only the crust," she protested. "It was Katie's preserves and she did the baking."

"It was a most excellent pie," Reverend Polchek interceded. "Accept praise when it is given properly."

His smile eased the admonishment. She smiled back. "Thank you. I am glad you all liked the apple pie."

"Got any more hidden talents we oughtta know about?"

Cristeen glanced sideways at Matt and smiled slyly. He

laughed warmly, rocking back in his seat. She found she liked eliciting that reaction. His eyes crinkled at the corners and light shimmered in them. He had a broad smile that let you know he was laughing with you not at you.

She liked that he included her in discussions, helping her feel at ease. Like one of the family. That thought stilled her heart a moment. *Family. Where is my family? Do I have a family?* The pain squeezed at her very soul. Matt glanced at her, concern in his gaze. She smiled tentatively, letting the pleasant company push away her fears.

Paul was discussing the virtues of the Scotch Highland cattle they raised on the ranch. Reverend Polchek was unfamiliar with the breed. As Paul continued speaking, Cristeen found herself becoming sleepy. Not wanting to appear rude, she stifled the first yawn. Matt noticed and quietly suggested she lean on him to rest.

The description of the cattle breed was quite interesting and Cristeen truly wanted to hear it all. Longhaired and long-horned, gentle yet tough, disease resistant and requiring little in way of shelter. It all sounded too perfect to be real. Her eyes drooped and she pictured the calves romping in the pasture, their shaggy hair flopping over their eyes. Her giggle was interrupted with another yawn. Matt's upper arm was looking more and more attractive as a pillow. She squirmed a little, snuggling against his arm to find the most comfortable position.

"You didn't take a nap today, did you?" His voice sounded soft and far away.

Opening one eye she saw he had leaned quite close to whisper to her. She was drifting off to sleep. And he was right; she had forgone her usual afternoon nap in order to make the apple pie.

"Nope," her one word answer was a bit slurred.

"Excuse us, Paul," Matt carefully picked up Cristeen. She was too tired to protest. "I think someone stayed up past her bedtime."

"I'm not a child," she complained weakly.

"I wouldn't know."

It was a gentle probe for her age. Cristeen wasn't so sleepy as to misunderstand that. She studied his face as he walked. The hallway was shadowy, lit by the lamp beside the front door. He was smiling just slightly, his lips curving upwards at the corners. His eyes were focused forward, taking care not to misstep and jar her. She wrapped an arm around his neck to hold herself up and snuggled her head into the hollow of his shoulder.

"I'm twenty-two."

ELEVEN

"Good morning, Miss Cristeen."

"Good morning, Henry."

The boy greeted her just as she entered the broodmare barn. Cristeen was sure he had watched her cross the yard as he leaned on the manure fork. With his lop-sided grin and tousled hair he looked carefree and irresponsible. She knew from dinner conversations that the men considered him anything but. Still, his boyish charm was most apparent.

"Get along good on dem crutches, I see."

"So I'm told," she smiled at him. "Your father made these, didn't he?"

Henry beamed with pride. "Ayup, he's good at dat kinda ting."

She tilted her head. Curious accent, almost German but mixed with a Western drawl. A nice combination, she decided. She liked Henry at once; this was their third conversation and already it was the longest.

"Ya' want to visit with the mares?" He nodded over his shoulder to indicate the horses inside the barn.

"Sure," she moved inside. It wasn't exactly why she had come down to the barn. But then she didn't really know why she came. She just liked being near the horses.

"Mr. Donovan said you might come down today."

"He did?" Cristeen was mildly surprised. It made her feel good to know someone anticipated what she would enjoy.

"Ya'. He said I should watch out for you."

"Oh? In what way?"

"Mr. Donovan says you get tired easy, what with dem crutches an' all. So I gotta watch for when you need to rest, an' be sure to find a comfortable place fer you to set." Henry was quite pleased to have remembered all these instructions, and proud to have been given the responsibility.

"Matt, I mean, Mr. Donovan told you all that?"

Cristeen was flattered that Matt cared enough to prepare for her to visit the barns. It gave her a sense of belonging, of security. Someone was watching out for her well being; taking care that she enjoyed her days. Moreover, she felt comfortable with Matt, with all of them. No one questioned her wanting to be near the horses. No one scorned her seeming lack of domestic tendencies. If housework wasn't her cup of tea, so be it.

She wondered how much of that was due to her still being treated as a guest rather than a member of the household. Matt always included her in discussions about the ranch, drawing out her opinions and ideas related to the cattle and the horses. But he did not ask for her input when it came time to make decisions.

She was becoming part of the family dynamic by the sheer fact of her presence. It was clear Katie enjoyed her company and friendship. And Ty continued to flirt with her at every opportunity. Even Paul was beginning to warm towards her. Matt was the one she couldn't quite read. He always treated her respectfully and with dignity. When she felt weak and vulnerable he was tender and kind. He asked questions that made her think, never pushing for the answers. Surely he must get angry; Katie spoke of arguments.

He still hadn't told her why he had stopped going to church. Katie had confided that fact to her while they were baking on Sunday. Two days had passed, and the subject lay dormant. It was just as well, for Cristeen wasn't sure what to tell him about her returning memories. Yet, the longer he waited the more curious she became. Silly, how we want what we don't have and covet even more what we can't have.

And he hadn't commented at all about her age. Did he think her an old spinster? Or, paradoxically was she too childish for her actual age? Probably it just didn't matter her age. She was just a guest under his roof, and each day brought her closer to the time she must leave. To go where? She sighed deeply. Where, oh where, that was the question she had been avoiding.

"Miss Cristeen?"

She realized Henry had been talking to her and she hadn't heard a word of what he said. "Hmmm?"

"Are you tired now? I fixed up a trunk against the wall out in da sunshine, for ya' to set down an' rest."

"Thank you, Henry. I would like that." He pointed to a large wooden trunk, on top of which he had placed enough hay to make the seat soft. "Would you sit with me a spell?"

He seemed happy to have been asked. With a glance at the stalls and the manure fork, he shrugged and sat beside her. "Guess it won't be no harm if'n I take a short rest."

"No, no harm," she reassured him. "You're just watching out for me like Mr. Donovan told you to."

His smile was genuine. After moment's pause, Cristeen asked, "Henry, don't you go to school?"

"Naw. I did when I was a young 'un. But Pa needs me to work, an' 'sides, the teacher up an' quit."

"No school for anyone?" She was incredulous. "How old are you?"

He puffed up his chest. "I'se eleven."

"Almost a man," she smiled. "Still, schooling is very important for a young man, if he wants to get ahead in life. Maybe have a ranch of his own one day."

She could see Henry did want a ranch of his own. He would need to learn so much about ranching itself.

Academics would be just as important as vocational training. Maybe she could contribute something to this outfit, after all.

"I could teach you some, Henry." He was surprised. "I went to school quite a bit when I was young. There are many things you need to know that you cannot learn on the range."

"Can you learn me to read good?" He barely contained his breathless excitement.

"I'm sure I can teach you to read well."

He looked down and kicked a clod of soil. "Reckon I ain't got time enough for dat."

They silently contemplated how to get around Henry's work schedule. Cristeen was fairly sure Matt would endorse her idea of teaching the boy. Henry, too, was becoming part of this family. And this family looked out for its own. Matt would want to give Henry every opportunity for advancement. He would also want the work done that Henry had been hired to do.

Standing still, Cristeen could balance and pivot her upper body. The concept crept into her brain; she could help clean the barns. And she could feed the mares, check on their well being. In fact, she suddenly realized she knew a good deal about horses. She could probably evaluate the health of each better than Henry, and maybe as well as Ty. With some practice and finesse, she could even turn the horses out into the paddocks.

Cristeen's heart beat faster. She was flush with her own excitement. She could collect eggs, scatter corn for the hens, and milk the cows. Well, maybe not milk the cows; she wasn't sure about sitting on such a low stool with one leg stretched out underneath the cow while milking. Standing again would be the trick. Perhaps milking was best left to Henry. After all, she couldn't do all his work. They would just share, freeing enough time for Cristeen to begin schooling Henry.

Henry was equally excited about the idea. How to present

it to Matt was the next question. "Leave that to me," Cristeen confidently told Henry. But as she crossed back to the house she wondered exactly how to go about this task. It would be unwise to trick him; perhaps as unwise was the thought of discussing it at dinner that night. She did not know how he liked to be approached on ranch business. Should she ease into the subject, or just blurt out her request?

She nibbled at a slice of beef by way of lunch. She had butterflies in her stomach. It was an odd feeling. Nevertheless she passionately believed her idea was right. Cristeen left Katie on the pretext of taking a nap.

Once in her room, she sat at the desk. Her room. That was indeed how it felt now. Looking around, she took in the wall-paper with it's rich tapestry of mauve roses and gold ribbon; the oval braided rug that kept her feet warm when she got out of bed. The heavy mahogany furniture with brass drawer pulls. The dainty if practical pitcher and basin sitting on the dresser. The bed quilt that bore the loving touches of a mother. All the qualities that made this room feel like home.

On the desktop the Bible lay invitingly. Matt's mother's Bible. Cristeen had been reading through the chapters and the handwritten notes along the margins. Mary Donovan had been a devoted Christian, a loving wife and mother. It showed in her notes. Someday, Cristeen would get up the courage to ask Katie, or maybe even Matt, about Mary Donovan. Until then, she was grateful to have this Bible to read from.

Beside the Bible lay her own book, the copy of *Oliver Twist* with the loving inscription on the inside cover. Who was this father who had given her a book she apparently cherished? She could remember reading the book, and so many others. She recalled diligently working at her own schoolwork and also helping someone else. Who?

TWELVE

It had been a long day and Matt was tired. Tired and hungry; what he wanted most right now was a hot meal and some sleep. They spent the past two days cutting the yearlings from the herd, bunching them in a makeshift corral. Several stray steers had been spotted meandering the eastern slopes; they needed to be rounded up as well. All in preparation to trail the yearlings to spring pasture.

Highland cattle are usually quite tractable. Yearlings can be like a breed unto themselves; rebellious, defiant, and resistant to leadership. The very characteristics that made the Highland breed so attractive for a mountain ranch became a detractor with yearlings. Thickets of thorny shrubs would be effective fencing for another breed. To the Highlander a thicket was simply a source of food; they ate the tender new leaves then pressed on by, moving ever onward.

The three men had worked hard to bring back these stray cattle, before they crested the hillside and headed down onto the Montigny spread. They wouldn't be the first Donovan cattle to make it to Montigny land. Nor was it uncommon to find the Montigny running M brand mixing with the Donovan herd. The Montignys were good neighbors and Matt wanted to keep it that way.

It was coming on twilight. Matt led his horse into the dark shadows of the barn. Ty went before him, Paul followed behind. Silently each man went about caring for his mount.

Matt stripped the saddle off Gid and gave the buckskin a brief sackcloth rubdown. The horse nudged him as he paused by the stall door; Gideon was impatient for his supper.

"Patience, Gid." Matt gave the gelding an affectionate thump on the neck. He poured a scoop of grain into the feed bucket and received a soft nicker as thanks.

April was drawing to a close. The day had been warm, the evening promised to continue the trend. Long shadows stretched across the park as the sun finished its descent behind the great mountains. A soft breeze played with Matt's hair as he slowly crossed the yard. Paul and Ty had already reached the porch when Matt began his trek across the open expanse. Deep in thought, his stride was a slow amble.

The young steers were making a break for greener pastures. It was past time to trail them up to the higher meadows where the grass would be plentiful. The newborns needed a few more weeks yet before tagging along with their mothers to the high green valley that was their summer home.

Matt glanced off towards the fenced meadow where the first calf heifers were bedded. In the dusk he could barely make out the dark forms of cattle. All the heifers had calved; it was time for them to rejoin the older cows. The three of them could drive the heifers down the valley, then trail the yearlings out to spring pasture. Starting at first light tomorrow they could be back in time for church on Sunday.

Church. The thought elicited a heavy sigh from Matt. He removed his hat and ran a hand through his hair, as if trying to stimulate his brain. He still owed Cristeen the explanation he had promised about his lack of church attendance. He did want to tell her, needed for her to hear the story. If he could only explain it in such a way that she saw the importance of turning to God, of putting her trust in Him.

Twice now she had demonstrated that she at least in principal believed in the Lord. But she did not trust the Lord. By definition belief and trust went hand in hand. To believe means to have confidence, to trust. And trust means to believe. Cristeen could not truly believe until she could trust.

He needed her to truly believe. It would be the key to her absolute healing. Moreover, the idea that an evil lie in wait for Cristeen had settled firmly in Matt's mind. When she left this valley she would need the protection that only God could provide. Matt could not in good conscience let her go without knowing she had a place set aside in the kingdom of Heaven. If she stayed...he needed her to believe.

Light spilled out the kitchen window. Matt could see Katie moving about the room as he stepped up onto the porch. Opening the door brought a wave of warm aromas washing over him: the sweet odor of fresh baked bread, the sharp bite of fried onions, and the mouth-watering smell of cooking steaks. How wonderful to return home at the end of the workday to a house filled with such delicious scents.

Katie stepped quickly from the table to the stove, rapping her wooden spoon across Paul's knuckles. "Git," she scolded him as he attempted to sneak onions from the pan. Paul retaliated by kissing her; she laughed.

Cristeen balanced on her crutches as she set the table. Ty dried his hands and moved to her side, a moth drawn to the flame. He flirted incessantly, much to her delight. She laughed lightly at something he said.

Matt took in the scene dreamily. This was his family. When his father passed away, Matt donned the mantle of leadership easily. He had been prepared, groomed, trained to step into his father's shoes. In the ten years since he had given it very little thought. Tonight he saw the gift he had been given; the warmth of happiness and love filled his home.

This was why Paul was anxious to marry Katie. To have a family of his own. When that happened, Matt's family would be forever changed. In just a few short months this house would be a dark, cold, odorless building to which he returned each night. He really should hire a housekeeper;

maybe he could get her to bake bread now and then just to have the aroma to come home to.

"Don't you ever want to marry? To share your home and your life with someone?" Katie's words echoed in his mind. He turned his back on the room to hang his hat beside the door. Yes, he did want to get married someday. Not to someone who could cook for him and clean his house. For that he could hire a housekeeper. He wanted someone to share his life, and that meant a woman who could love this ranch as much as he did. Aside from his own sister, he had come to believe that woman did not exist.

"As soon as Matt is ready, we can eat." Katie's statement cut through Matt's thoughts, bringing him back to the present.

Matt threw a quick smile over his shoulder at his sister, moving to wash up before dinner. When he again looked at his family, they were seated around the small table waiting for him. Ty sat at Cristeen's side; he said something that caused her to laugh. Matt caught her eye, a rosy blush crept up her cheeks but she held his gaze. The laughter stayed in her eyes.

The talk during the meal was of moving the herd. Matt contemplated aloud whether Henry should go with them. Cristeen sat quietly, offering no opinion one way or the other. More than once he started to ask her what she thought of his plans, but stopped short. Although she was becoming part of the family group, she still viewed herself as just a guest. Asking her opinion might make her uncomfortable.

As the dishes were cleared, he noticed Katie nudge Cristeen several times. Cristeen would swat at Katie, much as one swats at a pesky fly. Finally Katie hissed, "Now, Cristeen! Ask to talk with him in private."

Try as he might, Matt could not entirely hide the fact he heard the command. Cristeen seemed extremely nervous, · not looking at him as she requested a private audience. Her request stopped Paul and Ty in their tracks, increasing her tension.

Matt was as curious as she was nervous. "Library good enough?" She nodded and followed him down the hall.

He sat and waited for her to begin. Cristeen paced, in a manner of speaking, as much as a person can on crutches. After a moment she perched on the edge of the window seat and toyed with her sleeve cuff as she spoke.

"First, I want you to know that I would never presume to undermine your authority or question the way you run your ranch."

Interesting start, Matt thought. Where could she possibly be going with a beginning like that? He let her continue.

"I was talking with Henry today," she glanced up briefly, adding, "and don't think any of this was his idea. He's a great kid and a hard worker."

Matt smiled and nodded. Cristeen took a deep breath and plunged in. "I think he should be getting some schooling. Henry tells me the teacher quit, and he needs to work. I thought that I could teach him, at least some things, so he would have a chance to get ahead in life."

Matt leaned forward, putting his elbows on his knees. He wrapped his right hand around the fist of his left, then rested his chin there. "Well, the idea has some merit." She smiled tentatively. "What about his work. As you said, he is a hard worker and I have come to rely on him."

Here's the tricky part, Cristeen thought. "I could help him with his work." Seeing a protest forming, she rushed on. "I can collect eggs, feed the mares, and help clean in the barns. I can milk, but I haven't figured out how to position this leg."

Matt chuckled. *He hates the idea,* Cristeen groaned inwardly. *Hates it and thinks I'm silly to have even thought it.*

"I'm not laughing at you, stop looking so upset."

"You aren't? Then why are you laughing?"

"You've thought of everything. How long have you been hatching this plan?" He sat up and smiled broadly.

"Just today. Are you angry?"

"At what? That you care enough about someone else to try to help?" She cocked her head to the side in question. "I too would like Henry to get some schooling. It was something I'd pushed to a back burner. So you are presenting me with a solution to a problem."

She liked being part of the solution and not the problem. His next words caught her by surprise. "What makes you think you are qualified to teach him? Not to say you aren't a very intelligent lady. Teaching is more than just knowing facts."

Teaching was not the facet of the plan she had anticipated him to balk at. Feeding the animals, working around the horses, these were the aspects she had been prepared to argue for. She had given no thought whatsoever to her qualifications, or lack thereof, to teach Henry. Looking the issue squarely in the face now, Cristeen simply knew she could do this.

"I just know. I can't explain it anymore than that."

Matt nodded. "Maybe you were a school teacher."

Why do I gotta learn this stuff? A vaguely familiar voice whined in her memory. "I don't think so," she mused. "Although I seem to remember helping someone else with school work."

She gave herself a mental shake. "Perhaps teaching Henry will allow me to learn."

"About yourself." He finished the thought. "Perhaps. I believe you are qualified to teach him. However, I'm not quite so comfortable with the idea of your working in the barns."

"Oh please say yes," her well thought out arguments evaporated in a moment of desperation. "I really want to do something to help out around here."

Matt rose and moved to the open doorway between the library and parlor. He could just make out the photographs on the mantle; he did not need any lamplight to see them in his mind's eye. Every detail of his mother's face was etched in his memory. He felt her smiling at him across the dark room.

For a moment Cristeen thought Matt was leaving the room, walking out on the discussion. She felt confused; he said he wasn't angry but she saw how his jaw tensed as she made her last plea. His approval was paramount. This ranch belonged to Matt; he was the one who ultimately paid the price for a bad decision.

"I can't teach Henry any other way. He has to help out at home in the afternoons." Her voice grew softer. "That said if you don't want me working out there, then I won't. I will not go against your decision."

Cristeen was giving in, just like his mother had always capitulated to his father's wishes. Matt fought against the anger burning within him. The feeling of injustice was childish; Mary and Peter Donovan had a deep and abiding love for one another. For the sake of that love, Mary had given up the material trappings of wealth for a dirty, dusty life as a rancher's wife. It was a place she did not love and a way of life she only endured. Yet she cherished the people of the West.

If only his mother had stood up for her own wishes. Peter would have stayed in the East with her. *But then Father would have merely endured his life.* Neither choice seemed fair, and Matt long ago reconciled himself to the fact it was not his to decide if Mother made the right choices. Especially considering had she chosen differently he might very well not be here to wonder.

Cristeen should not back down so easily. Frankly he worried about her low self-esteem. Left to her own devices she seemed confident enough to do anything, including climbing the staircase against his better judgment. But when faced with a human obstacle she seemed prone to retreat. His anger was not going to help, particularly when she had nothing to do with its cause.

Matt curbed his anger as he spoke, although he did not
yet turn to face her. "I never said you couldn't teach Henry."
Cristeen exhaled loudly. "I just don't want you to get hurt,
again."

"How could I possibly get hurt?"

Slowly he turned to look at Cristeen. Her expression of
genuine bewilderment caused him to chuckle. "Could it be
that you have forgotten about your broken leg?"

"Oh, that." She waved her hand in dismissal. "I can do
so much still."

"Yes," Matt conceded. "Yes you can." He sat in the chair
across from her. "I'll be honest, Cristeen. I've been wanting
to bring Henry on full time, and this could just be the incen-
tive to convince his parents to allow it."

"I don't understand."

"Henry works to help put food on the family table. If he
hired on full time I could pay him more without insulting his
Pa."

"I understand," Cristeen smiled. "And then I'd have
more time to teach him."

Matt laughed. "I misjudged you. There's no back-down
in you, is there?"

She considered that a moment. "I suppose that's one way
to put it. I just really want to do something useful."

"Are you absolutely sure you want to pitch in out there?"

"Positive. It's where I feel the most," she searched for
the right words. "Comfortable doesn't seem to cover it. It's
more like being at home."

"You come from a ranching background." Matt had suspected it for some time; this seemed to confirm it.

Cristeen sighed deeply as she resumed picking at her
cuff. "I'm not that simple."

"Exactly what is that supposed to mean?"

Matt looked offended. "No, no," Cristeen rushed to
explain. "I didn't mean to imply ranchers are ignorant. I meant

my past is more complicated. I have lived in many places."

"You remember?"

"Not really."

One minute of quiet stretched into two. Matt tried to wait patiently for further explanation. When none seemed to follow he finally broke. "Well, are you going to explain?"

Cristeen shrugged. "I can't."

"Try, please."

He sounded like he really wanted to know. Like he might understand. She looked into his eyes, seeing kindness and empathy.

"I remember bits and pieces. Winters in Massachusetts, the fast paced hustle of Chicago, and cattle grazing on a flat expanse that stretched all the way to the horizon." She began to twirl the Celtic cross. "Memories of feelings hit me at odd times."

"Do you mean you remember getting hurt?"

"Sometimes. Oh, not the gunshot." Matt's brow creased in puzzlement. "For instance, one night I dreamed that everyone I have ever known just went away."

"I should think abandonment would be a natural feeling given your situation."

"Then explain this. As I watched the horses pulling the buckboard Sunday, I was overwhelmed with heartache. I miss being around horses, working with them, riding."

Using the crutches Cristeen pushed herself up and again paced about the room. Matt remained silent; a quick glance showed his empathy was still there. She was grateful he could be patient as she struggled through her explanation.

"Everything I do with Katie feels, novel. There is no sensation of having ever done household tasks. At least not regularly."

"Not even making a pie?"

"My first."

"You're a natural."

"Thank you," his approval felt good. "The first time I went into the barn it all felt somehow familiar."

"Ty said the mares took to you, too."

"I don't understand this feeling." She returned to the window seat. "I just know I know horses."

"Like you know teaching."

"Yes, exactly." Cristeen felt a great weight lifted from her. She had finally verbalized what had been eating at her. Moreover, Matt seemed to understand.

Matt studied Cristeen a moment. Relief showed in her eyes. "I think you should begin teaching Henry and doing some light work in the barns." He stressed light. "Perhaps it will help you to truly remember."

"Thank you," she whispered.

"You do realize you just called my bluff. Again."

He liked the way her mouth contorted as she tried to grasp his meaning. And the slow shake of her head was a small victory in this game of words they shared.

"I said that if I answered your question about church, you would have to tell me what you've been remembering."

"Ah ha! You have to answer me now."

"Will you accept my promise to tell you later?"

"That depends on how much later."

"Saturday."

She gave a low whistle. "Must be quite a story if it takes all week to work up to."

Matt laughed. "Well, as a matter of fact, it is. But that's not why I'm putting you off that long."

"Explain."

"I'm not ready tonight. And I won't be back 'til Saturday."

"Back?"

"We're trailing the yearlings..."

"To spring pasture." She completed the statement. "When do you leave?"

"First light," on a whim he added, "will you miss me?"

"Yes." Cristeen was startled by the sincerity of her answer. To cover she quipped, "Now who can I bother with questions about the meaning of life?"

Matt was also startled by Cristeen's positive answer. He laughed at her question, as much at the humor as to move the conversation onto a safer plateau. "Ask me something that philosophic in the morning and I'll give you a nonsensical answer."

"Promise?"

THIRTEEN

It is held by some that Irish fairies, the daoine sidhe, are fallen angels not bad enough to be lost nor yet good enough to be saved. Ever creatures of whim, fairies are in general good to the good and bring evil to the evil. They are capricious and quickly offended, therefore one must not speak of them as anything less than gentry. As the people they once were, the daoine sidhe spend much of their time with feasting, dancing, and merriment. And, oh the ceol-sidhe, the fairy music; in our dreams alone can we go amongst the fairies and dance to their beautiful music.

In the soft light of the late afternoon sun it was of this ceol-sidhe Cristeen dreamed. She watched through half opened eyes as dust motes floating in the beams of light took on the forms of seventeenth century royal court dancers. The ladies in extravagant gowns that billowed out from their waists and whirled around their legs as they pirouetted across the dance floor. They were accompanied by gentlemen in equally elegant garb of lace and ruffled waistcoats in satin and taffeta. These tiny dancers twirled about the room in a minuet.

A smile tugged at Cristeen's lips. She was still not quite awake yet aware enough to realize it was a trick of the mind that made the dancers appear before her. She was floating in that place between dreaming and wakefulness, a part of her longing to join the dance. When she closed her eyes she could hear the piano music and more clearly see the marcra sidhe, the fairy cavalcade.

Stories of fairies, elves, and princesses were the fodder of Cristeen's childhood imagination. Her mother, born and raised in Ireland, loved to pass on the traditional stories of her homeland. Tales of magical, mystical times and deeds, when everything was possible, love conquered all, and good always overcame evil in due time.

Mother, such a powerful and potent word. It evoked in Cristeen feelings of love, security, warmth, and tenderness. Images of a beautiful, lithe woman sprang into her mind. Memories of being held in her mother's arms, or rocking on her mother's lap.

Cristeen's memory was returning. Like a child's jack in the box, emotions and images popped into her thoughts at random and when she least expected them. The flashes of memory were occurring with more frequency over the past three days. To some extent more predictably as well. The images and memories began to make lasting impressions. They were like puzzle pieces finally fitting into place and creating a recognizable picture.

Remembering did help ease some of her anxieties. Along with the tender, happy memories came the unwanted, long suppressed feelings of sorrow, hurt, and disconcerting self-consciousness. Nonetheless Cristeen accepted the bad with the good with a happy heart. Whatever painful memories arose, she had lived through it once and she'd get through it again.

The music stopped; the dancers became dust motes once again. Cristeen was fully awake and only reality filled the room now. Disoriented by sleepiness, she glanced around. There were the floor to ceiling bookcases; the sunlight fell in a straight path across the polished hardwood floor, as though directing one to a secret treasure. The sun's warmth caressed Cristeen's face. She had fallen asleep at the window seat in the library, her back nestled into the angle created by the window and a bookshelf. As she sat up, knotted neck muscles reproved her choice of napping places. The book she had been reading slid to the floor.

Footsteps quickly crossed the adjoining room, accompanied by a rapid swish-swish. Katie slid open the paneled door dividing the library and parlor. Concern wrinkled her face.

"Cristeen? I thought you were upstairs. Did the music wake you?"

"You heard it too?" Cristeen was incredulous.

"Of course. I was playing it." Katie looked closely at her. "Did you think you dreamed it?"

"Yes."

Katie smiled broadly. "Well I hope it helped you have pleasant dreams."

Cristeen wasn't quite ready to share all her memories. They were part of what made her who she was and she was reluctant to bare her soul just yet. Moreover, though the events and people she remembered were from long ago they were as new again to her. For just a while she wished to savor them, keep them selfishly to herself like a child with a new toy. Still, the memories made her whole once more and she did desire to ease Katie's concerns.

"I liked the music. It reminded me of my mother."

"You remember? Oh, Cristeen, how wonderful!"

A frown flickered across Cristeen's face. "Yes, I suppose it is good."

For indeed the memories were bittersweet. Sitting on her mother's lap, gently rocking, a cooling summer breeze whisping at the curtains, and listening to her mother's melodious voice retelling a favorite fairy princess tale. Remembrances of a love that wrapped Cristeen like a cocoon, filling her with a sense of safety and contentment. With these sweet memories came, unbidden and unwanted, the vivid memory of watching the doctor pull the sheet over her mother's still and lifeless body. And other grief ridden memories.

Katie was at her side. "Some of your memories are less than pleasant? Our pain defines who we are as much as our joys. It is only the sudden return of those memories that makes them quite so painful."

"Don't forget," Katie continued, "that no matter how unbearable they seem right now, you got through it once and you will again."

Cristeen smiled weakly. "Yes, and this time I'll have help."

Katie gave her friend a quick hug. "Is it memories of your mother that makes you so melancholic?"

"Both of my parents."

"Are you an orphan?"

"No, not really. My mother died when I was seven. My father," she searched for the right description. "Well, he became someone else."

"Grief can do that."

Cristeen did not respond. Instead she turned her head to watch the sun finish its long slide behind the mountains. As a young girl she had gazed longingly at the peaks of the Berkshire Mountains. Those were like mere foothills compared to these rocky heights.

Katie respectfully let the quiet continue. Just another reason for Cristeen to be thankful to have found such a good friend.

"Whatever did I do to deserve you?" Cristeen asked softly, turning a smiling countenance to Katie. "I mean all of you, but most particularly you and Matt."

"Maybe the Lord knew you needed some good friends."

"Perhaps. I certainly wasn't doing too well on my own." She considered a moment before continuing. "Have you always believed in God?"

"Yes," Katie's smile reflected warm happy memories.

"When I was little it was Mother who taught me the Bible."

"Your mother had a strong faith." Katie smiled in agreement. "I could tell from her Bible."

Cristeen turned her gaze once more to the mountain view. "When did she pass away?"

When Katie did not answer, Cristeen looked to see her eyes filled with tears. "Oh, I am sorry Katie. It's too painful for you. Of all people I should have known better."

"I miss her."

Cristeen let the silence stretch out, waiting for Katie to choose when to continue.

"She died a little over a year ago. She had been sick for a long time."

"You don't have to talk about her if it hurts."

"I want to. I can talk to Paul, of course, but I try not to talk too much about Mother. I don't want him to worry about me."

She paused, contemplating her next words. "I really need to talk to someone, though. Matt, well, he doesn't want to talk about Mother."

"You can talk to me, Katie. It's the least I can do, listen I mean."

Katie smiled. "I have this theory, you see, that Mother actually became ill when Father died. She loved him so much. When he died she could have gone back East, but by then she had become accustomed to western life. Plus, I think being here let her feel close to him still, like he wasn't really gone."

"Your father loved the ranch?"

"He loved this land, these mountains," she made a sweeping gesture at the view. "Without Father, though, it was hard on her. I was young but I helped whenever and wherever I could. And of course there was Ty; seems like he's always been here."

"Where was Matt?"

"Virginia, at college. He wanted to come home, quit

school. Mother wouldn't hear of it."

"Why?"

Katie rose and lit the lamps. After adjusting the wick in the second lamp, she explained. "Matt going back East to college was a compromise between my parents. Father always planned for Matt to take over the ranch and he taught him everything he knew."

"Mother dreamed of Matt becoming governor," Katie chuckled. "Maybe every mother has that dream for their sons."

"But why Virginia?"

"I think she secretly hoped he would fall in love with Virginia. That's where my mother was from. Mother never really liked the idea of Matt taking over here. She wanted him to have an easier life than what she perceived my father's to be."

"What about you?"

"I was only twelve when Father died. Maybe she dreamed I would meet a successful businessman and move to some place cultural, but not too far away." She gave Cristeen the look of a child patronizing a parent. Cristeen giggled. "Thankfully, by the time I met Paul, Mother had come to understand that I, too, love this ranch."

"Anyway, when Father died some of Mother's vivacity died too. When Matt graduated he came home to stay. She seemed resigned to his decision, yet not long after her health began to decline."

Cristeen stared at her hands, imagining how Mary Donovan felt when she lost her husband. And how saddened she must have been to realize her dreams for her children were for naught. The lady died heartbroken.

"Matt blames himself for breaking her heart," Cristeen whispered without realizing she spoke aloud.

"What?" Katie was incredulous. "Did he tell you that?"

"No," Cristeen turned away from Katie's scrutiny. *I've*

136

overstepped my bounds. What do I know about him to make that judgment? Yet she knew in her heart it was the truth. Matt cared deeply for his family, maybe too deeply. Their interests and well being came before his. She had seen that in the way he treated his sister, the way he let her believe his life would not change when she married Paul.

Cristeen could feel Katie's eyes on her, as if trying to see into her very soul. The hairs on the back of her neck prickled with unease. *Why doesn't she say something? Tell me what a ridiculous idea, that Matt would think that. And how foolish of me to think I could know a man's heart after only ten days of friendship.*

But Katie did not reproach Cristeen. Nor did she ridicule the insight. For at that moment Katie began to see her brother for who he truly was. She was aware that Matt spent a good deal of time talking with Cristeen. Almost every evening it seemed he found time to chat with their houseguest. Until now she had thought he was being polite, charming but polite. She had no idea what the two discussed, although there were times she overheard them laughing together. And of course she had heard about Cristeen's challenge for Matt to give his reasons for not attending church.

Come to think of that, Matt had not become angry at the challenge. Many an argument between Katie and her brother was ended by Matt simply walking away. Yet he had not walked away from Cristeen even though it was a very sore subject. She realized Matt did want to talk about certain topics just not with his sister.

This revelation of a tender, thoughtful brother surprised Katie. He had always been kind to her, in a gruff big brother manner. He kept his emotions tightly checked, leaning on Paul's impish sense of humor to keep family gatherings lighthearted. So why had he suddenly opened up to a complete stranger?

Who was Cristeen?

Agonizingly long minutes passed. Cristeen desperately wanted to flee, but her handicapped leg prevented her. At last she could withstand the stare no longer.

"Please don't be angry with me."

"Cristeen, how could I be angry?"

"Offended?"

"By what? You saw what was there all along but I was too close to see. No, I am not angry nor offended. I am thankful that you have shown me the truth about my brother."

Cristeen chewed at her lower lip. As was her habit when nervous, she began to twirl the Celtic cross. "Will he be angry?"

"Not if we don't tell him." Katie laughed. "Maybe he'll be relieved that I know the truth and he didn't have say a word."

Cristeen's head sank. "I don't think he'll be happy. He's quite private."

"Now that's something I already know."

The lightness in her tone made Cristeen glance sidelong at her. She was grinning. Cristeen began to relax, though she was still somewhat concerned. Katie would act differently, or say something that revealed her knowledge of Matt's feelings of guilt. The very last thing Cristeen wanted was to lose Matt's friendship. That fear also caused worry; more often than not in her life she lost that which was important to her.

Katie placed a comforting hand on Cristeen's arm. "He doesn't stay angry long, Cristeen. I have a sneaking suspicion Matt will forgive you far quicker than he would me."

A tentative smile played with Cristeen's lips. She glanced up, meeting Katie's eyes. Light danced in them,. *Just like Matt's eyes when he smiles,* the comparison sprang into Cristeen's thoughts. She felt the warmth of a blush creep up her cheeks.

Katie rose. "Come, Cristeen, let's have a light supper

while we finish this chat."

As they moved down the shadowy hallway, Katie spoke over her shoulder. "You know, I've always wanted a sister. But I was stuck with a brother. Maybe as my wedding gift Matt should give me my wish."

"A sister? Is your brother some sort of a wizard and you've been keeping it a secret?"

Katie snickered. "Don't be silly. I may not be able to have a real sister, but I could have a sister-in-law."

They reached the kitchen. "So you're trying to marry off your brother in a purely selfish move? Shameful."

"Not entirely selfish." Katie dished stew into bowls. "Someone has to take care of him when I've moved out."

Cristeen began slicing the bread. Katie's words were far from subtle, and the bread knife far from dull. Cristeen jumped back as she accidentally drew the blade across the end of her thumb. Instinctively she put her thumb in her mouth, even as she windmilled her other arm to catch her balance. Katie stepped in to assist. Her thumb was barely cut and the bleeding stopped quickly.

"In case you are hatching any grand plans," Cristeen smirked. "Count me out. I can't even seem to take care of myself these days."

"Matt seems to enjoy taking care of you. Keeps him out of trouble, too."

Cristeen, you really must learn to stop blushing. You are only encouraging her, not that it is an unpleasant topic of conversation. Cristeen snorted at herself and Katie took that to be a reply. This conversation was pushing Cristeen out of her comfort zone. Something had to be said to halt Katie's apparent line of thought.

"Katie," Cristeen plunked herself down on the hard wooden chair. "I enjoy your brother's friendship, and I hope he reciprocates the sentiment. Friendship, Katie. That's all, nothing more."

Katie's eyes narrowed and for a moment Cristeen feared she had finally said the wrong thing. Then Katie smiled smugly, as if she knew something no one else did.

"Can't blame me for trying," she said. "If I have learned anything from my brother, it is knowing when to end a discussion. Pick a subject, Cristeen, and I promise not to chase you off the way I do Matt."

Much later Cristeen found herself lying awake, utterly unable to sleep. She stared at the embers in the fireplace, recalling the conversation of earlier. She did enjoy the friendship she had with Matt. And a small part of her dared hope that perhaps he could be interested in more. The logical part of her ridiculed the idea. She was little more than the poor waif Sarah had called her. She had lived in so many different places she couldn't say where she was truly from. There was no family heritage to which she could lay claim. She didn't even have any skills useful to making her way in society. The most promising future Cristeen could hope for was to find a secluded mountain valley, far from civilization, where she could live off the land. By herself. Alone.

She missed Matt.

FOURTEEN

M att trotted across the expanse between the barns and the house. Behind him, Ty's watchful eyes went unnoticed. Ty turned back to the horses as Matt reached the porch steps. It was the first time in his long memory that the boy had been in a hurry to return home from the highland pastures. Matt's distraction had become blaring clear to both Ty and Paul over the course of the drive, though neither said a word to him about it.

Matt took the porch steps in one stride. He was unaware of how apparent his preoccupation was to his friends. However, he did recognize the difference in his thoughts and feelings during this trail drive. At first it started with the calves frolicking as they drove the small herd down valley. *There's a sight that would get a giggle out of Cristeen.* From there the list grew of things Cristeen would enjoy, or sights he would like to show her. Yet it wasn't until sometime during the second day when he realized what he was doing.

For the first time in his life, Matt had been impatient for the drive to be over. So that he could get home. At last he understood how Paul had chafed all those times Matt found excuses to stay out in the mountains longer. Poor Paul. If this was how much Paul missed Katie, Matt was a heel for keeping them away so long.

Henry sat at the table in the kitchen, studiously applying

himself to a writing task. As Matt stepped inside, Henry glanced up and grinned.

"Hi, Mr. Donovan. Da women vill be right glad y'all is back."

"It's good to be back, Henry. What're you doing there?"

"Miss Cristeen vants me to practice my readin' an' writin'. See, I'se gettin' real good." Henry proudly displayed the writing tablet he had been laboring over.

Across the top of the page spelled out in meticulously neat print were the words *reading* and *writing*. Henry had been copying each word, trying to faithfully reproduce the clarity of Cristeen's handwriting. The last pair of words he had written were a close proximation, at least clear and easily recognizable.

"Very good, Henry." The boy beamed at Matt's praise. "Where is Miss Cristeen now?"

Before Henry could answer, Cristeen called from down the hall. "Henry, could you please come help me? I can't quite reach that book."

Matt stopped Henry when the boy began to rise. "I'll go. You keep practicing."

Cristeen stood with her back to the door, glaring at the desired book as if condemning it for being placed too high. Matt leaned a shoulder against the doorframe and watched her for a moment. She glanced at the chair beside her, then back again at the book shelf. Matt could almost hear her thought process; move the chair closer to the shelf so that standing on it she might reach the book herself. He couldn't help but smile at her determined independence. When she actually moved as if to pull the chair, his smile disappeared.

"Don't you dare," he chastised. "You could get seriously hurt."

Cristeen jumped with alarm, spinning around quickly at the sound of his voice. He was crossing the room, intent on stopping her from standing on the chair. As she focused on his face, she took a step back. In her fright the crutches were forgotten and she began to fall. Matt caught her and carefully helped her to sit in the previously offending chair.

For a moment Cristeen clenched her eyes, her breaths coming in short gasps. Matt feared she had re-injured her leg. He hovered close, waiting for her to open her eyes and let him know she was alright. He was caught completely off guard when her eyes opened and she slapped him. Luck alone put him in the position that her flat palm smacked soundly against his chest

"You scared me!" This time she thumped his chest lightly with the side of her fist. The move was followed with a fit of giggles.

Confused, Matt remained motionless. Was she still scared, and this was hysterical laughter? Or was she truly angry? Tears rolled down her reddened cheeks.

"Cristeen?" He asked tentatively.

"Oh, I'm sorry," she gasped. Another deep gulp of air finally stopped the giggling. "I was so focused and your voice startled me. Then I couldn't for the life of me figure out who you were."

"Didn't know, oh, the beard." Matt sank into the other chair, stroking his chin and laughing. After a moment of shared merriment he said, "The first thing Katie will say is go shave."

Cristeen giggle again. "I'll bet you won't, at least not for a few days."

His eyes danced. "Not for a few weeks."

"Oh Matt, you are cruel."

He rubbed the stubble on his cheek. "It's hardly a beard with only three days growth. And she's so much fun to rile."

"Let it grow, then." She cocked her head. "Besides, it looks rather nice on you."

"Katie won't be happy. Especially that you chose my

side."

Cristeen flushed. "She owes me."

Now what's that about? Matt wondered. Cristeen was obviously uncomfortable as an awkward silence was developing. *Something has changed.* He let it go for now, choosing instead to put Cristeen at ease.

"Which book were you trying to get?" He moved to the set of shelves she had been eyeing.

"*A Christmas Carol.*" Matt pulled the book from amongst the other Charles Dickens works. Cristeen sighed. "Sure, make it look easy."

She was smiling. Even so Matt could hear the frustration edging her voice. After nearly four weeks handicapped with her broken leg, Cristeen was growing impatient. He wondered how she dealt with such anxiety; would she get cranky or would she withdraw?

"Growing weary of your handicap?"

She shrugged. "It is unwise to look a gift horse in the mouth."

"You are anxious to be able to do for yourself."

Her eyes flashed with defiance, "I can do for myself. But it would be nice to walk unassisted. And reach a book barely above my head."

"Cristeen, I had to stretch for the book. You were not going to get this down without climbing a ladder."

"Yes, well, be that as it may, neither can I climb a ladder. In the meantime, I have a student to teach."

Matt helped her up. "Let me walk you to class, Miss Cristeen. And I'll even carry your books."

The dimple in Cristeen's cheek deepened and her eyes crinkled with her smile. "How gallant of you, Mr. Donovan." After a moment of thought she added, "You know, I don't think anyone has ever carried my books for me."

"Really? A pretty girl like you, and none of the boys offered to carry your books?"

"I was different." There seemed to be more to that statement, but she did not elaborate. "Do you mean that?"

"What?" Realizing Cristeen had stopped, Matt turned to look back.

"You called me a pretty girl."

"I just figured you were a pretty girl at school age," he stepped closer, "because you are a beautiful woman now."

Cristeen felt her face grow hot. *Serves you right, fishing for that compliment.* Though disconcerting, the compliment sent a thrill of delight through her. Looking up into Matt's warm brown eyes, Cristeen felt hopelessly lost. She couldn't remember ever being unable to come up with a witty retort whenever necessary. Truly speechless she was, and becoming somewhat alarmed by these unfamiliar emotions. Those gentle eyes began to smile.

Matt was enjoying Cristeen's discomfiture, if only because of the rosy blush it brought about. There was a fine line between teasing and tormenting; Matt had no desire to cross that line.

"Have you nothing to say, no witty comeback?" He joshed softly. She shook her head slightly. "Do I get to claim victory this round?"

Cristeen lowered her eyes. "Is that why you said it?"

"I only say what I mean." He started once more for the kitchen. "You really must learn to trust me, Cristeen."

His lighthearted tone kept her from despair. With some difficulty she caught up to him and they entered the kitchen together. Matt set the book on the table and gave Henry a pat on the shoulder. The boy was still diligently writing; he grinned up at Matt.

"I must get back to work," Matt winked at Henry. "Miss Cristeen should also."

Cristeen watched Matt stroll jauntily across the yard. Slowly his last comment sank in; he had come to see her first upon returning home. A slow smile crept across her face.

You are lining yourself up for a world of hurt, girl. She chose to disregard the warning.

* * *

"Please tell me you are going to shave before church."

It was Katie's second such plea. The first had been answered only with a laugh. As Matt did this every spring, Katie accepted the laughter as tradition. Now she would demand a verbal response. Matt had an annoying habit of ignoring her whenever it fitted his convenience.

They were sitting around the table in the kitchen. Dinner was essentially over although none made a move to leave. For the men it was the good food and fresh coffee that held them fast. For Katie it was the company; she wondered if Cristeen felt the same or if the other woman stayed put simply because walking away was difficult. Watching the way Ty treated Cristeen like royalty convinced Katie that she stayed for the company. And more than once she had caught Cristeen furtively glancing at Matt.

"Matthew!" Katie spoke sternly. "I won't take that chuckle as my answer."

Matt glanced at Cristeen and grinned. "She must be serious now if she's using my full name."

"Poppycock," Katie fought to keep her cool, knowing her brother was trying to get her goat. "You want full name, I'll give you full name, Matthew..."

Matt cut her off. "Dirty pool, Katie!"

"...James Donovan." She finished with a smug look. Matt greatly disliked being addressed by both his first and middle names. Katie suspected it made him feel like a child, hence it became a powerful tool.

Matt groaned.

"Gotta answer her now, Mattie-boy." As per usual, Ty added to Katie's arsenal. "Are ye or ain't ye gonna shave."

"He's not." Cristeen answered for Matt.

A surprised hush came over the group. Katie stared long at Cristeen. Matt noticed the now familiar blush steal across Cristeen's face; she held Katie's gaze nonetheless. Katie addressed her friend, seemingly oblivious to the presence of the others.

"And why ever not?"

"Because he doesn't want to." Her chin jutted out defiantly. "Besides, he's rather handsome with a beard."

Paul coughed. Katie glared at him, as if he had committed a horrible offense. She saw the look that passed between her brother and Cristeen; Matt mouthed the word *touché*. Katie got the distinct feeling she was on a sinking ship.

"Well," Matt leaned back in his chair, savoring Katie's shocked expression. "I have always been out-numbered, what with Ty taking Katie's side in any argument. Naturally, Paul, I expect you'll agree with your fiancée."

Paul nodded. "Of course. Does seem to put us at an impasse, don't it. Two to two. So Ty, you gotta be the tie breaker." He chuckled at the pun.

Ty squirmed. "Ye cain't be aiskin' a man to choose like this."

"Choose, Old Man." Paul's grin was growing.

"There just be no way to choose betwixt the two most beautiful girls I have had the honor to know."

Cristeen grew redder at the compliment; Katie knew better. "Ty, you can't charm your way out of this. Whichever side you choose, I'll always love you."

"That tis the problem, Katherine dear." Ty contrived to look woeful. "Your love I am assured of. Cristeen, now she's not knowing me so well, nor I her. Cain't be so sure of her devotion."

Katie sighed. "You're siding with her, right?"

Ty nodded and Matt sprang from his chair. "I knew you would, Ty." He slapped the elder man good-naturedly on the back. "You're smitten."

"You'd be a wise man to leave that there word out o' yer vocabulary, boy."

"Ya', Matt." Paul added. "Ever hear the one about the pot calling the kettle black?"

Once again Cristeen came to Matt's rescue. "Oh my, look at the time. Let me help you clean these dishes, Katie."

She was up and moving to the dishpan before anyone could respond. "Would you men please help by bringing the plates over? And Ty, would you be a dear and fetch the kettle?" The last was said with a hint of humor.

The table was cleared, dishes washed and dried. Katie said very little. Just when Cristeen feared she had damaged their friendship, Katie grinned at her. When the last plate was put away, Ty gave each a kiss on the cheek before retiring to the bunkhouse.

"Yer both me favourite," he said with a wink as he left.

As the door closed, Katie turned to Cristeen. "Traitor," her smile softened the implication. "Did you mean it?"

Cristeen moved to the table, keeping her back to Katie. "Sure, I think Matt should keep the beard if he likes it."

"You know that's not what I was referring to."

"You mean the handsome part?"

"Don't pretend you don't know."

"What of it?"

Katie sat so she could look directly at Cristeen. "What happened to the just friends, nothing more attitude."

"I think Ty is adorable; doesn't mean I wanna marry him."

"You're exasperating!" Katie cradled her head between her hands. Without lifting her head, she looked at Cristeen. "Do you have any idea how much you and my brother are alike?"

"No." The impish look came into her eyes again. "His hair is a different color than mine. He's a mite taller than I. My eyes are not brown."

Katie groaned. "Never mind."

"I'm more pleasant in the morning."

"I said," she stopped. The jesting had left Cristeen's tone. "Yes, you are more pleasant in the morning."

"But Matt is more pleasant in the evening."

Katie considered that. "Perhaps. He is more pleasant in comparison to his bearish morning self."

Cristeen giggled. "Bear, good word. Covers all that growling."

As they descended the stairs, Matt and Paul heard the pair giggling.

"Now what do you suppose they are up to?" Matt asked naively.

Paul studied his friend for a moment. "You really have no idea, do you?"

"About what?"

Paul shook his head. "Nothing."

"Don't be so cryptic. I would like an explanation for that smug look."

"Not smug, just perceptive." Paul did his best to blank his expression. "Best for you to figure it out on your own."

Matt frowned. He did not enjoy being the butt of one of Paul's jokes. Paul was being serious, though, and that in itself was cause for concern. Pride further aggravated Matt's irritation; he liked to believe he had a handle on everything that went on around here. That he was in control. Now it seemed like everyone else was keeping a secret from him.

Paul chuckled. "Don't look so angry, Matt. You'll figure it out, sooner or later."

The laughter from the kitchen had stopped. "Paul, is that you?" Katie called.

"Ah, the sweetest voice calls." Paul thumped Matt on the back. "See, I caught on eventually. You will too."

Matt remained at the foot of the stairs while Paul trotted away. Yes, he would catch on. Quickly, too. He saw what

Paul was getting at, what Ty had implied earlier. Was he smitten with Cristeen? He enjoyed her company. It was nice to have someone to talk to who didn't lecture, criticize, or otherwise try to tell him how to lead his own life. Someone who actually listened to his ideas, even sought out his advice. With Cristeen he enjoyed an easy friendship.

Matt spun on his heels and retreated to his study. This room was where he went to think. Admittedly he also came here to escape, usually from Katie. He paced the open space in front of his desk. Tonight escape would not be possible, for it was from himself he would be fleeing.

Cristeen was a friend. With that he felt comfortable. *Paul is your friend, too, yet you don't miss him so deeply after only three and a half days apart.* So what was different? Perhaps it was simply that this friendship was still new. There was still that eagerness to learn all about his new acquaintance.

Matt stopped pacing and leaned his forearms along the mantle. He stared into the flames, remembering the very first night Cristeen spent under his roof. No, she was not just an acquaintance. Nor merely a friend, though he could not find the right word to define that extra step. He was not in love. Not yet, but that was what had him spooked. The more time he spent with Cristeen the more he realized how much she fitted his idea of a perfect wife.

What did he really know of her? *She's intelligent, witty, independent, persevering, loves horses, feels the pull of the mountains. She is caring, compassionate, intuitive, thoughtful, funny. And beautiful.* And still a complete mystery. For all he knew, she was a married woman.

The knock startled him. "Go away Katie."

"I'm not Katie, but I'll go away if that's what you want."

Cristeen. Great, he couldn't dismiss her. Nor was he ready to face her. *Dear Lord, if ever I needed your guidance now is the time!*

"I wanted to take a walk, if that's what you call it." She

snorted. "Katie said I shouldn't go out alone."

The question went unasked. Matt turned his eyes heavenward; strolling on a pleasant spring evening. In the concealment of darkness, he could handle a conversation with Cristeen.

FIFTEEN

"The breeze feels so soft," Cristeen spoke as softly. Matt leaned on the paddock fence, watching the shadowy forms of the horses as they moved across the meadow. He stole a glance at Cristeen; she too stared across the field. The moon was hiding behind a bank of clouds. Even in the dark he could sense her pensiveness. This wasn't a casual walk nor conversation.

"What's on your mind Cristeen?"

"Everything, nothing," she sighed. "Is my horse out there?" She pointed to the shadows coming closer. Now the hoof falls could be discerned.

Matt chuckled. "Yes. Can you tell which one?"

"It's too dark to pick out even such a light color as palomino."

"You remember?"

"Yes. But not everything makes sense yet."

"How much do you remember? When did your memories return?"

She giggled. "You're worse than Katie. Let's see, most of my life, and over the past three days. Did I answer sufficiently?"

"No." Cristeen looked sharply at him. "I want to know who you are, where you are from, what happened to you. But I'll wait until you are ready to tell me."

Cristeen breathed a sigh of relief. She wanted to tell

Matt everything, answer all his questions. Some answers she just did not know yet. Others she was afraid to give. Her life had been very complicated, it would not be easy to explain. Moreover, she knew now why she felt more at home in the barn than in the kitchen. Surely once she revealed that truth their friendship would begin to wither.

Ironically, not having friends taught Cristeen the value of friendship. A friend was more than just someone you knew. A friend could be trusted. Going through life never trusting anyone had worn Cristeen to exhaustion. She began to distrust even herself at times. Life was too short to go through it so miserably.

"I need to sit." Cristeen moved away from the fence line. Matt followed her to the trunk seat Henry had rigged up beside the barn.

"What's this?"

"Henry fixed me a spot in the sun, to rest whenever I'm down here." She plunked unceremoniously onto the seat.

"He did? That was rather thoughtful of him."

"You told him to watch out for me." Cristeen wriggled around to get comfortable then leaned back to gaze at the silver edge clouds. "Tell me about Virginia."

"Who?"

"Not who, where."

In the half-light it was hard to see her smile but Matt could hear it.

"Katie told me you went to college in Virginia. What's it like there? Do they have mountains?"

"Yes, and they are beautiful." He leaned against the barn. "I don't want to talk about me, I want to hear more about you."

"Tough. I want to talk about you."

"Are you accustomed to getting your way?"

Cristeen ducked her head. "It's easy enough, once you learn to ask for the right things."

The way she said it, subdued and meek, told Matt she was not a spoiled child. "What do you mean?"

She closed her eyes and sighed. The emotional turmoil of her childhood had molded her into a lonely adolescent. From it she had emerged a self-reliant, independent adult. How did she explain that without sounding morose?

"When my mother died, what I wanted more than anything was to have her back. I was too young then to understand the foolhardiness of that desire. I wasted a lot of time and energy wishing, and on the subsequent anger at not getting what I wanted." She paused, taking a shaky breath before continuing. "After a while I realized that I was asking for the impossible. I learned to ask for the probable, and so avoid the pain of denial."

The moon finally broke free of the clouds that had obscured its silvery beam. Cristeen returned to staring at the orb; it seemed to hang just beyond the reach of her fingertips. Matt searched her face; no trace of emotion revealed itself there. It was as if she were speaking philosophically about events unrelated to her life. Watching closely he at last detected her clenched jaw, saw the measured way in which she breathed.

"So you figured by asking for what you were likely to get anyway you would successfully get what you want."

"Getting what you ask for isn't necessarily the same as getting what you want."

Her lower lip trembled and she bit down on it. With the moon now lighting the night, Matt could see the tears glistening in Cristeen's eyes. This was more than just a little girl's wish to have her mother returned to life. He knew something about that kind of grief; this was deeper, more complicated. A quagmire of grief, anger, guilt, and hurt. It probably started with her mother's death, each destructive emotion building on the other. Until she shut out the world.

No wonder she was so fiercely independent. She wasn't

trying to prove anything to him, or anyone else for that matter. She simply could not risk needing someone. That would open her up to the endless possibilities of hurt. Matt closed his eyes and inwardly groaned. That she was letting him see this meant she was either beginning to trust him, or had not yet fully remembered to distrust. He hoped it was the former, but he had best be prepared to battle the latter.

Cristeen hugged her arms in an effort to stop her shivers. Matt sat down beside her. "I'm sorry you lost your mother."

"I'm sorry you lost your mother," she echoed back with sincerity. Her lip trembled as her teeth began to chatter.

"Won't you at least admit that you're cold?"

She shook her head in denial even while a smile fleetingly stopped her chattering teeth.

"Come here," Matt pulled her against him, wrapping an arm around her shoulders and rubbing her arm. Cristeen went still, for a few seconds even her breathing stopped. Gradually he felt her relax, her breathing returning to normal.

"Why aren't you cold?" There was just a hint of whining in her question.

"I just spent three nights sleeping out in this, remember. I'm just used to it."

"Oh, ya." Her teeth chattered.

"Time to go back to the house. Up you go," he pulled her onto her feet.

"I'll walk," she took the crutches from him when he would have carried her. "Thank you anyway."

Neither spoke as they crossed the yard. Inside, the stove still warmed the kitchen. Cristeen stood soaking in the heat. She was cold and tired. As the warmth seeped into her flesh she grew sleepy. But she fought it, stifling a yawn.

"Is my company dull?"

She glanced up quickly, unaware Matt had seen the yawn. "Of course not. I'm just a little tired is all."

"Early for you. You been working that hard these past

few days?"

"Harder than the previous three weeks," she smiled. "I just didn't get much sleep last night."

She ducked her head, but not before he saw the truth. "More bad dreams?"

She shrugged. "It's not that bad, really."

Matt cupped her chin, forcing her eyes to meet his. "Bad enough you aren't looking forward to sleeping tonight."

She dropped her eyes as Matt removed his hand. "I thought that remembering would take the fear away. Instead it worsens."

"I don't suppose you'd care to tell me about it?"

She shook her head. "Please don't be upset."

"I've had my share of bad dreams, Cristeen. Oh yes," he chuckled at her surprise. "You tell me about it when you feel up to it. I will give you this bit of advice, though. Telling someone takes away most of the fear."

He turned away from her, taking two mugs from a shelf. "Have some coffee and warm up. We can talk as late as you want."

"Here?" She pointed to the hard wooden chairs.

"No!" He nodded his head towards the hallway. "The parlor is much more comfortable."

Matt carried the coffee cups. Moon lit the house much as it did the landscape outdoors. Once in the parlor, Matt directed her to sit on the sofa. After lighting one lamp he chose the chair directly across from her. Cristeen held the hot coffee mug with both hands, still feeling chilled.

"What shall we talk about?"

"Well, I still owe you my explanation about church."

"You don't have to tell me, if you don't want to."

"Not interested anymore."

"Interested, yes. But it can wait. I, too, can be patient."

"I admire that."

"Stop smiling at me."

"I admire your blush, too."

Cristeen took a gulp of coffee, mostly to hide her face behind the cup. Even Matt's eyes smiled. She was really starting to like him a great deal. That frightened her almost more than the nightmares. She was asking for trouble. Letting herself feel this way could only bring her heartache. For once in her life she threw caution to the wind.

"Change the subject, please."

"You can be quite demanding," Matt chuckled as Cristeen glared at him. "Very well, only remember you asked. What were you and Katie giggling about after dinner?"

The question brought the smile back to Cristeen's eyes. It was all the reward Matt wanted.

Her good spirits didn't end with a smile. "Are you sure you want to ask that?"

"Positive." Well, perhaps not quite positive, but too late now.

"Katie compared you to a bear." She paused for effect. "And I agreed that you do growl at times."

He walked into that trap. Of all the animals Katie could have picked, a bear was at least complimentary. "She's compared me to worse animals."

"I know. Most often I believe you are either pigheaded or as stubborn as a mule."

It had been a very long three days. Matt saw now that Cristeen and Katie were thick as thieves when it came to this subject. How much had Katie told Cristeen? Did Cristeen understand that some if not most of it was merely Katie's point of view? Then the worst revelation hit him; with her keen insight, Cristeen likely had gathered more information than Katie thought she was imparting. He was on dangerous ground.

Cristeen laughed. "Don't look so worried. Katie also said I'm just like you."

"Stubborn?"

"I think that was her chief complaint."

"Hmmm," he stroked his chin. "I'm inclined to agree."

She feigned offense, turning her nose up disdainfully. It lasted only thirty seconds before she giggled. A yawn interrupted the laughter.

"It feels good to laugh."

"You're getting more tired, though, right?"

Cristeen considered the last sip of coffee in her cup. "I'm just not ready to talk about it."

"Then don't. Tell me something else."

"Like what?"

"What's your name?"

The question caught her off guard. Not that she was trying to keep her name from him. It simply had not occurred to her that she had anything more than a first name. Tentatively she spoke her full name, trying out the sound of it, "Cristeen Ciara Latham."

Matt digested the information. "Ciara, is that your middle name?"

"Yes. It was my grandmother's name, my mother's mother." She grasped at the Celtic cross. "This was hers also. She gave it to my mother, Mother gave it to me. Family tradition."

"You are Irish, just as Ty said."

"Is that a bad thing?" Anxiety laced her voice.

"Of course not, Cristeen. Ty is so Irish he bleeds green. My family is also of Irish decent, though my mother's family is French."

Relieved by his words, Cristeen elaborated on her own family. "My mother was Irish. She came to America as a young woman. My father fell in love with her at first sight, so they both said."

"Sounds like your parents were very much in love."

"Oh yes," a wistful smile played on her lips. "Our house

was a very happy home. Until..." her voice trailed off.

"Your father must have been devastated by your mother's death." Matt recalled his mother's despair when his father died.

Cristeen lowered her head, unwilling to let Matt see the pain evoked by his perceptive comment. Devastated didn't seem a sufficient description. Shattered, disconsolate, utterly destroyed. He had loved her mother with all his being; he died with her. The man that went on surviving was not her father, the change was too complete.

The voice of caution was warning her again. *Opening yourself up to love someone opens yourself up to be hurt. The only way to keep from being hurt is to keep detached.* The memory of her father's desolation proved the wisdom of that sentiment. Loving someone could only bring heartache; even friendship would only leave her disappointed and hurting.

"I should go to bed now." Cristeen stood abruptly.

Her brusque manner confused Matt. He followed her into the hallway. "Did I say something wrong?"

"No." Her voice sounded husky.

Matt stopped following. He had said something to trigger this change in her attitude. Of that he was certain, yet he was at a loss as to what. Standing in the darkness, watching her disappear into the kitchen, Matt understood how Katie felt whenever he walked out on a discussion. Chasing after Cristeen would only harden her resolve. He would have to let her go, for now. And somehow figure out what he had said to set her off.

SIXTEEN

"Tell me again why I agreed to this." Mike Reardon hissed at his deputy. "We don't do missing persons."

Rory Johnston grinned. He could tell that his boss was mostly upset that he wasn't the one to discover this lead. "Ease up, Boss. You know I'm right this time."

Mike growled an affirmative. They were headed for the Rossiter House, the fanciest hotel in the city. Some said it was the most elegant hotel west of the Mississippi. Certainly it catered to a very well-to-do clientele. And George Edwards was undoubtedly of the right class to be staying there.

"Run down the facts, convince me I'm not wastin' time."

"You want me to tell you what you already know, too? Okey-doke. Hank Crespin got blown away, his partner has vamoosed, and the physical trail washed away. Sums up that part, right?"

Again Mike nodded. "Next you figure out where Crespin's last been seen alive and talk with everyone at The Cherokee Inn. Seems two strangers had some sort of dealings with Crespin and Marks out there. But now you can't find them strangers."

Mike stepped off the boardwalk, heading at an angle across the busy street seemly oblivious to the carriages that stopped short to let him pass. Focused as he was on his mission, he did note the traffic enough to cross safely. Rory stuck close, still rattling off the stats of the investigation.

"One of them strangers was riding a palomino. I run into this here Mr. Edwards who's looking for his niece who just happens to have also been riding a palomino."

"I still don't see why you are so convinced this is the big break I've been looking for." Mike held the door for Rory then stepped into the hotel.

"Don't you see, Boss, all we gotta do is find out who took the girl's horse an' we find out who shot Crespin." Rory's voice hushed as he glanced nervously around the opulent foyer.

Oriental carpets, crystal chandeliers, and polished brass made a none too subtle statement about the social status of the Rossiter House patrons. In their dusty jeans and rumpled shirts, boots coated with mud, Mike and Rory stood out like the proverbial sore thumb. Before the desk clerk could object to their presence a large man strode forward to greet them.

"Sheriff Reardon, I presume?" The man extended his hand and Mike shook it firmly. "George Edwards. Glad you are willing to take time out of your busy work schedules to help me."

George Edwards was a tall, broad shouldered man, with a thinning patch of gray hair covering his head. He was dressed like the affluent businessman he was. Mike knew the name; Edwards had a successful hardware company based in Denver and had recently been elected to the state legislature. Mike came prepared to meet a pompous, self-centered ignoramus. Instead he found Edwards to be an honest, down-to-earth kind of man. Friendly and obviously concerned for his niece.

A uniformed bellhop led the three men down the hallway to a private meeting room. Edwards politely requested tea be brought in, then asked if the other gentlemen might prefer coffee. Mike declined both. As the door closed, George Edwards motioned for the men to be seated.

"I'll be frank, Mr. Edwards," Mike opened the conversation. "We don't generally investigate so-called missing person cases. I'm sure you are aware that here in the West things are different than on the east coast. People are free to come and go as they please, no questions asked, so long as they abide by the law."

"Sheriff Reardon," Edwards considered his words. "I have lived in Colorado for most of my adult life. I am quite familiar with the unwritten code of ethics we all live by. Nevertheless, this is my niece we are discussing."

Mike ran a hand through his hair. "I apologize. I by no means meant to imply that she took off on her own without notifying you."

Surprisingly, Edwards laughed. "That notion never crossed my mind, Sheriff." A tap at the door drew his attention. "I believe I am the one who should be apologizing. Please, let me introduce to you the reason I know my niece did not skidaddle of her own accord."

George Edwards went to the door. He greeted the young woman standing in the hallway, gently drawing her into the room.

"Don't be nervous, my dear. These men are going to help us find your sister." Turning to the men, Edwards introduced her. "Leigh, this is Sheriff Reardon and Deputy Johnston. I want you to answer their questions."

Mike stood as Leigh was introduced. "Ma'am," he nodded his head in greeting. She was obviously uncomfortable. Her gaze swept the room, measuring the distance to the door and escape. She did not look at Mike directly, instead focused on the top button of his shirt.

After a brief moment of hesitation, Leigh turned to Edwards. "I don't feel comfortable with this, Uncle George."

Her tone held uncertainty and was not assertive. She seemed to look to her uncle for reassurance. Mike wondered what she was hiding. Or perhaps she worried about his reliability and trustworthiness. Many a sheriff was known to be as willing to break the law as any criminal. And it stood to reason if she and her sister had been waylaid and their horses stolen, Leigh would naturally be suspicious. Especially if it had happened here in Fort Rossiter; logically she would not trust even the law here.

"Please, miss," Mike spoke soothingly, "you can trust us to see that any law breakers are punished. You sit down there and tell me what happened and I promise to do my best to help."

"Do as he says, Leigh." Edwards propelled the young lady towards the nearby chair. "I checked him out before we left Denver. You can trust him." Turning to Mike, he added, "No offense meant, Sheriff."

"None taken." Mike also sat down. He saw Edwards was a protective uncle. He tried to remember what little he had read about the man; there had never been any mention of nieces, or any close relations for that matter. Excepting Mrs. Edwards, whose past was mentioned briefly in a pre-election article. Caroline Edwards hailed from Boston and before that Ireland. Mike could not recall any mention of her family in the articles either.

"Sheriff Reardon," Leigh spoke in a quiet voice. "I want to find my sister, and Uncle George says you are my best hope. My only hope, he says. I have no where else to turn, and none but my aunt and uncle to advise me."

She gathered a wrinkle in her skirt and twisted it to hide her tension. The movement drew Mike's eyes and he studied her hands. Her fingers were rough and callused, not the hands of a well-off socialite. Hers were the hands of a char-woman, or a farmer's daughter. Yet her diction was that of a well-educated lady. She was dressed fashionably, seemed at ease with the heeled shoes and ruffled skirts. But her body language spoke of her unease in these surroundings. She had first identified her only escape route and now sat perched on the edge of the chair, ready to take flight. She behaved like a wanted criminal.

164

"My sister told me to go straight to Denver and wait for her there." Her voice became firmer. "Had she arrived I would not have ever considered speaking of this incident."

She hesitated over the word incident. Mike made a mental note of that. "I will need you to tell me everything that occurred, exactly as it happened, if I am to help you at all."

She looked away. When she looked back her eyes locked on his. "If she is not safe I will tell you everything. Should we find her alive and well, then it will be my sister's decision and responsibility to disclose those details."

Wonderful, Mike thought, *they want my help but I'm going to have to fight for the pertinent information. Why couldn't I have chosen an easier profession?*

He took a deep breath, letting it out slowly. "I think we are getting off to a bad start. I need you to trust me, without that I might as well walk away now."

Her eyes narrowed as she studied him. *Sizing me up,* Mike realized. She didn't trust her uncle's judgment any more than she trusted the sheriff. Edwards had a record for integrity. The only logical explanation for Leigh's distrust was lack of familiarity. She did not know Mike therefore she did not trust him. Likewise, she did not trust her uncle therefore she did not know him.

"You are not from Colorado, are you?" He knew he was right when Leigh inhaled sharply. "I'm guessing Kansas, Nebraska, or maybe Wyoming."

"Why?" She was cautious, yet intrigued.

"If you had come from much further away, say the East, you would have traveled by train directly to Denver, thus avoiding Fort Rossiter all together."

"So why those three states, Boss?"

Mike glanced at Rory; the man had a lot to learn about deductive reasoning. "She obviously doesn't trust the law; it's not personal against me, it's my profession." He looked again to Leigh. "In your experience, the law has either looked the other way or been paid off by the very criminals they are supposed to be apprehending."

She smiled begrudgingly. "Go on," she encouraged.

"So I figure you come from someplace nearish and full of dubious law enforcers."

Edwards piped up. "That pretty much includes most of the western portion of this great country, Sheriff Reardon."

"Sadly, Mr. Edwards, you are correct. However, again had she come from somewhere south or west, she would not have to pass through Fort Rossiter to get to Denver." He stopped, reconsidered his earlier conclusion and amended it. "Perhaps you've been in Kansas, but you came here by way of Nebraska or Wyoming."

"Very good, Sheriff." Edwards looked to his niece. "You were living in Kansas when first you contacted us."

Leigh smiled politely. "Yes, Uncle George. And you are correct, Sheriff Reardon. I lived sometime in Kansas, not too far from Salinas and Abilene, where cattlemen are kings and even the law bows to them."

It was a small victory, this acknowledgment. Mike would take it, and build on it. "I assure you I bow to none but the law itself. I respect your reluctance to believe what I say. It is wise to base your trust on actions rather than hollow words. Do you have the time to find out if I can be trusted?"

"No, Sheriff, I do not have the time. I fear my sister may already be out of time."

"Shall we begin then, Miss...?" He fished for her name.

Leigh sighed, deciding her sister's life demanded this man's trust. "Miss Latham."

SEVENTEEN

The drive to church was long and miserable. Neither Matt nor Cristeen spoke. In the sideseat phaeton Cristeen sat directly across from Katie and Paul. Matt drove, a duty, which allowed him to keep his back to Cristeen. It wasn't that he didn't want to look at her, speak to her. She made it clear she had nothing to say to him. And he certainly wasn't going to force her to speak, especially under Katie's watchful eye.

If Katie noticed the tension between the two, she said nothing. When the carriage stopped, Paul helped Katie down and they strolled to the church building. Cristeen sat still, staring back up the road they had just come down. She felt the carriage dip as Matt stepped inside. Out of the corner of her eye she saw him sit on the seat Katie had recently vacated.

"Cristeen," Matt spoke softly. "I don't know what I said or did that upset you so much, but I beg you to please forgive me."

She clenched her jaw. It had been a very long night, made longer as she discovered an apparent inability to cry. Her chest felt like a knife had been plunged into it, and now and again the blade twisted as if searching for her heart and the fatal blow. At times breathing became difficult. Sheer exhaustion finally did what nothing else could; she slept dreamless.

The stabbing pain returned. This wall her mind was trying to build kept crumbling. She did not want to get hurt again, and experience said it was only a matter of time. Matt wouldn't do it purposely, of that Cristeen felt sure. Something would turn him away, whether it was her history or her peculiar talent with horses. Maybe he would stick by her until she finally remembered how she got shot. One way or another, his friendship would be withdrawn.

She squeezed her eyes against the pain. *Trust him,* her heart repeated again and again. *Not everyone turns away; sometimes it is you that turns your back.* Was she so wrong to cut the ties before they ripped her heart out?

The buggy rocked as Matt moved again, this time sitting beside her. Cristeen so desperately wanted to trust Matt, to let go her fears and lean on someone else. All her life she was the strong one, burying her emotions. It was good protection against her father's drunken rages and depressed ridicule. She stayed calm, and even managed to appear happy, all to keep her sister from becoming discouraged. When she was unsure, she bluffed her way through. She pretended to know what she was doing until people believed her.

It was a lonely way to live that made her tired through to the bone. There had been times she wanted to simply give up. Let everyone be damned. So what if her sister became hardened and bitter. When she sank to the bottom of her despair, occasionally wishing she were dead, her ornery streak would reassert itself. She spitefully continued the facade until even she believed it again.

Matt watched the emotions playing across Cristeen's features. He, too, had once struggled with an internal conflict. He recognized the agony in her clenched jaw and clamped eyes. He reached over and turned her face to his.

"Please, Cristeen." She kept her eyes shut; he felt the tension in her jaw. "If you can't forgive me, at least yell at me. Scream, holler, call me names. Just talk to me."

A tear rolled down her cheek. Slowly she opened her eyes. The haunting fear was plain to see. Another tear fell, and another. Matt pulled her against him, turning her into his shoulder. He held firm when she tried to pull away. He felt her accept his comfort; she trembled as the tears finally broke free. The crying lasted briefly, ending with a shuddering sigh. Still she did not speak.

He brushed his hand down her hair. Cristeen sniffled; Matt handed her his handkerchief. She held it limply. As from far off, Matt heard the parishioners singing a familiar hymn; church service had begun. He sat still, one arm holding Cristeen against him while with his other hand he continued to stroke her hair. After what felt like an eternity, yet the hymn had not yet finished, she spoke.

"I'm tired," she managed a croaking whisper.

He laughed softly. "Bet you didn't sleep much last night."

"Nope," her voice was steadier.

"Do you forgive me?"

"I can't." His heart sank, only to lift again as she added, "You didn't do anything wrong. I just remembered that I had forgotten to remember what a dangerous thing friendship can be."

"You must be incredibly tired, because you are not making sense."

"I guess you just have to be me to understand what I mean."

"You aren't improving, either." She giggled. "At least that sounds better."

"Won't Katie hate me for keeping you away from service now that she finally got you going again?"

Reluctantly Matt pushed Cristeen away from him. He looked down into her eyes; there was still painful doubt in them, yet they had softened. "Katie didn't get me to come to church again. The decision was mine. But no, she won't hate you."

"I'll trust your judgment in that regard."

"Good. You should trust me more often." He smiled.

"Feel up to a short walk? I'd like to show you something."

The cemetery was directly behind the church building. The trees surrounding the small glade gave it a secluded feeling. Like being in a world apart from reality. There were quite a few headstones, more than Cristeen would have expected for such a small village.

"The settlement is fairly old," Matt explained. "Many men of my father's generation fought in the War Between the States, as well as in the numerous battles with the Indians hereabout."

He led her to a large gravestone in the far corner. A long reaching tree branch arched like a canopy over the plot. Cristeen read the inscription on the stone. Below the names and dates, the epitaph read, "Sorrow only lasts so long, Happiness lasts forever."

Cristeen tenderly traced the letters spelling out the name Donovan. "Your parents," she whispered.

"My parents." Placing his hand on her back, Matt steered Cristeen to a boulder just to the side of the family tombstone. "I come here sometimes, just to think. When I sit quietly beside them it's almost as if they hear me talking to them. Rather odd, I know."

He stopped talking. Cristeen sat on the rock and gazed up at him. He was looking at the headstone with an expression of tenderness and love. She grasped the Celtic cross pendant, realizing that this was her way of staying connected to her mother. Of keeping alive those happy memories of her childhood.

"I don't think you are odd to talk to your parents."

"Daft? Touched, perhaps?"

"Don't mock the love you feel." Matt looked sharply at her. "Just because I'm afraid to let myself care doesn't mean I don't know what love is."

He smiled. "Don't be afraid, Cristeen. If you never care, never love, then you will never truly live."

She looked past him at the epitaph on the stone. "Who wrote that?" His sheepish grin told her she had guessed right. "You did, didn't you?"

"Ya'. Don't go spreadin' it around that I have a sappy, sentimental side." His grin disappeared into his beard. "I have enough trouble keeping Sarah at bay as it is."

"What's her story anyway? Never mind, I don't really want to know."

"Don't care, heh?" He flinched as she slapped his arm lightly. "Sorry. But you're right; you don't really want to know about her. Let's just say I am not a poor man and Sarah is a woman who likes what money can buy."

"Already more than I wanted to hear." Cristeen smiled, hiding the tiny stab of jealousy she felt at his words. She knew it was a foolish emotion; even if Matt might someday want more than a friendship with her, he had made it perfectly clear he did not care for Sara one iota.

Oh it was so good to see Cristeen smile. Matt stared at her a moment, soaking up the joy of her grin. A moment too long, for she began to blush. That was fine by him; the rosy glow gave her a warm, happy appearance.

"Stop staring at me."

He was beginning to enjoy hearing those words, too.

"I'll make you pay for this."

He knew her just well enough to take the threat seriously. Today he was prepared to accept the challenge. "And what will be the punishment for my alleged crime?"

"Alleged-smedged. Remember when I said I could bide my time until you were ready to tell me why you stopped coming to church? Well, I lied. Fess up."

His eyes twinkled like the morning sun on dewy grass. "You didn't lie, Cristeen. I brought you out here for just that reason."

"Oh."

Matt offered her his hand. "That rock won't do, the

story's much too long."

He led her to a bench tucked unobtrusively beside the gate. Its wooden slats were grayed with weather, but much softer than the hard stone she had been sitting on. Matt sat beside her, leaning his arms on his knees. Cristeen sat as straight and proper as she could, being as she really had no idea what was proper. She waited patiently for Matt to begin.

"I've thought a lot about this over the past week." There was apprehension in his tone. "I have never talked about any of this to another living soul."

"Discretion being the better part of valor?" Cristeen tenderly jested. He snorted derisively in response. "I'm pretty good at keeping secrets."

Matt stood and paced a ten-foot square. Stopping at the open gate, he stared at the barely visible church. He was not seeing the whitewash clapboards nor the recently erected steeple that housed the bell. His vision looked far beyond the churchyard, all the way into his past.

"It started when my father died, I suppose. I was away when it happened, returning only for the funeral service."

Cristeen barely remembered her mother's funeral. Adults had deemed both girls much too young for the trauma surrounding a funeral. Her youthfulness had proven beneficial later; no one expected her to carry on daily life as if nothing had changed. How hard it must have been for Matt, having to return to every day routine so quickly.

"I'm sorry you did not have the opportunity to grieve."

Her words pulled Matt back to the present. He glanced at Cristeen, sitting perfectly still, her eyes focused on her hands where they lay in her lap. Of all the things she might have said she chose the words that went to the heart of his emotion.

Cristeen glanced up. Seeing Matt's eyes on her, she stated, "Katie told me you were in Virginia when your father died."

Matt nodded understanding. "Did she tell you how he died? He was thrown from his horse and tumbled down a ravine. He broke his neck."

Cristeen winced. No wonder Mary Donovan did not want her son to continue ranching. Such a mundane accident, it almost seemed insulting. Yet was there any good way to die? In the end, no matter the cause, the loved one was still gone.

Matt rubbed his beard, turning his eyes away once more. "I suppose Katie told you how much my mother wanted me to stay in Virginia."

"Yes."

"We discussed it often during the years I was in school."

"You did not let her down, Matt. You have to live your dreams, not someone else's."

This time her words brought a slow, wry smile to his face. He strolled back to sit beside her again. "How'd you get so wise in only twenty-two years?"

It was the first time he made mention of her age. Cristeen squirmed, uncomfortable with the assumptions she could see in his eyes. Someday she might be willing to tell him her own life experiences. For now she hoped it was enough that she had learned from those experiences.

"Do you realize it took me nearly six years longer to figure out what you just told me?"

"Sometimes it's easier to see the truth when you are not examining yourself."

"Are you telling me you aren't as wise as you seem?" She shrugged, grinning crookedly. He took a moment to absorb her reaction. "You are perhaps just a little too good at keeping secrets."

"Maybe someday I'll tell you one of my secrets. Then you can tell me the truths I have missed."

"Are you sure you want to make that offer?"

"No, but it's too late now." There was not the slightest hint of regret in her tone. "You digress, Mr. Donovan."

"My apologies, ma'am," he mocked. "Alrighty then, you

173

asked for it. Here's where I show you how right Katie is about my mulishness."

"Asserting your independence cannot be called mulish."

"Ah, you were an obedient and well-behaved child, I see."

"Far from it." With some difficulty, Cristeen managed to control her unease. "I broke no laws; let's just leave it there. And stop trying to change the subject."

Matt stood and moved a short distance away, keeping his back to Cristeen. He hadn't expected this to be such a difficult conversation. Cristeen's lighthearted interjections helped. Still it was with a fair amount of chagrin that he continued. With his back turned she would be unable to see just how ashamed he felt.

"Butting heads with my mother was the least of my problems, Cristeen." A deep breath and he plunged ahead. "Upon returning to the ranch, my ranch, I commenced proving to Mother, Katie, Ty, the whole world, that I was in charge of my life. I did things my way. It's a wonder I still have a ranch to run."

"I cannot imagine you making foolhardy decisions with regards to that ranch."

"Thank you. But your compliments should go to Ty, and my father. Without my father's teaching, and Ty's patience, I definitely would have acted with complete disregard for the future of the ranch. And my family."

"Paul and Ty respect you," Cristeen was puzzled. "Everyone here respects you."

"Because I am Peter Donovan's son." He sighed as he made the statement. "I'll grant that Paul's respect has nothing to do with my father. Ty, well, I think you mistake love for respect. He's been around all my life; he's more like an uncle than an employee."

"Kin by heart. He chose to be a part of the Donovan clan."

"I reckon that sums up Ty fairly." He smiled over his shoulder. "Most of the older residents of Glenpark remember my father. None of them, save the Reverend, have ever seen first hand just how pigheaded I am."

"And I suppose more'n just Sarah see your bank account."

"Possibly. They are decent, honest people Cristeen. Don't misjudge them; even Sarah is good at heart."

Cristeen chose not to respond to that.

After a short silence, Matt continued. "Anyway, my point is that I arrogantly went about leading my life believing I was in complete control. Then Mother became gravely ill. It should have been a wake up call. Instead I took it as a slap in the face, an insult added to injury."

Cristeen scrunched her face in confusion. "I don't follow."

Rather than explain, Matt took up pacing again. He removed his hat, smoothed a hand through his hair, replaced the hat. All the emotions were still there, he had simply learned how to keep them checked. Not without help, however. *Dear Lord, I need your help again. Help me explain what I went through in such a way that Cristeen will understand the importance of giving over control to you. She's so independent, Lord, and I fear what that misplaced self-faith might lead her into. Please give me the right words. Most of all please let her hear them.*

A peacefulness settled over him, calming his restless strides. He returned to Cristeen's side. "When your mother died, you were angry right? At her, and at God?"

"Yes."

"When you couldn't get her back, who were you most angry at?"

She broke eye contact. "Me."

"Why?"

With a slight tremor in her voice she answered, "It was my fault she was gone, and I wasn't strong enough or powerful enough to bring her back. My prayers meant nothing."

Matt cupped her hands in his, causing her to once more meet his gaze. "I was powerless to save my father. I deluded myself into believing he would be alive if only I hadn't been on the other side of the country. Eight years later, I wasn't thousands of miles away. I stood at my mother's bedside and watched her fade away, powerless to stop her pain or prevent her death."

Anguish washed through Cristeen. The horror wrought by his words was almost more than she could bear. Yet looking into his eyes, she saw an inexplicable peacefulness. His jaw muscles flexed; the pain was still part of Matt's existence. It could hold sway over his actions.

"You understand how I felt then, but you are still bewildered?"

"So much hurt," she whispered. "How can you look so..."

"At peace? This is the part I most need you to understand."

He took another deep breath. "Just before Mother passed away, I pretty much hit bottom. I turned my feelings of personal guilt into a furious rage at God. How could He allow my mother to suffer as she did when all her life she had been so faithful to Him? What kind of God did that? Do you understand?"

"Implicitly."

The answer gave Matt pause; this conversation was more crucial than at first he thought.

"So you stopped going to church services."

"Yes. What was the point?"

"What changed your mind?"

"Jesus. Don't roll your eyes." He smiled to temper the admonishment. "I was brooding, skulking about my house. Katie had gone over to the new house, and I was alone. Maybe I felt like irritating myself more. Whatever the reason, I went into Mother's room."

"And?" He had stopped, momentarily caught up in the memory.

"Her Bible lay open on the table."

Cristeen gave a start.

"Don't go worrying about ghosts. Katie frequented that room even before she had you to care for. I'm sure she left the book open, she does get scatterbrained on occasion."

"Anyway, I sat down and read the verses on the open pages. The words cut through my wrath, and I returned another day to read more."

"What did you read?"

"You won't understand why it meant anything to me."

"Fine, don't tell me."

Matt marveled at her ability to use words like a sharp weapon. The biting tone cut as efficiently as a knife. He was astute enough to realize the sarcasm was the result of emotional scarring. Cristeen struck first, and struck hard, all to keep from being hurt.

"Please don't be offended, Cristy." Matt noted the endearment surprised her but pushed that aside. "Although I read more, the verse that re-awakened my soul says, '*Search the scriptures...they are they which testify of me.*'"

She made a face.

"I told you, it was a message meant for me alone. You need only understand that those words drew me in, so that I read more. It is the more that truly made the difference."

"Okay, I'll bite," she responded defensively. "What more did you read?"

"John, chapter 15, verses 2-6." He drew a piece of paper from his vest pocket and carefully unfolded it. "I've memorized it, but I think if you read it for yourself the words will be more significant."

Cristeen took the proffered sheet of paper. "You wrote this out for me?"

"Last night. You and I are much more alike than Katie could ever know." Tenderly he brushed a strand of hair off her face. "I recognize your independent streak, and I know what kind of trouble it can cause."

Matt let her read in privacy. She looked at the paper. It was written in ink by a steady, firm hand. Each letter flowed into the other, forming a tapestry of words. Across the top of the page John 15:2-6 was written in beautiful script. She sighed; might as well read it and get it over with.

"Every branch in me that beareth not fruit he taketh away; and every branch that beareth fruit, he purgeth it, that it may bring forth more fruit... Abide in me, and I in you. As the branch cannot bear fruit of itself, except it abide in the vine; no more can ye, except ye abide in me...He that abideth in me, and I in him, the same bringeth forth much fruit: for without me ye can do nothing. If a man abide not in me, he is cast forth as a branch and is withered..."

Below the verses, Matt had added a personal note: On our own we can do nothing, we are powerless. Only by giving yourself over to the Lord can you accomplish anything, Cristeen. In Him you can trust. He will never let you down. He will not abandon you. He will protect you. No one else can.

Cristeen read again Jesus' words *"for without me ye can do nothing."* She read and reread Matt's words. Had she been leading her life much like him, arrogantly believing · that she controlled her own existence*? He will not abandon you.* But you did abandon me Lord, Cristeen wanted to cry out. He robbed her of her mother, leaving her to cope alone with her father's hardened heart.

She clamped her eyes against the unwelcome remembrances. Where was this loving God each time they moved, leaving behind any hope of normalcy? He had abandoned her to this cruel, harsh world. *You left me!* She raged silently against God. *You abandoned me, you did not protect me, you let me down!*

Matt watched with growing concern the emotional maelstrom. Cristeen had lowered her head so he could not fully see her face. Yet he saw that she read the words a number of times. Her free hand curled into a tight fist, her knuckles white. He could empathize with the anger she seemed to feel. But when Cristeen went completely still, he became alarmed.

"Cristeen, are you alright?"

"It doesn't make sense. How can you relinquish control of your life to a God that allows such suffering?"

This was an argument Matt had already worked through. "Do you understand the concept of pruning, say a grape vine? To produce a greater harvest, the farmer trims away wasteful, nonproductive branches. Sometimes it takes a deep cut to stimulate growth. So too with our faith. Us stubborn folks take a great deal of pruning."

She smiled wanly. "I guess I can be stubborn. What about my parents? Why did they have to suffer?"

"It was your mother's time to go home. And as devastated as your father was, at least he had you. I'm sure he was thankful for that."

"You're wrong about that." Anger flared in her eyes. "Maybe he was thankful to have my sister, but I was just a painful reminder."

Matt sat back against the force of her bitterness. She continued, barely noticing his reaction.

"You want to know what my mother looked like? Me. Everything about me reminded him of her. My hair, my eyes. She was tall and slender; I grew tall and slender. If I sang, he heard her. When I spoke Gaelic, they were her words."

She stopped and looked at Matt for a long moment. Years of pent up guilt shone in her eyes. "I wasn't even supposed to be me. I should have been Cristopher not Cristeen. No matter how hard I tried, I couldn't change the fact that I was born a girl."

She spat the words at him. He was unprepared for this revelation. The full meaning her words implied grew on him. Cristeen was more comfortable in the barn than the house because she had spent a lifetime trying to be her father's son. Right about now Matt held very little regard for Cristeen's father.

"Cristy, it's not your fault you were born a girl."

The defiant anger in her eyes faltered. She desperately wanted someone to tell her she was wrong about this feeling. Matt held her hands in his.

"I, for one, am glad you are Cristeen and not Cristopher."

She lowered her eyes. Matt fought against his assumptions, searching for a way to help her feel less unwanted by her parent. "Maybe you were a painful reminder at first, but surely with time, as his grief subsided, your father was grateful for such a beautiful reminder."

Her expression softened just a little. The tired smile did not extend to her eyes. "Nice try. Might have worked out that way, too, if he hadn't crawled into a bottle and never returned."

She sighed and let her head droop. He gently pulled her to lean against him.

"So there's one of my little secrets. What truth have I missed?"

He chuckled softly. "If that's a little secret, what are the big ones that you're keeping?" She tensed. "I'm teasing, Cristy."

Matt wrapped his arms around her, encouraging Cristeen to relax against him. "Here's what I think," he spoke softly. "You shouldn't feel guilty about not being a son. If your father never appreciated what a wonderful daughter he had in you, then it was his loss and I pity him for what he missed."

After a long silence, Cristeen responded. "I want to believe you, that God can be trusted. I really want to."

"That's a good place to start."

"I envy your peacefulness."

His smiling eyes held hers. "It took me nearly a year to reconcile the previous ten years of my life. You aren't going to change twenty-two years of ingrained experiences in a few short hours."

EIGHTEEN

"Ty, can I talk to you?"

"Whene'r yer heart desires, sweetheart."

Cristeen giggled. He had taken to using various terms of endearment rather than her actual name. Early in her recovery she had caught on to the truth about Ty. Without the Donovans he would be a lonely old man; Matt and Katie were the closest he had to a real family. Cristeen felt honored that he so readily absorbed her into his family.

Ty had been pumping water into the trough for the livestock. Cristeen's words stopped him, and glad he was for the break. Not just because she was pleasing company, but also because his arm had begun to ache. His old bones were wearing out.

"What can I do for my colleen today?"

"You really are incorrigible," her smile deepened.

"Aye, that I am. Do most anything to get a glimpse o' that dimple."

They strolled to the broodmare barn. Only Grizzy remained inside, even her colt had been turned out. The mare had a stone bruise, causing her to be slightly lame. Restricting her activity had to be enforced, as the mare enjoyed pacing about in her paddock. Ty reached out to pat her neck, and the ornery beast laid back her ears.

"Och, behave now, Griz," Ty scolded.

Cristeen reached passed him to stroke Grizzy's muzzle.

The mare lowered her head, her ears pricking forward as Cristeen spoke to her.

"Mhuirnin," she spoke softly, "dia daoibh."

Grizzy stepped closer to Cristeen, nuzzling her cheek. Ty watched in wonder. Upon reflection, he realized this was the first time he had been close enough to actually hear what Cristeen said to the horses.

"Where did ye learn Gaelic, child?"

Cristeen gave Griz a loving pat before turning away. She indicated the other doorway, wishing to look out over the meadows while they talked. As they moved in that direction she answered his questions.

"My mother taught me some, but I know little of the tongue."

"Is this what ye be wanting to talk aboot?"

She nodded. A fence line separated the barns from the pastures; Cristeen leaned on the top rail, casting a longing gaze on the grassland. She had been considering this conversation for a few days, ever since speaking with Matt at the cemetery. If she was to continue their friendship, she needed to know how her gift would be received.

"It's not just the language I want to ask you about," she looked at Ty as he also leaned on the fence. "But that's a start."

Ty pushed back his hat, squinting as the sun beat on his leathery skin. He could guess what troubled her about the words; people didn't much like anything different. "Had yer share o' problems usin' such words, have ye?"

She snorted. "You have a gift for understatement."

"Don't you worry yer purty head none over that here, a run mo chroi." The endearment rolled sweetly off his tongue, uh Roon mo khree - love of my heart.

Cristeen's smile lit her face. "The words sound like music when you speak them."

"Practice, mhuirnin, practice."

"I pronounced it correctly? I called Griz sweetheart also."

"Ay, you got it right, woor-neen." Ty smiled in return. "You talk to the crathurs a lot. That there is what yer real worry is."

She ducked her head. "Yes, that is."

"You done it all yer life? Or did someone taich you?"

"Teach me what?"

Ty's gaze searched the area. Cristeen had no idea what he was looking for until he came right out and asked, "Where's Mattie-boy?"

"Off with Paul somewhere, I guess. Why?"

In answer, Ty cupped her elbow and carefully steered her down the fence line. In a pasture removed from the mares, a small bunch of horses grazed. These were the working horses, the remuda. Cristeen knew most of them by name, thanks to Henry. The Count kept himself apart from the group, behaving much like a wild stallion.

"Call him over here," Ty nodded his head at the stallion.

Cristeen was uneasy, but also curious. What was Ty trying to prove, and why had it mattered where Matt was? She gave a shrill whistle; a dozen heads shot up and looked to her. The Count eyed her, but did not approach.

"He'll be needin' some coaxin'." Ty lifted the rawhide loop that held the gate, swinging it open just enough for the two of them to enter the pasture.

Cristeen began to understand why Matt's presence was not desirable. The geldings crowded close to both Ty and Cristeen, seeking attention and perhaps a treat. Ty gently pushed them aside, making a path for Cristeen. Once through the herd, she found that The Count had come closer though he remained at a wary distance.

"Hold these, please," she blindly held the crutches out for Ty to take. Without them she would be unable to get away when the stallion become unruly.

Cristeen closed her eyes and inhaled deeply, letting the

air out slowly. When she looked again, the big horse had taken two steps closer. Habit took over; she began to speak to The Count in a soft, soothing voice, a mixture of English and Gaelic. She made no movements, her arms hung straight at her sides.

Ty watched as curiosity overcame the horse and he cautiously approached Cristeen. The stallion snorted in her face, blowing warm air through her hair. After a few moments longer, she reached out and touched his muzzle. He lowered his head; she said something more and the horse stepped forward and to the side. Cristeen grasped a handful of mane and using the big stallion for support she hobbled back to Ty.

"Better'n I expected," Ty kept his words of praise quiet, not wanting to startle The Count. He glanced again at the barns. "Let 'im free now, an' come on out o' here, 'fore Matt sees you."

She whispered something to the horse and released her grip. The big stallion moved away, looking back once before loping across the grassy meadow. Ty returned the crutches and watched as Cristeen listlessly exited the pasture. She waited as he closed the gate; the light was gone from her face, her eyes now a dull blue-gray.

Ty noted the change in Cristeen's demeanor. He was fairly certain of the cause; a little chat should settle her. He offered her his arm, a gesture that at least brought a ghost of a smile to her lips. She shook the crutches to explain her refusal.

"Dearest Cristeen, would you honor this auld man by joining me for a drop o' coffee?"

Cristeen glanced at the house. "We'd be in Katie's way."

"I was thinkin' o' the bunkhouse, where we would also be able to talk privately. That is, if you trust this auld reprobate."

"Of course I trust you."

The bunkhouse was like a small home, not like the dormitory style housing familiar to Cristeen. The door opened onto a combination kitchen-dining area. Against the far wall stood a pot-bellied stove that served as both cook stove and a source of heat. A small round table was centered in the space just to the left of the door. Beyond the table, behind a partitioning wall, she could make out the frame of a bunk bed.

"Sit, be comfortable."

Cristeen looked to the right where Ty pointed. A cozy sitting area had been set up, including a worn, once plump armchair. The oil lamp on the side table was a testament to evenings spent reading.

"If I sit there, where will you sit?"

"Sit," he said with mock sternness. "There's chairs at the table."

Cristeen eased into the armchair and watched Ty go about the business of making coffee. The little house had a cozy feel and Ty was obviously at home. The small space meant everything was within easy reach; soon the kettle was warming and two cups sat on the table waiting to be filled with the steaming liquid. Suddenly Ty gasped in dismay.

"What's wrong?"

"I just remembered that you take cream in your coffee, but I don't keep none down here."

"Don't worry about that." She smiled her reassurance. "Given the choice, I prefer a bit of cream but I can make do without."

Ty absorbed the statement, turning it into a question. "Have you often had to make do without?"

Her smile faltered and sadness flickered in her eyes. "More often than I care to speak about."

"Fair 'nough," he pulled a chair out from the table and straddled it, placing his hands lightly on the back. "Let's talk horses then. You always been able to do that?"

"I wasn't around horses much till I was ten, and then it was mostly draft animals." She looked at Ty, "they don't really count, 'cause a workhorse like that is so agreeable anyway."

"When did you first start whisperin'?"

Cristeen sighed. "I thought I had forgotten that term. You understand, don't you Ty? It's not magic words that make the horses behave the way they do."

"Aye, that I do child," he studied her closely. Whispering was the common term used to describe someone who seemed to communicate directly with a horse, calming even the most savage of beasts. Her vehement denial of any mystical powers revealed the source of her trepidation. It was an apprehension with which he could empathize.

"I've known of a few horse whisperers, all of them uneasy with the treatment heaped on them by society." He cocked his head, considering a new thought. "And they were men. Being female certainly adds a twist."

"I s'pose so," her voice was hollow. "I never gave it much thought."

"You didn't make much ado 'boot it, but everyone else did?"

"Ya'" she said it with such lackluster. "And the girl part, well that was only part of the problem."

The coffee was ready. Ty went about preparing and serving a cup to Cristeen. What she said hinted at a complex history that had sculpted her personality. More accurately, what she didn't say spoke volumes. That she had gone through some unpleasant and disquieting times, but also that she had learned to cope.

"Did yer Mum and Dad disapprove of the whispering?"

"My mother was dead by then. My father didn't find out for nearly two years, and then he used it to his advantage."

Ty moved to look out the window. He could wonder what she meant, but life was too short for that. "Used it to his advantage how?"

She did not answer for quite some time. When she did her tone was resigned. "He tried his hand at being a conman, the details of which I would really rather not discuss. When that finally dried up, I was left with only one skill with which to make my way in the world."

After a brief pause, she asked, "Ever been to Kansas, Ty? Rough, dusty kind of place."

"Plains are beautiful, though."

"I guess. I'm not much for flat land, more of a mountain lover."

"You changin' the subject on me?"

"In a round about way," she flashed a smile. "All done talkin' about history. I'm a whisperer. There, I've said it."

"An' you be worried how they will take that information?" He pointed his chin towards the big house.

"Yes. Will it change how they treat me?"

"Well now, that's an interesting question." He moved away from the window, giving himself time to formulate his answer. "Any time we interact with each other, that very interaction changes what we think an' sets the tone for the next time we meet."

Cristeen felt her heart sink. Just as she feared, once again she would be the oddity. An outcast living on the fringe of normal society. *Better to have learned now,* she told herself.

Ty pulled his chair closer to her. He sat and took her hand in his, giving it a loving pat. "Don't fret, love of my heart. If our feelings n'er changed, we would not be able to learn to respect one another. Our care grows deeper, it changes. Yes, knowin' this will change how Matt and Katie treat you. You will gain esteem. And friendship grows from sharing."

Cristeen stared at his hand holding hers. With a great deal of effort, she worked up the courage to voice the fear in her heart. "Why did you tell me to come away from the horses before Matt saw me? Would I be stepping on his toes, making friends with The Count?"

Ty was pleased she trusted him enough to ask. It was the fear he suspected he saw in her earlier dejection. The question also confirmed his belief that it was Matt's approval she sought, not anyone else's. Good, the boy was finally interested in a woman and it looked like she might reciprocate.

"Dear, sweet colleen," he smiled broadly. "If Mattie had spotted you there, unaware of your particular gift, he would likely have had me tarred and feather. Then run out o' the state."

"You're being silly." Yet she wasn't entirely sure.

He chuckled. "Perhaps I exaggerate a mite. You are not the only one who prefers to remain in his good graces."

She blushed. "He would not be that angry."

"Oh, he's got a nice even temper'ment, till he perceives someone he cares for as being in danger.

Cristeen went from beet red to pale. "Then you think he will not want me to work with the horse?

"Of course he will, mhuirnin, it's what makes you happy. He just needs to first understand that The Count is no danger to you."

NINETEEN

Cristeen sat on the trunk seat, leaning back against the barn. The late afternoon sun was warm and she closed her eyes drowsily. The book she had been pretending to read closed around her finger. It was another afternoon when the only thing she could do to help was stay out of the way.

At least she had Henry. Teaching came naturally to Cristeen. After all, her father had been a teacher; an English professor and later a private tutor. It was ironic that only after his death did she finally follow in his footsteps. Like a good son would do, the son Cristopher Latham had wanted.

Cristeen dismissed the bitterness that leapt sharply into her mind. *Foolish to cry over spilled milk*, she repeated the familiar cliché to herself. She could not change her past but she could control how it effected her future.

She could control; back to that now tired internal debate. Over the last four days she had grappled with the concept of control. After an exhausting review of her memories she was forced to admit she had a need to feel in control. It had begun early, when she started dressing as and acting like a boy in an effort to regain her father's favor. By masquerading as the son he desired she thought she could control how he treated her.

Later the control compulsion manifested in her aloof and unapproachable personality. Distancing herself from would-be friends was the only way she could prevent, therefore control, the anguish moving on brought about. If she never cared for the people around her she could not miss them when they were gone.

The concept was intricately woven into her being, difficult to detect. Even now she was doing it, closing her eyes as she thought. To look at her, one would think she was napping in the sun. She manipulated daily situations in order to keep her true feelings hidden, thus safeguarding her heart. And saving herself from the embarrassment of thinking someone thought more of her than they really did.

If Matt was right, she had been missing out on a lot of living. Her sister Leigh came to mind. In many ways Leigh was the complete opposite of Cristeen. She enjoyed the company of others, whether or not they would be long-term friends. Leigh frequently wore her heart on her sleeve, letting people know how she felt. Many was the time that Cristeen found herself comforting her younger sister when a supposed friend turned out to be disinterested.

Yet Leigh quickly rebounded and found new friends, better friends. Everywhere they lived, Leigh made friends. Thinking on it, Cristeen could not recall a time when her sister did not have at least one close friend. The younger girl was full of life and vitality; people were drawn to her energetic life force. She once said that getting to know new people was exhilarating.

Was this what Matt meant when he said if Cristeen never loved she would never truly live? It was nearly the most frightening thought. What scared her more was his suggestion that she absolutely must relinquish control of her life. Yes she believed in God, believed that Jesus had been sent to save mankind. But God was so distant; He had a whole world to deal with. How could He take care of her at the same time? If she was right, giving up control of her life to a God that hardly noticed her was reckless.

But if Matt was right? Not submitting was more than

reckless, it was suicidal. So it came down to the most basic question, who was right?

Cristeen read the entire book of John. Tuesday afternoon she discovered the concordance. Together with Mary Donovan's handwritten notations, this guide led her to numerous verses supporting the view held by Matt. Chance, or perhaps divine providence, led her to Luke 12:27-28: *'Consider the lilies how they grow...Solomon in all his glory was not arrayed like one of these. If then God so clothe the grass...how much more will he clothe you,...?'* The more she read, the more Cristeen realized that God did care about her.

A sharp whistle opened her eyes. Turning her head she saw Matt stride out into the yard. Fen and Coop danced around him, anxiously vying for the stick in his hand. He held the stick above their heads, building their excitement before throwing it. The dogs streaked across the open expanse. Cristeen saw Cooper reach the stick first; both dogs rushed back to Matt. He took it from Coop and repeated the game.

She sighed; Matt was right. She'd been making a mess of her life trying to control everything herself. She needed to hand over control to the Lord. The decision brought on an interesting new fear. With Matt she had a comfortable friendship. Was that all she wanted? Was it what he wanted?

When Matt came into the room her world seemed brighter. He smiled and her heart beat just a little faster. He was fun to tease, and to be teased by. Yet he could be serious, sympathetic and thoughtful. Her opinions and ideas seemed important to him. He took the time to talk with her, and he really listened.

Fen grabbed the stick and bounded gleefully back to Matt. One more time he drew back his arm and sent the small branch sailing across the yard. Cristeen admired the fluid motion. His head was bare and the sun was picking out the lighter strands in his otherwise dark hair. He had been shoeing the draft horses and his shirt was just now drying where perspiration had run down his back.

He really is a very good looking. Cristeen looked away at that thought. Any moment now Matt would turn around; she did not want him to see her staring. Instead she resumed watching surreptitiously through half closed eyes. Once more manipulating the situation, creating the illusion that she was nodding off. Just in time, too, for Matt did turn and walk straight toward the open barn door beside her.

As he drew closer, Cristeen shut her eyes completely. She started when he said, "If you're not careful, you'll really fall asleep sitting there with your eyes half closed like that."

She peered cautiously; he was gone. Irritating, his knack for seeing through her facades. Today Cristeen found it endearing. All the more reason to take care not to lose this friendship. She had to tell Matt about being a whisperer. Waiting would make it harder to tell and more difficult for him to hear. It was still the most difficult thing she had ever faced.

"You gonna talk to Matt or just fret about it till you get sick?"

Paul was leaning against the doorway. Cristeen was alarmed that she had not heard him approach. At the same time she wondered how long he had been standing there, and what it was he saw that brought on his question.

He moved to sit beside her, glancing at the book long since ignored. "Ivanhoe?" He raised an eyebrow. "You read much of it yet?"

A slow smile stretched across her face. "I read it all. Four years ago."

"Just hidin' behind it today, eh?" He looked across at the house, then leaned closer. "Katie's lookin' out the window. I'm gonna be in big trouble if you don't say your piece to Matt."

"What does anything I may or may not want to say to Matt have to do with you?"

"That's all Katie has talked about since Sunday. Seems she thinks you two had a little tiff."

Cristeen was touched that Katie cared that much.

"And Ty? What's he been saying?"

Paul snorted. "He only makes it worse. Keeps saying we gotta be patient, bide our time, let his colleen alone."

After a moment, he added impishly, "Why don't I go get Ty. Maybe he can make Matt jealous..."

"Leave Ty out of this!" Cristeen cut him off. She wasn't really angry, for Paul was jesting.

"Ah, you care for Matt too, then?"

"You are Puck reincarnated."

"Is that a bad thing?" She slapped his arm lightly. "Ow. All right, I'll let you be. As much as Katie worries about you, I worry about Matt. Just talk to him. He won't bite."

Footsteps sounded behind them. Paul rose to leave. "Talk, Cristeen," he admonished before striding across to the house.

Matt stepped into the waning sunlight. "What was that all about?"

Cristeen looked away. It was now or never, for her courage would not get this high again. "I need to talk to you."

Matt perched on the edge of the trunk. "Yeah? I need to talk to you, too."

"You first." She seized the opportunity to stall.

"I'm going to have to put an end to Henry's morning school hours."

"What? Why?" She searched his face. How could he be smiling after a statement like that. Teaching Henry was the only useful thing she did around here.

"His parents agreed to let him hire on full time. I want him to come with us on the drive to summer pasture, but he has a lot to learn. You can have him later in the day; I need the sunlight hours."

The words took a moment to settle. When they did,

Cristeen returned his smile. "So I can still teach?"

"You can still teach. I wouldn't take that away from you. It makes you happy."

Her breath caught. Ty said Matt cared about her happiness. Now Matt was saying it himself.

"Thank you."

A quiet stretched between them. At last Cristeen got up the courage to approach her thoughts. "I have an idea to help Henry learn about working cattle."

Matt considered her for a moment. Cristeen had demonstrated in the past that she knew about ranching. "Go ahead, I'm always willing to hear your ideas."

"Let him ride Sky. She knows what to do, and Henry will learn quickly from her."

"Sky?"

With a sheepish grin she explained, "Sky is my horse. Henry told me you rode her, so you know I'm right."

Now that's confidence, Matt thought. *She doesn't speak so confidently about herself. That horse really is special to her.* Aloud he said, "She's a good mount. Well trained."

"Thank you," she beamed. "She's got good cow sense. Easiest horse I've ever trained."

"So you are the one who trained her." Matt watched as Cristeen chewed on her lip; any moment now he expected she'd start twirling the cross. "That what's bothering you?"

"Sort of." Cristeen twirled the pendant.

Matt looked out over the pastures. He recalled now that she had been talking with Ty yesterday afternoon. He overheard a few words in Gaelic pass between them. Cristeen had alluded to an understanding of that ancient language so he had given it no further thought at the time. Now he wondered.

"What were you talking to Ty about yesterday?"

Cristeen closed her eyes with a sigh. There was just no easy way to tell someone you speak another language that you've never really been taught. And worse yet, she only spoke that language to horses. She might as well just plunge ahead.

"Have you ever heard of the term horse whisperer?"

"Sure, Ty talks about them occasionally."

"I'm one." She risked a quick glance to gauge his reaction. Except for an expression of mild surprise she could not tell what he thought.

Matt was surprised. Not that Cristeen was a whisperer, for all the signs were there pointing to her being more than an average horsewoman. He was taken aback that this was what she had been so afraid to talk about. After all, half of the ranch income came from the horses they raised. Just being a whisperer couldn't explain her trepidation.

"Do you like being a whisperer, Cristy?"

She shrugged. "I like being with the horses. They don't judge me."

"Unlike the people you have encountered?" Her nod confirmed his suspicions. "You were a lonely kid, weren't you."

Cristeen shot an inquisitive look at him. He was watching her, his expression a mix of concern and tenderness. She could find no sign that he scorned her talent. In fact, he took it in stride almost as if he already knew.

"I'd rather not talk about my childhood."

Matt smiled softly. "Tough, that's what I want to talk about."

She heard the echo of her own words. Well, she had that coming, now didn't she. "I guess I owe you some explanation."

He rubbed her arm. "I don't want much, honest. Just tell me why this bothers you. This is your big secret, isn't it?"

She stared long and hard at him. Just the hint of a smile lifted the corners of his eyes. A kind of indulgent expression, as if he didn't see anything wrong with the very thing she felt most awkward about. But he wasn't laughing at her.

"Please, Cristy, talk to me about being a whisperer."

"You don't think me bizarre?"

"Of course not!" He cocked his head to one side. "Is that how most people treat you, like an oddity?"

"Usually," she sighed heavily. "Not in Kansas, though. At least not at first."

"Do go on," he softly encouraged.

"They gave me Sky, kind of a bribe to keep me on the ranch." Cristeen glanced across the meadow at her horse grazing on the horizon. "She was three, as unpredictable as a funnel cloud. Partly, too, she was a challenge. There were bets made, money won and lost."

Matt was a bit shocked at that. "Men bet on you?"

"It was all in good fun. There." She looked over at him. "I'd been the subject of betting before. That part really doesn't bother me, 'cause I won all my bets."

He laughed. "You bet on yourself? That's confidence." His smile faded as he added, "cowpunchers don't much like losing bets to a girl."

It was Cristeen's turn to laugh. "Tell me about it. But they didn't know that little bit of irony for another three years."

"What?" He stared at her, once more hearing her words from Sunday, *no matter how hard I tried, I couldn't change the fact that I was born a girl.*

"Oh Cristy, that's what really worries you, isn't it?"

She turned away at her revelation. Certainly she had not intended to tell him she spent much of her life masquerading as a boy. She held her breath, waiting to hear his condemnation. When it did not come, she glanced sidelong at him. He still had that tender concern in his eyes.

"No wonder you enjoy being with horses more than people."

"Still don't think I'm an oddity?"

Matt wrapped his arms around her, pulling her into his hug. "You are perhaps the most unique person I have ever met."

He held her close when she tried to pull away. "I meant it as a compliment, Cristy." She stopped trying to pull away, but still she was tense. "How'd you pick a name like Sky?"

The question caught her off guard, and she answered without thinking, her tone wistful as she remembered. "She reminded me of the golden sun in a clear blue summer sky."

"So why not Sunshine, or Sunny?"

"Sky seemed poetic." She relaxed, realizing that Matt accepted her for the person she had become, with no reproach for who she had been.

Feeling the tension leave Cristeen, Matt relaxed. He recognized this conversation as a big step towards her trusting him. For that he was grateful.

TWENTY

A lot has been written by the Eastern press about the so-called Wild West. If these accounts are to be believed, the Western man spent his days fighting. The dirty, dusty boomtown streets were filled with drunken cowhands and zealous gamblers wreaking havoc and shooting it out. According to the alleged civilized East, western towns overflowed with irascible, irresponsible, inconsiderate dregs unfit for civil society.

Most of the stories were bilk. Certainly there were towns plagued by rowdies; men blowing of steam after a long cattle drive or a long day working the mines. And perhaps western law was more lenient than its eastern counterpart. When it came to settling a dispute often it was with a gun. Yet at heart, the people of the West were decent, honest folks taking what life gave them and trying to make something better.

In the short time Mike Reardon had spent in Boston he had seen more crime than in the sum of his years. A man, or woman for that matter, had a better chance of being assaulted on the east coast than in the supposed Wild West.

In general the people of the West respected each other's privacy. Unlike the gentry of the East, Westerners minded their own business, tending to be tight-lipped regarding other's affairs. Usually this unspoken code of ethics was something in which Mike took pride. Not today.

By it's very definition investigation required inquiries.

He had to dig to get the answers; often it was just a matter of asking the right questions. Mike stuck to it with dogged determination. He might have met his match in Leigh.

"Miss Latham, if you want my help you are going have to answer my questions."

"I never said I wanted your help. Uncle George insisted." Leigh lifted her chin defiantly.

"Uncle George is a smart man."

Leigh agreed. "That's why he saw fit to leave the room."

Not long ago Mike thought Leigh Latham was a quiet, insecure young lady. After only twenty minutes he learned else wise; she was strong willed, self-confident and a little brash. She spoke in an easy gregarious manner with Rory, deferred politely to her uncle's requests, and artfully dodged Mike's questions.

What little information he had gleaned from her came only after George Edwards and Rory left. Leigh had relaxed some with her uncle's departure, still she was reticent with her answers.

Mike was certain she was hiding some key bit of information, perhaps to protect her sister, or even herself.

A soft rap at the door interrupted. "What do you want?" Mike snarled.

"Mr. Edwards thought y'all might like some tea."

Mike opened his mouth to dismiss the man when Leigh jumped up. "Oh, yes, Malcolm. Tea would be wonderful." She dashed to the door and admitted an older, uniformed gentleman.

"Splendid. Put the tray there, please. You are a dear." She chatted easily. "If Uncle George doesn't tip you handsomely, Malcolm, you be sure to let me know. I'll take care you get what you deserve for spoiling me."

Mike sat back, watching the byplay. Leigh was most comfortable with those that society considered second class. He needed to rethink this interrogation. Perhaps a more personal approach, befriend her first, gain her trust. She was thanking Malcolm as the man left; he was at ease with Leigh as well, not stiff like most of the hotel employees seemed to Mike.

"Have you been here long, Miss Latham?"

"We arrived yesterday about midday. Why?" She tasted a crumpet while fixing a cup of tea for herself.

"You seem very at ease with the staff." She held up the teapot, "No thank you."

"Coffee, then. I insist."

Seeing she would not take no for an answer, Mike accepted.

"To answer your question, which by the way you neglected to ask, I understand the staff far better than I do the patrons."

"Because you don't come from a wealthy background?" She nodded. "You are George Edwards' niece, aren't you?"

"By marriage. Caroline is my mother's sister." Leigh chuckled. "I never even knew she existed 'till three years ago."

"You didn't know you had wealthy relations? Did your mother not get along well with the Edwards'?"

Mike accepted the cup of coffee Leigh handed him. She returned to her chair, carefully holding the saucer for her teacup. She contemplated his question, considered how to answer.

"It wasn't really up to my mother," she began slowly. "You see, Aunt Caroline married and moved away before my sister was born. So she wasn't even around when my Mom died."

"I apologize if I've brought up a painful subject."

She shrugged. "Water under the bridge, as they say. I barely remember Mom; Cris used to tell me stories about her."

"Cris? Your sister?"

"Ya', though she hates being called Cris. She tolerates CeeCee."

"She is older, younger?"

"Four years older. How 'bout you, Sheriff, any siblings?"

"Please, Miss Latham, call me Mike."

"Only if you call me Leigh," she smiled broadly. "Now you are the one not answering questions."

She was charming. Mike almost forgot he was trying to get information for a homicide investigation. "Caught me there," he returned her smile. "I am the second youngest of seven."

"Wow! Bet you got bossed around a lot."

He laughed. "My two oldest brothers were killed in the war, so I never really knew them. But, yes, my older sisters did their best to run my life."

They shared a laugh. Leigh sipped her tea, thinking about her own childhood. "Cris wasn't really bossy. Mostly she kept to herself. She helped me with my school work, which I despised at the time, and did her best to keep Daddy pacified."

"When it was just the two of you doing something, was she usually the one in charge?"

"Naturally. Well, she thought so anyway."

What a coy smile, he thought, bet Leigh got into plenty of mischief. And Cris had to get her out. Now the tables were turned. Or were they? Had Leigh gotten into trouble and her sister tried to get her out?

Mike leaned forward conspiratorially. "Leigh, I really would like to help you find Cris. I need to know what happened."

She put the teacup down a bit too forcefully. "I can't tell you."

Won't, you mean. Out loud he said, "How about I tell you what I know, and you fill in the gaps? You aren't protecting her by keeping silent."

"Who says I'm protecting her?" Leigh whispered.

She was on the verge of tears. To his relief, Leigh took a deep breath to gather herself and kept the tears in check.

What she wasn't saying Mike could almost read in her eyes. This conversation was derailing; he needed to redirect it.

"Why not take the train?"

The question puzzled Leigh. "What?"

"Why ride to Denver, from...?"

Leigh smiled wanly. "You really do want to help?" She sighed when he nodded yes. "Cris would probably lecture me about being too trusting. That is, if she were here."

Mike let her sit in silence. He could afford to be patient. She had finally decided to trust him; he need only wait.

"We were three days in Julesburg, as we telegraphed Mrs. Swanson and waited for her reply. Cris had promised to let them know how we progressed. Our telegraph stated we would next wire from Denver, in a week or so."

"Tell me what happened after Julesburg."

"Nothing much, except I used up the last of our ammunition while hunting. So we had to stop for supplies."

"And you stopped at the Cherokee Inn. Did you meet Hank Crespin there?"

"We didn't meet anybody. I told you we didn't know anyone in Colorado."

"I meant, did he talk to you there, did you see him at all?"

She met his gaze, "Oh, sorry. There was a man there who fits the description you gave me; he spoke to us."

"What did he say?"

"I can't repeat it," her eyes dropped and the barest hint of pink tinged her cheeks. "He was rather rude."

Mike's snort startled Leigh.

"Rather rude? That is perhaps the politest thing I have ever heard anyone say about Crespin."

His words relaxed her once more. "Cris would have found a more eloquent way of putting it. Just as she eloquently dismissed this Crespin fellow, and the other one, too."

So Evans was with Crespin. "She put him in his place? Did she have any idea what kind of trouble he could be?"

This time it was Leigh who snorted. "You have to know Cris to understand." She considered her sister a moment before explaining. "When she gets her back up, well, she just doesn't see that she can be stopped. Telling her she can't do something just about guarantees she will do it."

Mike leaned back in his chair, keeping his groan to himself. Crespin wouldn't take well to being told off by a woman. "You said you stopped to get supplies. Did you have much money?"

"Cris said we didn't, but I reminded her of the cash Kyle gave her before we left Kearney."

"Nebraska?" Leigh nodded. "Did you remind her within Crespin's earshot?"

Leigh thought a moment. "Don't remember that well. He hadn't said anything to us until after we bought stuff. Do you think he heard me?"

Mike saw she was teetering on tears again. "Don't worry about that. Tell me what happened when you left." Crespin followed them. Mike realized that, did Leigh?

"We traveled late. Cris wanted to make Denver by the next afternoon."

Mike knew the trail; it was two days minimum.

"The moon was pretty bright, we rode a long time. Finally I got tired and begged her to stop."

So neither one realized Crespin was following. Riding straight through from Julesburg, and probably those three days had been their first real rest, the two women were likely bone tired. Exhaustion has a way of dulling the senses.

"Then what?"

Leigh shook her head; she wasn't going to continue.

"Hard to talk about it? Let me sketch it out, you correct me afterwards." Mike waited for Leigh to nod in assent. "Crespin and his partner, whose name is Evan Marks, followed you. They lay in wait, caught you off guard. Took your money, maybe tried to do worse."

He could see by her pallor he was on the mark with that last comment. "I don't understand exactly who shot who, though. Did Crespin shoot your sister?" She nodded. "And you shot him in retaliation?"

"No," Leigh whispered. "You got it mostly right. That other guy had hold of me while this Crespin..."

"Assaulted Cris."

"Yes." Assault was a good euphemism. "Anyway, Crespin had already shot Cris in the leg. He strangled her, I thought she was dead."

Leigh could contain the tears no longer. Mike reacted quickly, grasping her hands and giving them a reassuring squeeze. "She wasn't dead, though, was she? Remember that." He rubbed his thumb across the back of her hand.

After a deep breath, Leigh continued. "He was coming at me, and I did the only thing I could think of. I hauled back, using that Marks guy as a support, and mule-kicked Crespin."

Mike couldn't help laughing at the image brought to mind. Under different circumstances he would have paid good money to see Crespin's face at that moment. "He deserved it, go on."

"Cris got up. I don't know how, she should have been dead. She told him to leave me alone."

"Did she have a gun to back up her words?" Crespin wouldn't have listened to anything less.

"Yes, a Colt Calvary; she'd used it plenty of times on small game and snakes."

Mike envisioned what occurred next. Crespin probably laughed, possibly dismissed Cris altogether. His weapon had been drawn, so something in her manner must have convinced him she was serious.

"Cris shot Crespin."

"Yes," Leigh felt the weight on her conscious lighten. "Then we taken out of there, Cris saying we should split up 'cause it would confuse that Marks character. I agreed, thinking he would follow me as I went straight down the trail, plain as day to follow."

"He didn't follow you?" That did surprise Mike, at first. Then he realized the logic in following Cris. She was the one who had insulted them, she was the one who killed Crespin. And she was wounded to boot, surely an easy target.

Leigh figured that out, too. By the time the sun came up she realized Marks had gone after Cris. But she believed Cris was not too badly injured, mostly because that was what Cris had told her. So Leigh continued to Denver, making the distance in near record time.

"She said not to go back, she'd meet me in Denver. I believed her; I waited. I still just can't believe she lied."

Mike didn't want to tell her that Cris probably hadn't lied. She had probably died. Leigh had charmed her way into his heart; he liked her enough to keep that truth to himself.

Leigh pulled her hands from Mike's, and walked over to the fireplace. "I know what you are thinking. She's dead. Uncle George thinks so, too. Only Aunt Caroline believes me."

"Why are you so sure she isn't dead?"

"I just know!" she said emphatically. "That and last week I rode back up the trail a ways, and I couldn't find Sky."

"You've lost me with that bit of logic."

"Cris's horse, Sky. Where Cris is, Sky is. Since I can't find Sky, they must have made it to safety somewhere."

There were so many holes in that logic Mike hadn't the heart to point out even one. The horse might also be dead, up there in the harsh cold mountains. Marks may have taken the horse after killing Cris. Or Cris did make it to safety. To consider that possibility; it would have taken a miracle. Mike saw the amount of blood she lost just in the clearing; she would have continued to bleed as she rode away. Even with the pressure bandage Leigh applied.

"I see you side with Uncle George," her tone was

resigned, but her stance was defiant.

"If I do, you're going up the mountains on your own, aren't you?"

"Yes I am."

"Tell me something, Leigh. Is Cris as stubborn as you?"

"Who do you think I learned from?"

He sighed, "What direction was she headed when you parted?"

TWENTY ONE

The trouble with letting herself care for Matt was that she missed him terribly when he was gone. Cristeen squinted as she searched the northwestern horizon.

"You know what they say about a watched pot."

She started at the sound of Katie's voice. "Why is this drive taking so much longer than the first?"

Katie stepped out onto the porch. If Cristeen had bothered to look she would have seen the broad smile on her friend's face. In years past it was Katie who had paced impatiently while waiting for Paul to come home. Cristeen's irritation actually lent Katie patience.

"You know why, Cristeen. The herd is larger, the distance longer, and they need to brand the calves." She put an arm around Cristeen's shoulders. "Matt has been doing this for years, he'll be fine. Stop worrying."

"I'm not worried."

"You've got that defensive tone you use whenever you aren't quite telling the truth."

"Well, I'm not worried."

"You miss him." Cristeen nodded; Katie's smile deepened.

"I don't think I have ever been as happy as I have been these past few weeks." The fear nagged at her thoughts. She had been cramming a lifetime of happiness into the short time remaining that she could stay at the ranch.

Katie studied her friend's expression. Anxiety showed in her eyes, uncertainty wrinkled her brow. Katie wondered if it was haunting memories or an uncharted future that had her bothered. Cristeen dropped her eyes. Katie looked across the valley, thinking again how pleasant it would be if Cristeen simply stayed.

"You can stop missing Matt."

The definitive statement brought Cristeen's eyes up once more. "They're back!"

Four riders approached. Ty and Henry broke away, heading to the barns with the pack string. Matt and Paul continued straight on to the house. Cristeen stayed on the porch as she watched Matt ride in. He sat tall in the saddle, his shirt ruffling in the slight breeze. The beard he had kept neatly trimmed for the weeks prior to leaving had grown. As she watched he tipped his hat back and grinned.

Matt spotted Cristeen as he rode past the out buildings. As they drew closer he could see her smiling.

"Well, looks like it's not just me that gets welcomed home from this trip."

Paul's words set Matt to grinning. He pushed up his hat brim to see better.

Before the horses stopped, Katie had left the porch. Cristeen moved to the steps, suddenly feeling unsure. She wanted to run out to greet Matt, tell him how much she had missed him. The feelings were too unfamiliar, somewhat uncomfortable. Hesitantly she hobbled down the steps, going only a short distance into the yard.

Matt stepped down from the saddle, letting the reins trail on the ground. He overlooked Cristeen's hesitation. Her past had not taught her to show affection, in fact she had learned to keep her feelings buried. She was here, waiting for him, and that was enough. His stride ate the distance between them.

"Miss me?" She looked up into his eyes and nodded.

"Good, 'cause I sure missed you."

He wrapped her in a hug, and was pleased when she hugged him in return. She rested her head against his shoulder and sighed. Glancing down he saw her smiling.

"You were gone too long," she complained softly.

"Maybe next time you'll be healed enough to go with me."

Her heart leaped. Was it possible he wanted her to stay? Could this happiness continue? Surely something would happen to bring it all crashing down like a house of cards. Prior glimpses of joy caused Cristeen to tense with apprehension.

Matt felt Cristeen tense up. He held her close as he caressed her back. "I'm sorry. That was a bit forward of me. I just thought you might enjoy riding into the mountains."

She closed her eyes, listening to the warm resonance of his voice. His hand moved lightly across her back, gradually easing her fears. She sighed and relaxed into his embrace.

"I would enjoy that very much."

He leaned close to her ear and whispered, "Stop worrying about what might go wrong and just enjoy the moments." She shivered as if a chill ran down her spine.

"Are you happy here, Cristy?" He searched her reaction.

She smiled warmly. "Yes. I wish it didn't have to end."

He dropped an arm around her shoulder and steered her towards his horse. "Me, too." He glanced over his shoulder at the porch. "Where are your crutches?

"See, you were gone too long," she grinned. "Doc has me walking now, to strengthen the muscles."

"Is your leg healed?"

"Nearly so, but it is still weak and I must be careful with it. Maybe I could ride Sky soon."

Matt reached over and tousled her hair. "Nice try. No horseback riding for you until Dr. Roberts approves."

She made a face at him. "I must like you, 'cause I'm actually going to take your advice."

"I wouldn't call it advice."

"You'd better, I don't take well to being told what I can or cannot do."

Light danced defiantly in her eyes. Matt considered that a moment. "Let's compromise." Placing a hand on either side of her waist, he lifted her onto his horse's back.

She shrieked and giggled. "I can't ride in this dress."

"Why not," he set her on the saddle sideways. "See."

"Oh, I've never ridden sidesaddle before."

"Have you and Katie been doing a lot of baking?"

"No, why?"

"You're heavier than I remembered."

"Matthew Donovan!" Cristeen kicked at him, throwing herself off balance. She grabbed the saddle horn.

"Careful," concern quickly gave way to amusement. "I think I like this. You better be nice to me, or you'll fall off."

Cristeen pouted. "I don't like this at all."

"That's just because you're not in control."

Her mouth snapped shut. He was right, of course. It was kind of a nice feeling, that he knew her well enough to understand. At the same time it was extremely annoying, both his being right and his being in control.

"Relax," Matt laughed. "I won't let you fall, and I'll let you get even with me later."

"Promise?"

"Cross my heart," his hand made an X over his heart. "I won't let you fall."

"I meant the part about getting even," she smiled wickedly.

Matt groaned, "How do I get myself into these situations?"

They reached the corral. Matt lifted Cristeen down, grabbing her wrist as she made to move away. She looked quizzically at him.

"Tell me what you were afraid of back there."

"Besides falling? Don't scowl, I know what you meant."

Her eyes held his. Ghostly shadows seemed to drift in their pale blue color. Confidence was reigning now though. He let go of her arm, releasing her to walk away. She smiled before turning toward the fence.

"I really missed you," she said over her shoulder. After a short quiet she added, "Ask me again later, when I have more courage or less discretion."

Matt led his horse into the corral and began stripping off the gear. She hadn't said it maliciously, yet her meaning was clear. Cristeen still did not fully trust him. Would she ever? He deposited his saddle on the top rail forcefully. The blanket slid to the ground unnoticed. After slipping the bridle off the gelding's head, he sent the horse away.

Cristeen was standing beside the saddle when he turned. "I didn't mean to be hurtful."

Letting out a long breath of frustration, Matt hooked the bridle on the saddle horn. After ten days of separation he had forgotten how easily Cristeen could get under his skin. She was looking earnestly at him; he couldn't stay angry. He ducked between fence rails to join her.

"I've been having dreams again," her eyes fell. "Sometimes you are in them."

To be told by the woman he loves that she has been dreaming of him would thrill most men. Cristeen's admission sent a cold shock wave through Matt. Her dreams were not typically joyful, nor romantic. When she dreamed often she woke in such a state of distress it took hours for her to give in to exhaustion and sleep again.

Still, the ones causing her pain in those nightmares were the people she cared about. If Matt numbered amongst them she at least felt some fondness for him. He would almost rather she despise him than to cause her this anguish. He had never felt so powerless to help.

"Is it the same dream?"

Cristeen nodded almost imperceptibly. Emotion choked her voice, "It has a new twist. Now instead of being stranded on an island, I find myself on a cliff. Everyone is slipping over the edge and only I can save them."

Unspoken was the true horror of the dream; she could not save them. Now Matt had joined the ranks of those whose lives she could not keep from danger.

"Oh, Cristy," words could not express how much he hurt for her. He pulled her against him, as if to shield her from harm. "I'm sorry I wasn't here when you needed to talk."

She buried her face into his chest and gave up her struggle against the tears. This was what she needed, to cry and maybe, just maybe, let it go. All of her life she had been the strong one, had kept a stiff upper lip and held it all inside. For this moment at least she was grateful to lean on Matt, let him be the strong one.

The cleansing tears were short lived. As she took a few ragged breaths, Matt whispered tenderly in her ear, "I won't ever leave you, Cristeen Ciara Latham. Not even if you send me away."

The hand that lay against his chest clenched, gripping the fabric of his shirt. She had no intention of letting him go, either. He smiled.

"Walk with me." He gently turned Cristeen away from him, steering towards the meadows. She clamped her hand around his arm, drawing his attention to her face. "Does your leg hurt?"

"No," she managed a weak smile. "Just not ready to let go."

"I can accept that answer."

* * *

The darkness encroached upon the waning lamplight. Her head drooped, then bobbed back up. Cristeen was losing this battle against sleep. She could not bring herself to disturb Matt, again. The clock downstairs had just chimed two and she had kept him up quite late. She couldn't be sure when he left because he stayed until she actually fell asleep.

The nightmare did not wake her tonight. Not the usual one anyway. She had slept dreamless for a short while. What she saw after that wasn't really even a dream. Her sister's image had simply floated through the amorphous space of her thoughts. At first Leigh was silent; when she began to call for Cristeen the agitation and anxiety in her voice swelled to a feverish pitch. That was what woke her tonight.

Cristeen nodded off again. Sitting up in bed was not working. The desk chair beckoned, its hard wooden seat surely less comfortable and easier to stay awake in. As quietly as possible, she moved the lamp to the desk, wincing as the glass chimney rocked while setting it down. She glanced over the three books on the desktop. Her own copy of *Oliver Twist* held her attention.

She had read the inscription inside the front cover numerous times in the past two months. In the beginning the words had been comforting. *To my dear Cristeen,* surely written by a loving hand. When at last *Father* meant something to her, the words lost their ability to comfort. The book was a gift on her eleventh birthday. She had read and reread the story countless times. The space between being ten and turning twelve was a brief happy time for Cristeen. It was wedged between her father's drunken grief years and the befuddled con years.

For a short eighteen months her father returned. He got a job teaching, albeit primary school in a small town. Cristeen made a friend; Leigh made ten. It had come to a crushing end like all the other times, over who knows what offense. It was just after Mr. Johansen's funeral. Though she outwardly believed her father got drunk and offended the wrong person, inwardly Cristeen blamed herself.

With the benefit of hindsight, Cristeen could see now how foolish that guilt had been. Yet it was her guilt, and at least it was one emotion she was allowed to show. Tonight she was free to show any emotion that moved her, nevertheless she was fettered by the past. She cursed her father and the bottle he seemed to love more than his own children.

No, that wasn't true. Except for the occasional extreme, Dad always had a smile for Leigh. Praises were heaped on her younger sister. Time and again Cristeen silently suffered her father's rages of *'why can't you be more like your sister?'* She knew why, but what could she do about the color of her hair and eyes. What little she could do to change her appearance she did, trying her best not to look like Mother.

Leigh, Leigh, Leigh. Cristeen wanted to scream the name. Leigh looked like their father's family - brunette hair, hazel eyes, tall but broad across the shoulders. She never blamed Leigh, for her sister could do little about her appearance either.

Cristeen got up to pace. Her leg was sore, the muscles not yet returned to even a semblance of their former strength. Also it felt like the actual bones ached, a deep, tired kind of pain. The crutches leaned against the bureau where she had abandoned them a week ago. Taking up one now, she resumed pacing.

"Do you not sleep at all anymore?" Matt's gentle question startled Cristeen.

"How do you do that, sneak up on me I mean?"

He held up one leg, revealing a bare foot. "Just took my boots off. Heard you thumping with that crutch."

She considered his answer. "So, you don't sleep much either?"

A soft chuckle was his only answer. "Shall we keep each other awake then?"

She gestured to the wingback chair. "Be my guest. Or, since this is your house, be your guest."

He sat in the designated chair. "You get very silly when you are over-tired. Sit, tell me what's bothering you."

He patted the edge of the bed. It was still far too comfortable and Cristeen far from ready to give in to her exhaustion. She reclaimed the desk chair.

"Dream?" She nodded. "Why didn't you come get me?"

"Wasn't that dream."

"Did I say wake me only if you have that particular nightmare?"

"Sorry, this one seemed too banal to disturb you."

"Yet it's keeping you up."

"Barely," she yawned.

"All the more reason to tell me about it and get back to sleep." She grimaced. "Talk, woman."

Cristeen giggled. "You aren't very convincing as stern and overbearing." His eyes narrowed as he glared at her. "Okay, okay, I give. I saw my sister, Leigh."

His smile turned to a questioning frown. "And? What happened?"

"Nothing, I just saw her. I told you it was banal."

Matt let the silence continue while he contemplated the dream. There had to be something more than just seeing her sister that kept Cristeen from going back to sleep. Some fear that perhaps even she did not recognize.

"You hardly talk about your sister. Why?"

She shrugged. "Don't want to worry about her, I guess."

"Should you worry about her? Do you know where she is?"

Without thinking she answered, "Of course I know. She's in Denver with Aunt Caroline, where she belongs."

That came too easily. "How can you be so sure?"

"Because that's where I told her to go, and I told her to stay there." *Don't come back for me, I'll catch up to you.* The remembered statement sliced through Cristeen's mind, chilling her so that she shivered.

Matt noted the shiver and knew he was on to something with this trail of questions. She was teetering on the edge of remembering the shooting, he could sense it in her actions.

"From what you have told me about Leigh, she doesn't always do exactly what you say. What makes you think she obeyed you so faithfully this time?"

"Because," it was a weak response, in meaning and in tone.

"Because what, Cristy?"

Cristeen squeezed her eyes against the memories. "Stop it," she whined softly.

Leigh had to be in Denver, it was the only acceptable hypothesis. The notion that her sister might be out wandering alone scared her to death. The fear went beyond basic concern over Leigh's abilities to cope in the wilderness. Deeper than merely worrying for her sister's safety in an empty land wrought with natural pitfalls. It was a mind-numbing, irrational terror.

Matt moved to her side. "I apologize. Please breath."

His gentle apology pulled Cristeen back from the edge of panic. She focused on his soothing drawl and took a deep breath. When she opened her eyes, his face was level with hers. His soft brown eyes delved into her soul, searching for answers she was unable to give. In their depths she saw a tenderness that threatened to swallow her whole.

"Go away," she whispered.

"No," his voice was also quiet. "I have a promise to keep."

"You are so annoying." She pushed against his chest.

Matt caught her wrists and pulled her onto her feet. "Ya', but you love me for it."

Cristeen rolled her eyes, "Annoying is not one of your more endearing traits."

"And what are my endearing traits?"

"You're not very subtle late at night."

"Can't afford to be. You are going to fall asleep."
She stifled a yawn and tried to pull free from his grip.
"No I'm not."

"Oh yes you are," Matt grinned. With a gentle tug he pulled her close and scooped her off her feet. She slapped a flat palm against his chest in protest. "I'm bigger and stronger, and more alert."

That last he added as the yawn Cristeen struggled against finally won. "I won't sleep," she argued when the yawn subsided. "I'll just wake up again in a short time."

He dropped her unceremoniously on the bed. She bounced and crawled to the edge.

"Uh-uh," he scolded. "Tomorrow we'll send word to your Aunt. You can let her know you are fine. Then you can stop worrying about your sister."

He turned to pull the wingback chair closer. Cristeen scooted her legs under the bedcovering but did not recline back. Once the chair was satisfactorily positioned, Matt retrieved the oil lamp. She watched his bare feet move soundlessly across the hard floorboards as she contemplated his offer. What a wonderful, considerate, compassionate man. And she did love him even when he annoyed her.

"What's wrong?" He noticed her tearful expression.

Unwilling to tell him they were happy tears, she grasped the first subject that came to mind. His bare feet. "Were you really just going to bed?"

He dropped into the chair. "What brought on that question?" She pointed to his feet. Laughing, Matt propped them up on the bed next to her. "I didn't say I was just going to bed. I said I had just taken my boots off. You assumed I had been awake."

"You fell asleep with your boots on," his grin confirmed it. "Do you often sleep in your boots, at home I mean?"

"Guilty." He dropped his feet to the floor, leaving his legs stretched out comfortably. "Some habits are hard to break."

Cristeen was aware that sleeping in one's boots out on the trail was a wise move. You never knew when it might be necessary to spring up, ready for action. Also snakes and other nefarious creatures were often attracted to the warmth of a recently vacated boot. If you took your boots off at night, you better make sure to check for unwanted guests before putting them back on in the morning.

There weren't any snakes in the house, though. She wondered briefly if Matt kept his boots on because she was apt to interrupt his repose. She decided to accept his explanation; after all, this was his first night under a roof in almost two weeks. She reclined, watching as he extinguished the lamp.

"You trimmed your beard."

"Yes. Stop babbling and go back to sleep."

"What about you?"

"The chair is comfortable." She snorted. "Well, I've slept in less comfortable places. Sleep!"

TWENTY TWO

They say behind every great man is a greater woman. While Mike by no means considered himself great, there could be no denying the greatness of his wife, Suzanne. She kept the household neat, tidy, and smoothly running all while raising their three rather energetic boys. Whenever Mike had time to spend with his sons they ran him ragged. How Suzanne kept up with them, let alone kept them out of mischief, was a mystery.

Added to her other mystical talents, Suzanne quietly supported Mike throughout his career. She never made judgments about his decisions, yet her opinions and ideas influenced his enforcement of the law every day. And the men, his deputies, adored her for her cooking, which she happily shared on every possible occasion.

She was a great comfort to him in times of need. After nearly ten years of marriage, he didn't think there was anything Suzanne could do that would surprise him. He was wrong. She had amazed him by volunteering to come with him today, to speak to Leigh Latham and convince the young lady to give up her search.

"So this is what the inside of the Rossiter House looks like," Suzanne smiled slyly at Mike. "I have been told there are three crystal chandeliers in the dining room."

Mike cupped his wife's face in his hands and planted a kiss on her forehead. "I promise I'll bring you here for dinner someday. Soon," he added as she raised an eyebrow. "You deserve at least a night out."

Suzanne smiled up at him. He felt his heart beat faster. Even after all these years together she still could make him feel giddy.

The door of the private parlor opened with a quiet swish as it brushed across the thick carpeting and Leigh entered the room. Her stride faltered as she spotted Suzanne, and a frown crossed her countenance. It was replaced quickly with a broad, welcoming smile.

"Hello," she extended a hand in greeting. "I hadn't expected anyone else to be here for this update meeting, particularly someone I have not yet met."

Suzanne accepted her hand, giving it a gentle squeeze. Leigh continued. "I realized at once I could trust you."

Mike's hands had moved from his wife's face to her shoulders as Leigh entered. He chuckled, seeing her trail of logic. He introduced the women, then stepped back to let them become acquainted. If anyone could convince Leigh to give up her quest, Mike felt sure it would be Suzanne. She possessed incredible patience and negotiating skills, which she accredited to motherhood.

"I've heard so much about you," Suzanne was saying. "I admire your fortitude."

Leigh turned to Mike. "You want me to give up, don't you."

He sighed. "Yes, go home Leigh."

"No."

"You have to accept the obvious. Your uncle's money can hire the best tracker in the entire country and he, too, will fail. There's no trail, Leigh. She's gone."

"Michael!" Suzanne admonished lovingly.

"I'm sorry. My tact up and left about a week ago."

Leigh giggled. "I'm good at exasperating people. Cris says so all the time."

"The fact remains," Mike went on, "the entire mountainside has been searched and no trace found. I cannot condone this fruitless use of my department's manpower any longer."

His words stung. Leigh felt tears welling in her eyes and hated herself for them. Why couldn't she be strong, like Cris? CeeCee wouldn't be so easily moved to tears, she would stand firm in her beliefs. Right about now Leigh could use one of her sister's witty comebacks.

Suzanne moved to the younger woman's side. "Leigh, why don't you sit down. I admire your faith, and your determination. I would like to think I, too, would persistently search for my sister if I believed she was alive."

"She is alive," Leigh weakly insisted, her faith waning.

"Think about it, Leigh. Honestly. Do you believe she is alive, or is it just wishful thinking? Life doesn't always come with happy endings."

The silence deepened, became almost deafening. It was broken only by Leigh's quiet sobbing as she accepted the inevitable conclusion; Cristeen was dead. Suzanne enfolded her into an embrace, gently rocking to ease the grief.

Mike leaned his head against his arms on the mantle. He ached for Leigh as well. She was a likable young lady and he had hoped things would turn out happier. Even Rory was distraught when Mike ordered his young deputy to stop searching. In the course of one short month, Leigh had developed a circle of friends, friends she would need now as she faced the truth.

A light tap on the door drew Mike's attention. Leigh continued to sob; Suzanne continued to comfort. Mike moved to see who was knocking. It was Malcolm.

"Begging your pardon, sir," the butler looked past Mike. "Is Miss Leigh alright?"

"She will be, Malcolm, eventually." The servant held a tray on which was a slip of paper. "Is that what you came for?"

"Oh, yes sir," Malcolm stumbled to regain his etiquette. "This just arrived for you."

Mike took the proffered telegraph, read the words silently. "Malcolm," he called after the man, "Miss Leigh is going to be just fine." Mike smile broadly, sending Malcolm away with a happy grin.

Suzanne looked up quizzically as Mike approached them with a smile. Leigh stopped crying, looking up as she sniffled.

"What is it, Mike?" Suzanne questioned.

"Uncle George wired you, Leigh." Mike smiled more deeply. "I think you should wipe your eyes and read this."

Suzanne took the slip of paper from him. "Handkerchief," she held up her hand while reading the telegraph. He produced the requested handkerchief, mildly amused at his wife's behavior, and watched with interest as she read the message.

"Oh, my," Suzanne exclaimed quietly. She handed the paper to Leigh.

CRISTEEN ALIVE AND WELL STOP I WILL BE THERE TOMORROW STOP

GEORGE EDWARDS

Leigh scanned the words again. After the fourth reading she leaped to her feet.

"I knew she was alive!"

TWENTY THREE

*S*treams of silvery moonlight poured into the clearing, highlighting the blood pooling under her leg. She clamped her hands over the wound, desperate to staunch the bleeding. A feeling of unreality settled over her; this simply could not be happening. She could see the blood seeping past her fingers, felt the pain of flesh torn by the passage of the bullet. Still she felt coldly detached. She watched in horror as he lowered himself over her.

"I'll learn you to mess with Hank Crespin, girly."

His breath reeked of alcohol and rotting teeth. His shirt clung to his torso with odious sweat. She tried to turn her face away as he leaned closer. His lips brushed her cheek, his hot breath hissed in her ear.

"I'm gonna enjoy this." His was a malicious laughter.

Excruciating pain shot through her as he viciously kicked her legs apart. With every bit of strength she could muster, she swung her fist, driving hard at his breastplate, hoping to stop his heart. Anger tinged his maniacal laughs as he caught her fist and pinned it down with her other arm. Buttons popped off her shirt; the touch of his hand made her skin crawl.

Fight Cristeen! His face loomed before her, so close...she held her breath, waiting, waiting. New pains shot through her as she slammed her forehead into his face. The force of the blow sent a dull, thudding ache through her *head. Shoulder muscles burned, her joints felt as though they would pop with the strain.*

And all her effort gained was inflamed rage. His eyes watered; the hit smarted but nothing more. He backhanded her face, swearing vehemently. As her head recoiled to face him once more she spit, more to clear the blood and dirt from her mouth than in defiance. Still, it drove him into a murderous frenzy.

He clamped his hand on her throat; she could feel her windpipe crushing. The world was shrinking in on itself. As the blackness enveloped her vision, his voice hissed in her ear once more. "I ain't gonna kill ya yet. First you see what I do to yer sister, then I'll take care of ya."

She gasped for air, desperately tried to call out a warning to Leigh. Her voice would not cooperate. She tried again, and again...

Cristeen sat bolt upright, taking deep gulping breaths. She was shaking, the sheets were drenched with the perspiration of fear. And she must have screamed, for she could hear Matt running down the hallway.

Her heart would not slow down. She was hyperventilating, unable to stop herself. Her trembling turned to shivering; she was as soaked as the bed sheets. Then Matt was holding her, rocking gently and whispering, "Shh, it's okay now." She cried.

Matt enveloped Cristeen, continuing to reassure her that she was safe, he would protect her. Gradually, over the course of several minutes her breathing became regular and her tears tapered off. Katie wrapped a blanket around Cristeen to stop the shivers. Even so she continued trembling.

When Matt shifted his weight, a wave of panic swept through Cristeen. She was insensible with fear, her only hope seemed to be his promise to protect her. She wrapped her arms around his, clinging as if to life itself. She whimpered and began to hyperventilate again.

"Honey, I'm not leaving you," he gently pried loose from her grip. "Wrap up in the blanket. That's it."

He kept one hand on hers as he turned to sit with his back against the headboard. Carefully he drew her into his embrace, resting her head on his shoulder. Her terror could be seen in her eyes despite the darkness. He could feel her heart beating double time.

"Look, Cristy, I slept in my boots again." He waved a booted foot, attempting to distract her from the lingering nightmare. She didn't even look.

"Matt," Katie spoke softly. "You can't stay here like this. Let me take over."

"No," Cristeen whined. Her fist clenched a handful of Matt's shirt.

"I stay," he spoke with finality.

Katie heard in his tone the futility of arguing. The intensity of Cristeen's reactions surprised Katie. She glanced back as she left the room, seeing her brother in a new light. Matt held Cristeen tenderly, his lips close to her ear as he continued to whisper soothingly. Katie could not hear his words nor did she need to; they were meant for Cristeen alone.

As dawn snuck through the bedroom window, Cristeen fell asleep. Matt felt her body go limp as she sighed. The hours had passed slowly; each time she started to sleep she gave a twitch to wake herself. Cristeen made no acknowledgment of the words of comfort he spoke, except to burrow closer against him. Her silence was disconcerting. Matt let it be, waiting for the daylight to chase away the lingering fear before questioning her.

The scream had brought him running. Cristeen crying out her sister's name over and over; the outcry stopped just as he burst into the room. The sight of her taking choking gasps of air chilled him even now, hours later.

Two days had passed since sending word to Denver. The action had seemed to settle Cristeen's fears. Now she was again stricken with fear over her sister. Why?

Matt let his head drop, resting his chin on his chest. He told Cristeen he'd slept in less comfortable positions than that wingback chair. Sitting with his backbone pressed against the headboard and nothing to rest his head on surely was the most uncomfortable position in which to sleep. Feeling Cristeen in his arms, watching her breath slow, deep breaths, made all the discomfort fade.

* * *

"She just sits there, not talking. Does she even know we're here?" Paul stood at the kitchen window looking out at Cristeen.

"I have my doubts that she sees any of us," Katie moved to stand beside him. "Except Matt."

Their voices were hushed. The western peaks had speared the setting sun. They watched as Matt crossed to sit beside Cristeen on the porch swing. He put an arm around her shoulders and she sagged against him.

"Never seen someone withdraw like that." Seeing his colleen so defeated broke Ty's heart.

"How much longer can it last?"

"On'y the good Lord can say."

Katie turned away. That Cristeen hurt bothered Katie, but it was Matt that had her worried. He was being ripped apart, trying to comfort Cristeen without knowing what haunted her. He had become a shell of his former self, snapping at Katie whenever she suggested he just let Cristeen alone. She decided she liked it better when Matt used to walk away rather than voice his anger.

The whole situation was made worse by the fact that none of the three, Cristeen, Matt, nor Katie, had gotten a full night's sleep in the better part of a week. Every night Cristeen woke screaming and took hours to calm. Matt had taken to sleeping in the chair beside her bed; when Cristeen did sleep he still got little rest. And all the commotion disturbed Katie as well.

Paul moved to follow his fiancée. Katie sank into a chair, too tired to think about dinner. She closed her eyes and gratefully accepted the shoulder rub from Paul.

"Something's gotta give."

"What Paul? What besides one of us?"

"Seems to me," they both looked at Ty, "this would be a good time to be prayin'."

* * *

Mike Reardon looked with disbelief at the telegraph copy George Edwards showed him. "She's in Glenpark." The irony was incredible; the message had come first to Fort Rossiter to be wired on to Denver.

"You've said that repeatedly, Sheriff. What significance is there in Glenpark?" George Edwards glanced at his wife as he asked the question.

Mike shook off his wonder. "I got friends up that way, Mr. Edwards."

"It's a small world, Sheriff Reardon." Caroline Edwards had a pleasant Irish accent.

"What does any of that matter?" Leigh burst out. "Let's just get packin' an' git on up there."

"Young lady,"

"Uncle George, meanin' no disrespect, but you can't stop me. Not this time."

"Leigh, she said she is fine. There's no need to rush."

Her eyes narrowed as she considered Mike's comment. What would Cris do at a time like this? Leigh frowned in concentration.

Mike, on the other hand, was determined to keep Leigh from rushing pell-mell into peaceful Glenpark. She was friendly, affable, and under control here in Fort Rossiter. He'd seen her fiery temper in action once or twice over the last month. Matt Donovan lived up there in Glenpark; Mike would contact him and get some more facts before letting Leigh ride in spitting fire.

"As I said, Leigh, I have friends up that way. Once we have a better idea of the situation, then you can go get Cristeen."

George and Caroline both nodded their understanding. "Leigh, honey," Caroline addressed her niece. "You don't want to ride into town thinking she's being held against her will. You might offend innocent people."

Leigh scowled. "And create a scandal, which Uncle George can't afford." She bit her lip. "I'm sorry. Cris always tells me how rash I am. Guess she's right."

Rory tapped on the office door. "Can I talk to you a second, Boss?"

"What is it, Rory." Mike had finally gotten comfortable.

Rory stepped inside. "Ma'am, Miss Leigh," he tipped his hat in greeting. He was keeping tight-lipped in their presence.

"Well?"

"We maybe got trouble brewin', Boss."

"Rory, there's always trouble brewing. It's what happens when you have so many drinking establishments in one city."

"Naw, I don't mean the usual stuff."

Mike glanced at Leigh and the Edwards. Maybe he should have held this conversation privately. He wasn't sure which was worse, the news to come or the ridiculous manner in which he had to drag it out of Rory. Rather than continue grilling his deputy, Mike waved his hand in a motion to indicate Rory should keep rolling.

"Evan Marks is in town."

The news drew a groan from Mike. "Why can't things be easy? Just once. What's the scuttlebutt?"

Rory fidgeted, glancing furtively at Leigh.

"Oh, tell him already!" Leigh exclaimed.

"He's asking about all your searching, Miss."

"Splendid," Leigh drawled sarcastically. "And what has he been told?"

Mike stood impatiently. "I am still in charge here." Leigh had the grace to look chagrined. He pointed to her, "You will stay put. I will go to Glenpark."

"Sheriff," Caroline interjected, "couldn't you simply arrest the man?"

"For what?"

"He's an accomplice for one thing. And a wanted man."

"Crespin was the front man; Marks has no warrants against him."

Like it or not, Marks had done nothing that could be corroborated that was cause for arrest. Leigh had not seen him well enough to swear to a description. The mere fact he was typically with Crespin was not enough. Cristeen surely would be able to positively identify Marks, though. That made her Mike's key witness, and Marks' key target.

TWENTY FOUR

"Cristy, I brought you a visitor."

Sky pushed passed Matt and blew softly on Cristeen. They were just outside the barn, Cristeen sitting in her customary place in the sunshine. As the palomino nuzzled Cristeen's face, Matt saw her lips twitch as if to smile. Her eyes focused on the horse as she responded to the caresses Sky bestowed upon her. Hope stirred in Matt.

A buggy rattled across the bridge. Matt glanced over his shoulder to see Dr. Roberts driving into the yard. He turned back to Cristeen in time to see a real smile dart across her face. Sky was puffing short breaths in her ear.

"Honey," Matt kept his tone gentle, reassuring, "I need to go talk with Doc. I'll just be right over there by the porch."

Panic briefly moved through her eyes, the color drained from her face. Despite this, she nodded. "Okay."

Seeing her uncertainty, Matt stood and whistled sharply. The dogs streaked across the open expanse to stand expectantly at his side. "Coop, Fen, stay." At his command, both dogs lay down and turned watchful eyes on the yard. "Better?"

"Better," she agreed weakly.

Cristeen watched Matt cross the yard, each long stride taking him farther away. She didn't deserve his care and attention, and she certainly wasn't worthy of his love. She was nothing more than riffraff. Child of an alcoholic father.

Artless. Disreputable. Graceless. Defiled, unclean, immoral.

Fear of losing Matt's love was more terrifying than any of the nightmares.

Matt greeted Dr. Roberts as the physician climbed down from the buggy. "Paul talk to you?"

"Paul and Katie. They are deeply concerned." Doc gazed at Cristeen. "Interesting choice of distractions."

Matt watched Cristeen and Sky for a moment before answering. "She has a special relationship with her horse, Doc. And it's working. This is the farthest I've been from her without causing hysteria."

"She can still see you."

"I just wish she would talk," his voice was heavy with despair.

"She says nothing?"

"She gives one word answers to simple questions. Ask if she's thirsty, she'll answer. Questions that require her to make a decision, well it's as if she doesn't even hear those."

Doc nodded. "She is suffering profound depression."

"Is that what you call it? All I know is when I look into her eyes I can't find Cristeen anymore. There's just this dull emptiness. Dead eyes." Matt scrubbed his palms across his face, trying to wipe away the visual impression. Everything about this Cristeen was lifeless. Except when the dreams woke her, then the terror was like a raging storm in her eyes.

Doc placed a comforting hand on his shoulder. "What she went through was overwhelming enough to shut down her mind. It is why she was amnesic. You have given her the strength and courage to face that fear."

"Marvelous," he frowned. "I gave her the strength to destroy herself."

Doc chuckled gently. "Patience, Matt. The flame is not extinguished. With your love and support she can get through this."

"How long will it take?"

"That is entirely up to Cristeen." Doc began walking towards her. "The best I can do is keep her from being a danger to herself, and you."

The idea Cristeen could pose a threat to him was absurd. "She can barely walk on her own, Doc. What could she possibly do to me?"

"If you don't get some sleep," Doc shrugged, letting Matt complete the thought. "Let me talk with her. I may yet have some medications that will help ease the situation."

Cristeen was idly scratching Cooper as she watched Sky nibble on a nearby patch of grass. She gave no indication that she saw the men approach. Doc stopped Matt from addressing her, stepping forward instead to speak to her himself.

"Good morning, Cristeen."

"Go away."

"Say it like you mean it and I will." She deflated.

Doc talked to Cristeen for a few minutes. She answered his queries with nods and occasional shakes of her head. Once or twice she spoke. As he questioned her, Doc performed a surreptitious physical examination. He grasped her wrist, as if to hold her hand comfortingly, but in reality he measured her pulse. Gently laying his hand on her cheek, he was able to look into her pupils and gauge their dilation.

When he was finished, Doc moved to speak privately with Matt. "She's exhausted."

"I could've told you that, Doc."

"It's a nasty, vicious circle. First the memories trigger nightmares, which disrupt her sleep as well as cause her anxiety. The sleep disruption further exacerbates the anxiety until it becomes full-blown depression. Depression leads to nightmares, and the cycle repeats itself."

"So how do we break the circle?"

"Sleep. Uh-uh, don't argue. I'll leave something with Katie to help Cristeen sleep." Doc looked closely at Matt. "You might consider taking the medication as well."

Matt watched Doc stroll away to the house before turning back to Cristeen. He saw her eyelids droop as she fought against the sleep Doc was so sure held the key to her cure. If only it was that simple. He stifled a yawn of his own. Well, no one said love was easy.

The morning sun was warm, the seat surprisingly comfortable. Sky was too well trained to wander far. Matt rested his head against the barn and drew Cristeen against him. Maybe the light of day would keep away the dreams.

"Close your eyes, Cristy. I'll be right here with you."

The dream came quickly. Barely thirty minutes had passed and Matt was just drifting into sleep himself. As he let himself relax he felt Cristeen stiffen. Instinctively he tightened his hold. She was breathing rapidly and he could see her eyes moving beneath closed lids.

When he pulled her closer, Cristeen shuddered. Without warning she took a swing at him, her fist grazing his chin. There was force behind the punch and her arm was recoiling to strike again. He grabbed her arm to stop the attack. Her eyes opened then, sending an icy chill of fear through Matt.

Her eyes were unfocused, darting rapidly, and over full with terrified hatred. She stared through him, still seeing the nightmare.

"Don't touch me!" She half commanded, half begged.

"Cristeen, it's me. Wake up." Matt shook her gently.

She whined softly as with anticipation of pain. With her free hand she clasped her shirtfront. "Please don't," she whispered a pitiful plea.

"Move away, Matthew, and let Katie talk with her."

Doc's voice startled Matt. "No," he had promised never to leave.

"You are causing more harm just being you."

"What?"

"Matt," Katie stepped forward. "It's not you personally. Right now Cristeen needs to hear a woman's voice."

Matt began to understand. Carefully he pushed Cristeen away, holding her just enough to allow Katie to sit beside her. To do so, he had to release her arm. Immediately Cristeen pounded her fist repeatedly against his chest, crying "I hate you, I hate you."

Katie soothed tenderly. "The bad man is gone, Cristeen. You can relax now."

Bad man, the words pounded Matt's mind like a bad headache. Is that what she thought of him now? So much for being her protector. The long nights spent comforting her, all for naught. She hated him.

"Matthew," Doc laid a comforting hand on his arm. "It truly is not you that she hates. You are simply a victim of bad timing in this instance."

"What does that mean?"

Doc considered Cristeen before answering. Katie's soothing words were showing effect; the hysteria was waning. He turned back to Matt.

"You have been there when she woke after each episode?"

"Yes. More than once I have even woken her when it seemed the nightmare had begun."

"Today was the first time you have been holding her during the nightmare. When it began, you instinctively held her closer?"

"Bad move?"

"You couldn't very well drop her. There was no way for you to know that your tightened grip would feel like being trapped. Nor reason for you to understand what feeling trapped means to Cristeen."

Matt stood back in agony. There was reason for him to understand why being restrained would cause Cristeen to panic. Recalled to mind now were the bruises on her throat, face, and wrists. The tattered shirt Katie had tried to hide. The signs, long forgotten, had been there all along.

Lord, I want the man who did this to Cristeen. I want to

*find him and...*his prayer stopped short. Seeing the man hanged didn't seem justice enough. He would have to trust in God to deliver justice in this case. It was a bitter pill to swallow, yet he knew God would mete out proper justice.

When Cristeen's whimpering subsided, Doc approached the two women. Matt was almost gladdened to see the fear flare again in Cristeen's expression as she tried to crawl behind Katie. Doc chose to overlook the reaction.

"No more unmedicated sleep for this young lady," Doc spoke to Katie, pointing to Cristeen. "A couple nights of good, uninterrupted sleep will do wonders for her sanity."

Katie nodded in agreement. Doc continued, "And you better talk some sense to her, too, Katie. It's time for her to tell you what happened."

Doc turned away from the women, leaving Katie to handle the situation. His gaze fell on Matt, who stood with his fists clenched as he stared at Cristeen.

"Curb the anger, Matt," Doc advised. "Until you know who you are looking for."

The situation was turned inside out now. Cristeen leaned on Katie, if only emotionally. When Matt so much as stepped into the same room, Cristeen paled and looked frantically for an escape. That she reacted the same way to Paul and Ty was of little comfort to Matt. Sure, it wasn't Matt personally she hated and feared, it was all men. It still spelled the end to any relationship he might have with her. Even friendship.

He spent the next day and a half moping around the house and barns. Paul complained to Ty that Matt was like a grizzly bear with a sore tooth.

"Can't argue with you there, boy," Ty smiled ruefully. "Just you remember that an' stay outta his path."

Matt felt like he was being torn in two. He promised never to leave Cristeen, even if she sent him away. Yet her irrational fear of him threatened her very survival. It took a lot of soul searching, and a good deal of prayer, to realize what he must do.

Late on the morning of the third day Matt announced his intention to ride into Glenpark. "Might as well send for Cristeen's aunt. Keeping her here is like torture, with us men scaring her half to death."

Matt loved Cristeen enough to let her go and hope that someday she might come back.

TWENTY FIVE

The windows on the east side of the bedroom caught the light of each dawn, inviting the new day into the house. By late afternoon the sunlight angling from the western horizon reflected through the north side window. During the day the room was well lit, though not brightly so, giving one the impression of a soft coziness.

Cristeen stood at the north-facing window. From this vantage point she could see half way down the length of the valley. To her left the mountains swooped skyward; to the right she could see Katie's house and the mirror like surface of the lake.

Swords of sunlight pierced the clouded sky, penetrating the stormy gloom. The world outside reflected Cristeen's mood, dark and brooding. Two nights of uninterrupted sleep left Cristeen refreshed. Doc's prescription had not been able prevent the dreams, but it had kept her from waking. Now she knew the complete and awful truth about her past.

Movement in the yard below drew her eyes. She watched Matt cross the yard and enter a barn. Even at this distance she saw his anger in his jarring stride. A few minutes later he rode out, bending low as he passed through the threshold. He nudged Gideon into a lope and disappeared from sight.

Cristeen placed her palm on the windowpane. "Goodbye," she whispered with finality.

Katie stopped in the doorway, watching Cristeen as she

said goodbye. Gideon's hooves could be heard pounding across the river bridge. Katie felt hot with anger. The two of them were so much alike, Matt and Cristeen. Both so stubborn, and yet here both were just giving up on the other. Oooh, it was so frustrating!

She took a deep breath to regain her patience, then crossed the room to Cristeen's side. Try as she might yesterday, Katie had not been able to get Cristeen to talk. Today she was determined to get everything out in the open. She whispered a quick prayer for wisdom and courage. Cristeen acknowledged her presence only in that she dropped her hand from the window.

"Do you love him, Cristeen?"

"It doesn't matter." Her answer was flat and toneless.

"Would it make a difference if you knew he loves you?"

"No."

Cristeen sighed and turned away from the window, no longer willing to torture herself wishing for what she could not have. There was a look of expectancy in Katie's expression. She wanted an explanation. No, she was going to demand one. Katie should to be careful what she wished for, she just might get it.

"My father told me once that my associating with strumpets would only lead to my becoming one." Cristeen crossed the room to sit in the wingback chair. She well remembered that rather heated discussion. Her angry retort of, *'and what do I become by associating with a drunkard like you?'* did not set well with her father. She narrowly missed his incensed slap, fleeing until his rage wore off.

She would have run away altogether if not for Leigh. Being the elder, Cristeen made it her duty to protect Leigh from their father's drunken rampages. Although he probably would never have lifted a hand against Leigh, his chosen child. His ire fell always to Cristeen. Blame for her mother's death seemed to hang on Cristeen like the Celtic cross she wore.

Indeed, she blamed herself for many years. If only she had been born male, then her parents would not have cared to have another child. And her mother would not have died in childbirth. The bitter irony was that the child who died with her was a boy.

Katie drew her back to the present. "Strumpet? I don't think so, Cristeen."

"For all that his wisdom came from a bottle, he was right. We are products of our environment."

"I disagree. Yes, our environment helps shape and mold our character, but to accept it as the sole determination of our fate is to deny the possibility of bettering oneself."

"You would see it that way. Your environment gave you privileges that bias your opinion. You were free to learn, to express your ideas. Your environment taught you to see the good in people, to trust and be trustworthy."

"Your father was a teacher, Cristeen. Surely you were free to learn."

"An assumption, Katie." She turned hard eyes on her friend. "Yes, when I was very young and my father was a prominent member of the University, I was encouraged to learn."

"And later?"

"I have lived all over, been exposed to innumerable environmental influences. I do not care to divulge them."

Katie smiled, despite the serious nature of their conversation. "So you are telling me there's a little bit of strumpet in you? What else?"

"You mock." Cristeen glowered. "Am I not teaching Henry?"

"Well, yes," Katie agreed reluctantly, feeling she was losing the argument.

"And where do you think I learned to ride, in Boston? Ha!" The logic of her argument pleased Cristeen. "I've been down the river, Katie. With men who thought I was a boy, so they felt no need to constrain themselves."

That bit of information raised Katie's eyebrows. Many an evening conversation amongst cowpunchers would not be suitable for mixed company. Rather than lessen her regard for Cristeen, the revelation made Katie wonder what kind of parent allowed such treatment of his daughter. Maybe Cristeen was partly correct about being the product of her environment. With no other example to show her differently, Cristeen could not be other than those with whom she interacted. Somewhere she must have found a better example.

Cristeen sat triumphant in her argument. Katie studied her friend. She saw an intelligent, well-read woman, quite capable of forming and expressing her own opinion. This argument was well thought out with each counterpoint anticipated. Cristeen went into this debate believing so strongly in her viewpoint, winning was a foregone conclusion. No wonder Matt enjoyed their talks; he loved a good debate.

In her blind faith, Cristeen overlooked a critical fact. She was not a loose woman, nor was she crude or socially inept. It might be true that her housekeeping skills were negligible. So what? No one had ever been condemned for being a lousy housekeeper.

"So, you believe you are the product of the environments in which you have lived? Do these environmental influences effect us throughout our lives?"

Warily, Cristeen answered. "I reckon they might."

"Supposing you are correct. What of this environment?" Katie's sweeping gesture took in the entire ranch.

"Ah, now I see your point. Given long enough exposure, perhaps a good environment could neutralize the effects of prior bad environments." Cristeen considered the idea. "Yes, it is a valid theory."

"Thank you."

"But it does not change the past. My past."

"Overcome your past, Cristeen."

"Not an option, I'm afraid. For what occurred I am entirely to blame."

Her conviction stopped Katie cold, her mind reeling. A vile and depraved man attacked Cristeen. That he probably had not completed the act did not lessen the crime. Katie had come to despise this nameless, faceless monster. Cristeen, on the other hand, somehow saw the blame as being hers. Katie felt a growing disregard for Cristeen's father. The man obviously instilled in his daughter a responsibility for all the ills and woes of the world.

Maybe Cristeen could justify her guilt, Katie could not. Without the facts, drawing any conclusion was wrong. Nonetheless knowing the truth wasn't going to change Katie's mind. Even strumpets did not deserve to be beaten and shot.

It would take a mightier advocate than Katie to sway Cristeen's mind.

Katie walked to the window, looking out at the majesty of the mountains. *Lord, give me the words that will open Cristeen's eyes,* she silently prayed. The Lord could heal Cristeen's heart, but only if Cristeen were willing. Katie could not make her accept His forgiveness. Cristeen needed to be reminded that unlike her earthly father, the Father in Heaven loved her and wanted for her to be happy.

"Cristeen, have you prayed about this?"

The question surprised Cristeen. What did she need to pray about? Her own actions and behavior had led to, even encouraged, her attack. She had endangered the life of her sister. She had taken the life of another person. *Thou shalt not kill*; no mistaking what that meant. She broke one of the Ten Commandments. Now it was time to be held accountable. She failed to understand how prayer might help.

Encouraged by her friend's bewilderment, Katie went on. "The Bible clearly tells us to bring our troubles to the

Lord. We need only ask and He will ease our burden."

"I don't see how He can ease this burden. What's done is done."

"In the first place, Cristeen, He wants to forgive you, if you'd only ask."

Cristeen lowered her gaze.

"In the second place, you are trying to figure this out all on your own. You can't. Only He can, and only if you let Him."

Only by giving yourself over to the Lord can you accomplish anything, Cristeen. She remembered Matt's words of advice. Jesus' words sprang into her mind, "...*without me ye can do nothing.*"

Cristeen was humbled. She was not abiding in the Lord. In fact, she had completely forgotten about Him. Her arrogance, as Matt so eloquently called it, was in believing that only she could get herself out of this situation. The only conclusion Cristeen could see had her suffering the same death she had meted out to her attacker.

Thank you, Lord, for not forgetting about me as I so often forget about you.

Katie waited patiently, sensing a change in Cristeen's attitude. When at last Cristeen looked up, tears were in her eyes.

"I have been shamed," she admitted softly.

"I know."

"You don't know the half of it."

"Tell me, Cristeen. Tell me the whole of it, and then we'll pray together."

She shook her head. "I can't. Maybe someday, not today."

"Can you tell me anything?"

"I will tell you that some of what you believe happened is true." Cristeen took a deep breath, releasing it slowly.

"Start at the beginning. Why do you blame yourself?"

That was easy to explain. "I have a sharp tongue. Maybe

you have noticed?"

Katie snickered. "My brother calls it wit."

"Whatever," Cristeen frowned at the reference to Matt. "I also have poor judgment when it comes to using that wit. I should have learned from experiences with my father to keep my mouth shut."

Katie looked closely at her. "He hit you?"

"Oh, he tried. I learned to be quick around him. Liquor clouded his judgment and slowed his actions. I guess I let myself believe I could out maneuver any man."

Cristeen paused, gathering her courage. "Anyway, I said some unflattering things to the wrong man. Thought I was putting him in his place."

"So he took it upon himself to put you in your place?" Katie saw the color drain from Cristeen's face and knew she was right. "That doesn't make it your fault. He was being rude to begin with, I take it?"

Cristeen nodded.

"You needed to say something to make him stop."

"I should have simply left."

"He would have followed."

"He did follow. I should have realized that, too."

"Still, he is the one that attacked you. You are not at fault."

Cristeen dropped her eyes. Her hand went to the Celtic cross at her throat. Desperately she wanted to believe as Katie did, that the attack was not her fault. Yet even if she accepted that theory, she was guilty for what followed.

"I killed a man, Katie."

The words were barely audible. Katie was startled. She had believed the source of the nightmare lay in Cristeen feeling vulnerable and helpless. And maybe that was what initially triggered her despondent, desperate fear. Cristeen was too independent and self-assured to feel helpless for long; too much a loner to feel vulnerable. No, the true nightmare lay in that Cristeen felt she alone controlled her destiny, and the course she charted that fateful night was overwhelming.

Cristeen took Katie's silence as incrimination. "As I said, you didn't know the half of it."

Katie crossed the room and crouched in front of her. "I saw what he did to you, Cristeen. I would like to believe I would be able to defend myself as well as you did."

"Killing him was not the right thing to do, Katie. He could have been stopped without taking his life."

"Oh, Cristeen," Katie hugged her friend. "Now I understand why you feel the way you do."

"You do?"

Katie rocked back, looking her in the eye. "Pray with me, and let the Lord be your judge. Then if you still feel guilty, I'll help you contact the sheriff."

TWENTY SIX

Mike Reardon rode into Glenpark feeling a bit like riding into his own past. In the years since he left, little about the town had changed. He knew that from conversations with Matt Donovan; now he saw it for himself.

He went straight to Horace Hatcher's office. Glenpark being the small hamlet it was, Horace served as mayor and constable, as well as editor and publisher of the only newspaper in town, which he printed on his own press once monthly. Horace knew everyone and everything in Glenpark. He made it his business, claiming it was for the public good.

"Sheriff Reardon, it surely is surprising to see you here."

The voice startled Mike, although he recognized it at once. "Mr. Donovan. What brings you to town?"

Matt laughed, for the first time in days. "Come on Mike, I live here. Better question is, what brings you to town?"

Mike dismounted and wrapped a rein around the hitching rail. "I was on my way to see Horace, but you can probably help me just as well. And you're more enjoyable company."

"Don't tell me you still hold a grudge over that whole thing with Sarah and Suzanne?"

"Naw, I got over that long ago. Suzanne far outshines Sarah. She did then, too." He looked closely at his friend. "Forgive my saying so, buddy, but you look like death warmed over. Sarah on your mind again?"

Matt guffawed. "Like you, I got over her long ago."

"I was glad when you came to your senses. What gives, then?"

"It's a long story, and I'm sure you came up here on business."

"Buy me coffee and a meal, and my business can wait."

They walked to Myrtle's Cafe. Myrtle Potter was one of those enigmas Mike had never been able to solve. She was old when he left, yet the past eight years hardly showed in her lined, leathery face. The only thing definite about Myrtle was her cooking; absolutely the best in the West.

"Michael Reardon!" Myrtle exclaimed. "Come home at last."

"Just visitin', Myrtle. How 'bout some coffee."

"And bring him a plate of today's special," Matt added.

"Two specials, comin' up."

"Just one, Myrtle."

Myrtle stopped to study Matt. She saw what she wanted and shook her head, making *tch-tch* noises with her tongue as she walked away. "What love does to ya', boy."

Mike looked at Matt. "What's she mean by that?"

"Just an old woman babbling."

"You answer a mite too quick, my friend. But I'll let it go for now."

"Good, I'm not in the mood to discuss it." Matt did his best to push aside his frustrations. "Now, tell me what brought you up here."

* * *

Matt rode in silence, aware of his friend's eyes upon him. Mike was here for Cristeen. It was still almost too incredible to believe.

Mike loped his horse to catch up. "Slow down, Matt. I can forgive you barely giving me time to choke down what I'm sure was a delicious meatloaf. Have mercy on my horse, man! He's come a far piece with little rest."

Matt reined back, slowing Gideon to a walk. "Sorry."

Mike studied Matt closely. Friends since they were boys, Mike understood Matt better than he did his own siblings. Matt had a tendency to be very closed mouth, especially about his personal feelings. The deeper the emotion, the quieter he became. His simple "I know where Cristeen is staying," as yet had not been explained. His silence spoke volumes. Mike knew the direction they were headed.

"So, how long has Cristeen been at the ranch?" Matt threw a quick, darting glance at him. It was confirmation enough.

"Two months."

"Why did she wait so long to contact her aunt?"

"At first she didn't remember her aunt. After that," Matt shrugged. "I don't understand what goes on in Cristeen's mind."

Mike chuckled and was rewarded with a dark glare from Matt. "Take a piece of advice from an old married man, buddy. Never try to understand a woman's thought process."

Matt smiled ruefully. "Where were you eight weeks ago when I could have used that advice?"

They rode on in silence. The ranch house could be seen now, partly hidden behind the trees that lined the stream. Matt felt a tightening in the pit of his stomach. He was dreading going home.

As he rode out only a short time ago Matt glanced up at the bedroom window and saw Cristeen watching. He wanted badly to just force her to talk to him, while at the same time realizing how detrimental that would be on so many levels.

At the bridge, Matt reined in Gideon. Mike stopped also, turning a questioning look on his friend.

"I don't know if Cristeen will talk with you," Matt looked at the house. "Go on to the house and see Katie. I'll take care of your horse."

Mike recognized the tortured expression on Matt's face. In ten years of marriage Mike had twice upset Suzanne enough that she stopped speaking to him. The first time lasted an agonizing two days. Mike learned his lesson and apologized quickly the second time.

"Love isn't always easy, my friend. But it's worth the struggle." Mike nudged his horse.

Matt reached out, grabbing Mike's arm to stop him. "I need to know, Mike. Cristeen won't tell me what happened. I need to know."

"You mean to tell me you have no idea what happened to her?"

Matt removed his hat and pushed a hand through his hair before jamming the hat back down on his head. His anger was tightly coiled. Mike could take Cristeen away, but not before Matt had a name for the man he intended to hunt down.

"Oh, I've got a pretty good idea." He turned cold eyes to Mike. "I just want to know who did it."

The look was chilling. Mike had seen Matt angry before; never had he seen such deadly intent in his friend's eyes.

"We need to talk, you and I."

Katie greeted them at the back door.

"Mike! How's Suzanne? The boys? When are you going to bring them up to visit?"

Mike laughed. "One question at a time. I've missed you Katie, and Suzanne has too."

Matt pushed by them. "Later, Katie. We have business to discuss." He strode purposefully down the hall, heading for his study.

"Bear," Katie grumbled.

Mike kissed her forehead. "Patience, Katie."

Mike outlined for Matt the facts as he knew them. "You heard of Hank Crespin?"

"Know the name."

"Cristeen and her sister had the displeasure of making his acquaintance."

Matt felt his anger rising like bile in his throat. Hank Crespin. Now he had a name on which to focus his rage.

"They ran up against him at the Cherokee Inn. Leigh says Crespin was rather rude." Mike smiled with the memory. "She has a gift for understatement."

Matt smiled despite his anger.

"She also stated that Cristeen eloquently dismissed Crespin."

"Oh no," Matt groaned. He knew how effectively Cristeen wielded her sharp tongue. Loosed on the wrong man, her brand of wit would only invite trouble, and trouble never turned down an invitation.

"Yeah, oh no is right," Mike went on. "Crespin apparently felt the need to avenge his reputation. Of course, it didn't help that Leigh reminded Cristeen of their money cache within Crespin's hearing."

"He ambushed them."

"Yup. The details are unclear. Leigh refuses to discuss the actual attack."

Matt ran a hand across his face. "I saw her wounds, Mike. It doesn't take much imagination to figure out what happened."

" 'Bout how I figure it," Mike finished up, "the thing that saved her was him figuring she was dead."

He stopped, staring past Matt. "Did I get it right?"

Matt froze, only now realizing Cristeen stood behind him. He cursed himself for not closing the door.

"So far." Cristeen answered shakily. "Tell him what comes next."

"Your sister mule kicked Crespin."

She snorted. "She would. I wondered why he was so far from her."

Cristeen moved around the chairs. Both men rose. Matt

studied Cristeen as she stood before him. She seemed rested, her reason returned. Yet in her eyes the demon still lurked. She held his gaze, neither smiling nor frowning.

"Hi," she greeted him softly.

"Hi," he smiled slightly. "Welcome back."

Mike eased out of the room, leaving them alone. He descended the stairs silently and found Katie in the library.

"Are they talking?"

Mike nodded. He looked closely at her. His friend's little sister, she was also like a kid sister to him. He could read Katie as well as he could Matt. Maybe better, as she didn't try so hard to hide her emotions.

"You know, don't you?"

Katie shuddered. "Can you believe Cristeen actually blames herself?"

"I talked with a doctor friend of mine. He said to expect it; apparently that is a fairly common reaction."

Katie twisted a section of her skirt. "Mike, will you have to bring Cristeen in? For killing that man, I mean?"

"No, Katie. It was justifiable, self-defense." Mike sank into the chair opposite her. "Will Matt be able to accept that?"

"I'm certain he will." Katie scowled. "I'm not sure Cristeen will accept it."

* * *

"I'm sorry for what I put you through."

"I'm the one that should apologize." Matt brushed a strand of hair off her face, letting his hand linger on her cheek. To his dismay she tensed at his touch. She closed her eyes, reaching up to pull his hand away.

"Please, don't."

Cristeen concentrated on breathing slowly. Looking into his eyes she felt her resolve melting. So tempting it was to lose herself in their depths. She must not; she must tell him her crime.

Matt misunderstood her reaction, reading it as apprehension. He fought the urge to wrap her in a hug, fearing another panicky outburst. Instead he said the words he had wanted to tell her before.

"Cristy, I would never knowingly do anything to hurt you."

Even his voice was soft and gentle. Full of tenderness. Cristeen trembled as a tear slipped passed her lashes. If only she could take back what she had done.

"Honey, you better sit." Matt became alarmed as the color drained from Cristeen. He risked placing his hands on her shoulders to guide her into the chair.

Cristeen hid her face behind her hands, ashamed of her tears. She had been resolutely determined to tell Matt that she had killed a man. And when Katie dashed into her room with the news that their sheriff friend was here, Cristeen knew God had sent him. Mike's presence was the sign Cristeen had prayed for; she would confess her crime and go away to face her punishment.

Again Matt misread her. The tears, her shakiness, hiding her face; the fear and vulnerability clashing with her need to be in control. His anger flared once more.

"I will find the man who did this to you." He promised through clenched teeth.

"No you won't."

Her certainty hurt. She did not believe him. What was it going to take for her to understand the depth of his feeling for her? When Hank Crespin assaulted Cristeen he could have no idea the far-reaching repercussions. Perhaps if she had died the man would have gotten away with his heinous crime.

"Cristeen, I can't let him go unpunished."

She laughed, a kind of unnatural, nervous sound. "You won't find him, and he hasn't gone unpunished. He's dead."

Matt was puzzled. Cristeen rushed into his silence before

her courage failed again. "I killed him. I'm a cold-blooded murderer."

She spat out the self-accusation. Matt continued to stare. Of course, he should have been able to predict this outcome. Cristeen was independent, self-reliant, determined, and stubborn. She had fought back, as evidenced by the numerous bruises on her face and body. There was no back down in her; she never gave up until her attacker was vanquished.

What confused Matt was her tremulous behavior; she knew Crespin wasn't coming after her and she had ultimately proven she could take care of herself.

Cristeen spoke again. "I am sorry I did not tell you sooner. Now that you know, you can understand why I must return to Fort Rossiter, to accept my punishment."

"Punishment?" Matt found his voice. "It was self-defense, Cristeen. You are not a cold-blooded killer."

Their eyes locked. Cristeen had that obstinate *I know I'm right* look that Matt had come to know. She truly believed in her guilt. Her eyes narrowed, grew colder.

"I could have stopped him without killing him. I never wanted anything so much as I wanted that man dead."

She shuddered at the vivid memory. Calmly looking down the pistol barrel, carefully finding the exact spot at which to aim. Precisely between the eyes, where the bullet would pass straight into the brain, wreaking havoc on its passage and swiftly ending life.

She had coldly calculated the shot in a split second. There were no reservations as she squeezed the trigger. She had not counted on all the blood and gore, though. Bone fragments, flesh, blood, blood, more blood.

The memory overwhelmed Cristeen. She became nauseous and light-headed. She was about to faint.

"Whoa, better get your head down, honey." Matt moved quickly to push her head down to her knees. He stroked her hair to help settle her nerves.

"I'm okay now," she declared weakly.

Matt crouched before her, briskly rubbing her hand as her color returned to normal. He smiled tenderly.

"Cristy, cold-blooded murderers don't faint over the memory of their kills."

"Please don't laugh at me."

"Oh, honey, I didn't mean to laugh." He squashed his chuckle.

"And stop calling me honey."

Matt stood, still holding her hand. "Now you're pouting. Come here," he pulled her to her feet and wrapped his arms around her. "Will you honestly answer a few questions?"

She nodded. He could still feel her tension in her rigid stance. He thought a moment before speaking. He needed to lead her to understanding, but she would have to make the correct conclusion on her own. Otherwise she would never believe in her innocence.

"He shot you first?"

"Yes."

"He hit you?" She nodded. "Then strangled you? You had every reason to believe he wanted you dead?"

"I guess."

"Did he assault Leigh?"

"No."

"What stopped him?"

"Me, but..."

Matt cut her off. "If you had only wounded him, what do you think he would have done?"

She shrugged. Matt knew the answer; he needed Cristeen to know also.

"Think, Cristy," he prodded. "What happened when you publicly insulted Crespin?"

"He followed us."

"And what would he have done had you not killed him?"

She buried her face against his shoulder, muffling her

answer. "Follow us."

"And?"

"I don't want to think about that."

"So, what was the correct choice, given the circum-stances?"

She didn't answer. Matt felt her relax as she accepted the truth; it was a justifiable homicide. He knew he had won her over when she thumped her fist lightly against his chest.

"I hate you," the words were said lightly, almost play-fully.

"No you don't." He let himself chuckle. "You just hate that I'm right."

She hit him again, leaning her head back to give him a crooked smile. "Not true. I just don't like being wrong."

Matt cocked his head to the side, soaking in her smile as he considered her words. There was a very subtle difference between the two statements. She was willing to accept his being right, even at the expense of her being wrong. She didn't like it, but she accepted it.

"I do like your smile," she blushed. "I like that, too."

Cristeen leaned into his caress. "You spoil me."

TWENTY SEVEN

Mike sat on the porch, patiently waiting with Katie. The sun broke free of the clouds just in time to set. Stepping out the door, Matt spotted them deep in conversation.

"Shouldn't you be making dinner?"

They stopped talking, Mike getting a quirky grin; Katie's expression waffled between concern and anger. Then Cristeen pushed Matt with the screen door.

"Give her a break, she's been worrying about you all day."

Katie darted across the porch to engulf Cristeen in a hug. "Everything is alright now?"

"No," Matt's answer surprised both women. "I am the brother here, don't I get a hug?"

Katie batted his arm. Turning back to Cristeen she said conspiratorially, "I can tell you two made up just by his irritating good humor."

Cristeen giggled. Matt enjoyed the sound enough to overlook his sister's words. Mike was at his side now slapping him on the back.

"Unless you do something about that friendship you are doomed, buddy."

Matt shrugged. "Too late, I'm afraid."

Mike turned to Katie. "May I burrow your co-conspirator?" He drew Cristeen away from Katie. "We have something to discuss."

Cristeen glanced at Matt, who nodded approval. Noting that, Mike requested Matt be part of the discussion as well.

"First of all," Mike began, "your sister is anxious to see you. I am sure she can be made to understand should you decide to remain here.

Cristeen felt her face grow hot as she flushed. She was not used to having her heart on her sleeve for all to see.

"That said," he continued, "I would like for you to come back with me, to wrap up a very loose end."

"What loose end?"

"Evan Marks."

Matt wracked his memory for who that was. "Crespin's partner?"

At the same time Cristeen asked, "The other man?"

Mike looked at each of them. "Yes, Leigh cannot positively identify him. You can."

The panic rose again in Cristeen. She clamped her eyes, as if to shut out the memory. "I don't know how I blocked that memory for so long."

She rubbed her shoulder where Marks' bullet had passed through in his attempt to kill her. Matt put his hand over hers, stilling its movement.

"Did he do this?"

She nodded. Taking a deep breath, she sat up straight and steeled herself. "I'll go with you."

Matt protested, "You would be safer here."

"What if he found me here? Would he hesitate to kill more than one of us?"

"How would he find you?"

"He did," she pointed to Mike.

"He had help from your aunt, remember."

Cristeen was vehement. "I will not be the cause of another killing, not when I can prevent it now."

Matt opened his mouth to argue her point, when Mike's chuckle stopped him.

"Face it, Matt, this is one argument you can't win."

Matt sighed his resignation. "Very well. When do we leave?"

* * *

Dr. Roberts was pleased to see Cristeen again. He watched her cross the room to greet him; there was still a pronounced limp to her gait, yet she moved easily and unaided. Very unaided, he thought with a chuckle, as Cristeen brushed aside Matt's attempts to assist her. It was clear she had regained her senses.

"Doc," she planted herself before him, "tell him I can ride."

Matt was mildly amused by her defiant attitude. "I never said you couldn't. I said Doc had to approve."

Her eyes flashed. Doc looked a little closer at the dynamo his star patient had become. He was relieved to see just the hint of a smile at the corners of her eyes.

"All right, then, let me take a look at that leg." Doc went into the consultation room. "Hop up," he patted the examination table. Cristeen swatted at Matt when he tried to lift her.

"You, out," she poked Matt's chest and pointed to the door.

Before Matt could argue, Mike stepped into the room, grabbing his shirt collar and pulling him away. Mike said something about giving the poor girl some privacy as he closed the door.

Doc shook his head with amusement. Cristeen took off her shoes and hitched up her skirt to reveal her healing leg.

"Some day, young lady, he may be more than just a friend." Doc carefully examined the leg, watching her facial reactions for signs of pain. "What will you do then?"

"Find a way to hide that." She pointed to the scar forming along her outer calf. She made a face, expressing her disgust in this healing process, then lay flat.

Doc was silent as he examined her leg. It was still tender; the muscles badly atrophied. "You would be in better shape if you had been walking on this over the past week." He tapped her foot, indicating he was finished. "However, I see no reason to stop you from riding."

Her joy was plain to see. She propped herself up on her elbows, smiling broadly at him. Cristeen had always been a pleasant patient; Doc could see why Matt found her attractive.

"You could distract him, you know."

"What?"

He winked at her. "Matt, keep him from seeing the scar by dazzling him with the beauty of your feet."

"Dr. Roberts!" She blushed. "You are as bad as Ty."

He laughed. "From you, I will take that as a compliment." He opened the door and announced, "She can ride."

Matt pushed the door fully open. Cristeen scrambled to pull her skirt back over her leg, hiding the aforementioned hideous scar. Matt ran a finger over her toes, setting off a wave of ticklish giggling.

He traced his finger along the top of her foot. "You have adorable ankles."

She felt a little thrill go through her unrelated to being tickled. She focused her eyes on the top button of his shirt, unsure of her ability to withstand the full power of his gaze. "You are exasperating."

"I know," he kissed the top of her head. "Here, Katie packed your bag."

He placed saddlebags on the table beside Cristeen. Oh it would feel so good to slip into her jeans, get free of the unwieldy skirt. She opened the flap, glanced inside. Her heart sank.

"My boots aren't here."

"Your boots could not be saved." One of them, anyway. Matt left that unsaid. "I know where there is a pair that should fit you perfectly."

"Where? Why should they fit me perfectly?"

"Because I had them made exactly the same size as your original pair. It didn't seem right to discard the ones you rode in with without having a replacement for you."

Cristeen knew he had done it even before she had regained consciousness. Another example of Matt's compassion. She bowed her head, unsure how to say thank you. He lifted her chin; the smile on his lips went to his eyes.

"Be dressed when I get back, or I'll tickle you again."

"Go away then."

The door closed once more and Cristeen slid off the table. She wriggled out of the dress and slipped the calico shirt over her head. Sitting in a chair, she pulled on her socks and reached for her jeans. Something about her right leg caught her eye; she looked at it closely, comparing it to her left leg.

"Doc?" He acknowledged her through the closed door. "One leg is smaller than the other. A lot smaller."

Doc's voice sounded closer when he answered this time. "Your muscles have atrophied, that is they shrank from lack of use. It is normal, and they will rebuild themselves with exercise."

The words were meant to reassure. Yet as Cristeen pulled the denim material over her legs, she thought again about the cause of her wounds. Unlike other flashes of memory, where the events had seemed slow and ethereal, today images flashed at high speed past her mind's eye. There was the bright flash and the searing pain of being shot. Crespin's face so close to hers she could have counted the whiskers on his chin. She felt the panic, the terror of knowing what would happen to Leigh if she didn't get up. Her hand seemed to jerk again as when her pistol fired. *What happened to me? What have I done?*

When Matt returned with the new boots, the consultation

room door was still closed. Mike shrugged when asked what was taking so long. Matt tapped on the door.

"Cristy, am I going to have to tickle you?" He got no response. "Cristeen?"

Opening the door slowly, he saw Cristeen sitting in the chair. She was bent over double, her hands cradling her head. Matt rushed to her side, calling out for Doc. When he placed a hand on her shoulder he felt her sobs.

"Cristy, what's wrong?" Matt crouched beside her.

She slowly raised her head to look at him. "I just felt a little overcome, and I remembered what you did for me the last time I almost fainted."

Doc brushed by. He looked carefully at Cristeen before making his prognosis. "Memory flashes will be likely to occur with varying degrees of severity for quite sometime."

Cristeen sat up, taking a deep breath and letting it out slowly. "Well, that was embarrassing."

Matt glanced over his shoulder. Mike had stayed out of the room, yet had clearly seen the episode. Matt turned back to her, kicking the door at the same time to swing it nearly closed.

"Just between us, okay?"

She knew he wasn't telling the whole truth, but she accepted it anyway. "Did you get my boots?"

He relaxed. "Yes, ma'am." He produced the footwear. "Let's see if they fit."

"Ha, the feet are covered."

"That won't stop me." He ran a finger along the bottom of her left foot, from heel to toe.

She writhed. "Stop, stop!"

Mike called out from the other side of the door. "Knock it off, Matt."

"Yes, sir!" Matt feigned obedience. To Cristeen he whispered, "Always did think he was the one in charge."

"I can hear you." The door was ajar. "And I can make life

very miserable for you, Mattie."

"Mattie!" Cristeen giggled. "I thought Ty was the only one who called you that."

Boots donned, Matt stood and pointed. "You will forget about calling me that, Cristeen Ciara Latham."

He opened the door fully. Mike stood with his arms crossed. Having waited patiently, it was time now for pay back. A slow smile spread across Mike's face.

"Uh-oh, you're getting that devilish look."

"Aye, Mattie." Mike mimicked Ty's accent, drawing a giggle from Cristeen. "And you, pretty lady, don't you forget I have spent the past month with your sister. I dare say there are things she has said that you wouldn't want passed along."

She shrugged, "Leigh only thinks she knows me."

"Ah, feeling invincible," Mike winked at Matt. "Then let's get you on your horse, Cris."

Mike did not expect the reaction his words caused. Cristeen stiffened, her eyes widening slightly as she inhaled sharply. She started to retort, then snapped her mouth closed and marched out of the office. Matt glowered at Mike, then rushed after Cristeen.

"Hey," he stopped her from mounting Sky, "he couldn't know how much you hate that name."

"Leigh told him." She shot an angry look at Mike.

"Yes, she did and I figured you hate it the way I hate being called Mickey."

Matt spun around, glowering intently at his best friend. "Because I know you could not understand how much that name hurts her, I'll excuse it's use. This time."

Matt turned back to Cristeen, prepared to help her into the saddle. She was one step ahead of him. Grasping the saddle horn and cantle, she bounced twice on her left foot, then sprang up and onto Sky's back. He gave her leg a pat in approval of her graceful mount. Then went back inside to make arrangements for Henry to pick up the buckboard later that day.

Mike watched the scene. When he first suspected Matt was falling in love, Mike thought perhaps it was a passing fancy. Cristeen had needed to be rescued; naturally she would feel something for her hero, and Matt for this damsel in distress. Seeing the two of them interact last evening, Mike began to understand the love was mutual. Today he finally realized that it was not an infatuation. Matt and Cristeen understood each other at a deeper level than mere friendship.

Woe be to Mike for having committed this injury to Cristeen. He looked up at her, sitting astride that beautiful golden horse. She was at ease in the saddle, speaking softly to the mare even as her eyes watched for Matt's return. Her copper-gold tresses fell in a braid down to her back, the afternoon sun highlighting the lighter strands. She squinted and raised her hand to shade her eyes.

"I'll be right back," Mike told her, though he doubted she listened. "Tell Matt to head out and I will catch up."

Mike did catch up with them, five minutes outside of town. Matt glanced back at the sound of galloping hooves. Recognizing the rider, Matt rejoined his conversation with Cristeen.

Mike reined in beside Cristeen. Sky continued to walk leisurely, Cristeen making no effort to slow her horse. Mike reached across to grasp her hand that held the rein.

Mike produced a hat and placed it on her head, removing his own hat in a gesture of apology. "I am sorry, Cristeen."

She rocked the hat side to side, back and forth, until it sat comfortably. "I accept your apology. Leigh thinks it's funny that I don't like that name. If you really must call me something other than Cristeen, I don't mind CeeCee."

Mike breathed a sigh of relief. Though he wanted Cristeen to accept his apology, he had mostly been watching for Matt's forgiveness. At her words, Matt nodded slightly, signaling that all was well once more. Mike shoved his hat back onto his head.

"I'll stick with Cristeen, if that's okay." She smiled approval of his decision.

The ride to Fort Rossiter was uneventful. Cristeen was aware that the men were protecting her; Mike riding in front, taking point, and Matt either at her side or slightly behind, checking their back trail. She did not protest. It was flattering to have the two of them showing so much care for her.

The distance between Glenpark and Fort Rossiter could be covered in one long day. The men both overruled Cristeen's desire to ride straight through. Mike claimed it would be best to break the trip into two days, so as to arrive in Fort Rossiter within optimal daylight hours. Matt was more forthright, telling Cristeen how tired she would be after two months of not riding.

He was right. Again, exasperatingly.

Mike chose to make camp in a stand of aspens. There was good grazing close by for the horses. Dry timber lay scattered all around; Mike built a fire beneath the aspens, so what little smoke rose would be dissipated by the leaves. The fire was small, just enough to heat the coffee. They ate jerked beef and drank strong coffee.

Matt rolled out Cristeen's groundsheet and bedroll, carefully selecting a smooth area free of rocks. Stars were just barely discernible in the twilight sky when Cristeen crawled into bed. As she drifted off to sleep, she heard Matt say he would take second watch. She smiled to herself; if she had a nightmare it would come late, during Matt's watch.

She did not have a nightmare. The crisp air was a refreshing tonic for her soul. She dreamed about riding through mountain meadows of knee high grass, beside bubbling streams that seemed to laugh at some private joke, across valleys speckled with the now familiar longhaired Highland cattle.

In the morning, Matt sat beside Cristeen, watching her sleep. It was not the first time he had done so, but it was the first time he had seen this look of tranquility. Her hair had escaped the plaiting, and fell willy-nilly about her face. She was smiling; he wondered what she was dreaming about.

"Quit gawking and wake her up," Mike complained from beside the fire.

Matt frowned, knowing Mike was right but not wanting to break the spell. Sometimes you gotta to do what you gotta do. He gently shook Cristeen's shoulder.

"Go away," she mumbled.

"Time to wake up, beautiful."

Slowly she opened her eyes. "What'd you call me?"

"Well, you told me to stop calling you honey." Matt walked to the fire, leaving her to make what she would of his comments.

Fort Rossiter was a well-planned community and as such the streets were laid out in neat, geometric blocks. Mostly, anyway. Where the lay of the land dictated, streets curved around lakes, streams, and other natural obstacles.

When Cristeen first glimpsed the city, it was still far off, looking like hatch marks on the landscape. A small glittering band of silver marked the site of the reservoir. As time passed and they rode closer, buildings rose up like a forest and eventually the busy streets began to look like flowing streams.

They rode down from the west, angling southward to skirt the reservoir. To the north lay mostly residential neighborhoods. In the distant northeastern corner of town grain elevators stood like sentinels overlooking the Colorado Central Railroad and its depots. The railway crossed the city diagonally from northeast to southwest, taking a sharp turn to head due south toward Denver.

Cristeen felt a nervous tension gnawing at her gut as they approached Fort Rossiter. At first she thought it was left over fear, or perhaps the anticipation of seeing her sister and meeting her aunt and uncle. Examining the emotion she realized it arose from none of these sources. She simply disliked busy, crowded city streets. Fort Rossiter aroused memories of Chicago, although this city was a much-scaled down metropolis.

Mike stopped them on the slope overlooking the south end of the reservoir. He seemed to study the lay out, checking to be sure all was in its rightful place. When he was satisfied he twisted in his saddle to speak to Matt.

"We'll head straight for the courthouse." Receiving a raised eyebrow as response, he explained, "I'm fairly sure Marks has been keeping tabs on Leigh. We'll pass through a smaller portion of the city, crossing from the reservoir to the courthouse."

Matt nodded comprehension. "Avoid the hotel district and the worst of the saloons, too."

"Yes. Once the horses are stabled I can check on things at the hotel."

Cristeen was content to let the men take charge. An odd feeling for her; less than three months ago she would have chafed, even raged, that they presumed she needed their protection. So much had happened since leaving Kearney. She turned her eyes to gaze beyond the city, towards the plains that stretched away to the horizon.

From Kearney to Julesburg, she had brought her sister through without difficulty. At the very outskirts of Fort Rossiter their situation took a drastic downhill turn. As is the way of troubles, one mistake snowballed into a giant obstacle. So many little things she could have done differently and thus avoided the calamity that occurred.

Thinking back, Cristeen reviewed each of her actions, or lack of action, gradually reaching the conclusion that she wouldn't change the past, even if she could. What happened had taught her too much: if you haven't anything nice to say, keep it to yourself; never tell Leigh how much money you have; some men just don't understand anything but the muzzle of a gun. She knew now that she could do whatever was necessary to defend herself.

More important, she had finally learned that she did need others in her life. She accepted the truth behind Jesus' words, *"He that abideth in me, and I in him, the same bringeth forth much fruit: for without me ye can do nothing."* Though she had long believed in God, she had never trusted in the Lord. When she put her trust in God, He provided her with the necessities of life. Which included close friends; for life truly was not worth living without the joy of friendship.

Cristeen looked again at the two men discussing the route to take through town. Matt shifted in the saddle, keeping balanced as his horse fidgeted. He glanced over his shoulder at her, smiling while continuing to talk.

No, she wouldn't change the events of her life that led her here. A warm happiness pervaded her soul. This love that had found her was worth the arduous journey. Matt's love didn't erase the pain, nonetheless it was worth the trials and tribulations she went through to get here.

TWENTY EIGHT

"Wait in here," Mike opened the office door. Cristeen walked stiffly past him; every muscle in her body ached. The room was small and cramped. Two desks, back to back, took up one side of the room, while a third lone desk sat crosswise in the corner opposite the door. Behind this desk was a padded chair, covered with soft leather that spoke of comfort. She crossed the room, drawn to the promise this chair held.

Matt followed her, choosing to sit on the deacon's bench that was pushed against the wall. She glanced at the desk top, noting its clean austerity. A desk blotter protected the wooden surface from the ravages of writing utensils and coffee cups. A circular mark off center showed where such a cup customarily rested. Tucked into the corner of the blotter was a telegraph with one word written at the bottom - Cristeen.

"Mike's desk?" She slouched in the chair.

"Yup," Matt leaned back, stretching to get comfortable on the hard bench. "You have a knack for picking the best seat in the room."

"I'm sorry," she sat up. "Would you like to sit here? You deserve a comfortable seat."

Matt laughed. "Ease up on the guilt, Cristy. Anyone can see how much you need a soft place to sit right now."

Cristeen grimaced. She removed her hat, placing it to the side on the desk, and ran a hand through her hair. It was at that aggravating length - long enough to braid, too short to remain braided for long. At least while riding she could push it off her face and contain it under her hat. Courtesy dictated removing her hat when indoors. She pulled the tresses to the back of her head. No sooner had she let go than they fell forward again into her face. She grabbed a thick strand, stared through it, contemplating the apricot color. Just like her mother's hair.

Matt watched Cristeen toy with her hair. Her agitation was growing. He wondered if she worried about a possible conflict with Evan Marks. She said little on that subject throughout their journey. Mike judiciously waited till she was fast asleep to bring it up last night. It was entirely conceivable that Marks would try to kill Cristeen. In fact, the probability of that reaction was governing their actions. Mike confessed that he almost hoped Marks would try something; "like to just shoot him and get it over with," he reasoned.

Cristeen abandoned her hair to pick up the Celtic cross pendant, twirling it as was her custom when nervous. She tilted it, finding different ways to capture the light in its reflective surface. Matt suspected the root of her concern.

"Was your mother close to her sister?"

His question hit the mark. He saw it in her clenched jaw, the way she stopped twirling the cross for just a second. Cristeen didn't like being in the city, the small room felt like a jail cell, and with nothing else to focus on she had finally begun to worry about meeting her aunt. Matt moved to sit on the corner of the desk.

"She will love you, Cristy. Because you are her sister's daughter. Looking like your mother will only endear you more to your aunt." He stilled her restless hands, holding them in his.

"How can you be so sure?" She looked up at him, seeking the tender reassurance she knew she would find in his gaze.

"She has fond, childhood memories of your mother." He

brushed the wayward hair off her upturned face. "Not the painful memories marinated in bitterness that your father clung to."

Cristeen searched his face, looking for signs he was deceiving her. What she found was open honesty, an offer of hope that not all her family would despise her. She leaned into the hand he cupped around her face, closing her eyes and absorbing the love and security his touch conveyed.

"Thank you," she whispered.

Matt leaned down and kissed her forehead. "Your happiness is all the thanks I need."

The office door opened at the same time as Mike tapped softly. Matt stood, not willing to cause Cristeen discomfort with a public show of his affection. He was pleasantly surprised when she grasped his hand, holding him at her side. Mike pretended not to notice.

"Things have been quiet." Too quiet, he thought. Rory reported that Evan Marks seemed to have vanished. "Your uncle has a room reserved for you. Perhaps you would like to freshen up before meeting them?"

"No, thank you." Cristeen smiled. "This is who I am. Besides, I don't think I could manage to get into that dress right now."

"Bit sore, are you?" Mike chuckled. "Let's get you over to the Rossiter House, then."

Matt let out a low whistle. "The Rossiter House? Mighty fancy accommodations."

Cristeen frowned. "I reckon Uncle George can afford it."

Her tone was disdainful. Mike looked at her, astonished. "You reckon?" he sputtered. "Do you have any idea who your uncle is?"

Cristeen shrugged, "A very rich man." She considered him for a moment before adding, "Please understand, Mike, most rich folks I've known have not been, shall we say, kind. Money doesn't make a man worthy; it's his actions that matter."

Mike stared in amazement. That philosophy pervaded the society of the West. Yet Mike had met very few women who believed in the sentiment. In his experience, women were attracted to the trappings of civilization and the pretty things money could buy. Even Suzanne, who supported him in every way; still she longed for a bigger house, better furniture, a brighter future for their boys.

Matt, too, marveled at Cristeen. She had never questioned his financial status; she had let his actions speak for him. No longer did he need wonder if she would care for him if he were not wealthy. He wanted to hug her and tell her how much he loved her. Instead he squeezed her hand, gratified to feel her squeeze his in return.

They walked the two blocks to the Rossiter House, Matt and Mike flanking Cristeen. Rory walked in front, far enough ahead as to not seem to be with them at all. Another deputy followed, slightly more conspicuously as his eyes darted from rooftop to alley. Both deputies disappeared at the hotel.

Cristeen gawked at the display of wealth. Wood surfaces gleamed, polished brass and leaded crystal abounded. The carpeting was oriental in style, and origin she was sure. Everywhere she looked, uniformed staff could be seen. Her stride faltered; only Matt's reassuring hold on her arm kept her from turning heel and fleeing. When Mike made to move ahead, Cristeen stopped him.

"Mike, I think now I want to know who my uncle is."

"Impressed?"

"Worried."

Mike chuckled, "Don't be worried. They adore your sister, despite her rambunctious nature."

Cristeen relaxed a little. Still, she really was nothing like Leigh. Matt rubbed her shoulders, silently telling her to stop worrying. Mike turned to face them both, relishing the reaction his words were sure to cause.

"Your uncle, Cristeen, is George Edwards."

Matt did not disappoint.

"George Edwards, of Denver?" Matt looked at Cristeen. "You are George Edwards' niece?"

"If you say so," she clearly had no idea the significance of her uncle's name. "I just know my Aunt Caroline is married to George Edwards. Besides the fact he has been quite successful in his business dealings, I have no idea who my uncle is."

"Caroline Edwards, of course," Matt slapped his forehead. "I'm so dense; I should have put two and two together."

"Well, are you going to enlighten me?"

"He's just one of the more powerful political figures in the state. There's talk of him running for Governor, or maybe United States Senate."

"Oh," she looked disappointed. "So he probably won't care for this socially inept, graceless, misbegotten waif."

"He will love his niece, because she is compassionate, considerate, intelligent, graceful, and beautiful." Matt put his arm around her shoulder, hugging her against him.

"You spoil me."

"So you say," he smiled indulgently.

Mike caught the attention of a uniformed porter. "Malcolm, please take Miss Latham's bag to her room."

"Miss Leigh has made purchases?"

"Not Miss Leigh," Mike laughed. "I'm sorry, Malcolm. Allow me to introduce you properly. Miss Cristeen Latham meet Malcolm, porter extraordinaire."

Malcolm flushed with the praise. "I just do my job, Sheriff. I am pleased to meet you, Miss Cristeen. Miss Leigh will be beside herself when she sees you."

He looked closely at Cristeen. "Never would have guessed you two was sisters."

The porter left them, carrying Cristeen's saddlebags as if they were the most expensive luggage he had ever handled. Mike led the way to the parlor where Leigh would be waiting. At the door he hesitated.

"This is kind of a family thing," Mike looked from Cristeen to Matt. "I'll wait outside and keep an eye out for trouble."

Matt found his curiosity growing. Cristeen spoke little of her sister; he wondered what Leigh was really like. The porter's comment was intriguing. As far as physical description, Matt only knew Leigh looked like her father's family. And he was more than a little curious to meet Cristeen's aunt and uncle.

Cristeen stared at the closed door. *Well, it's now or never. I have to meet them sometime; at least Matt is with me today.* Her hand strayed of its own will to the Celtic cross. She was grateful when Matt turned the doorknob and pushed the door open. She allowed him to steer her into the room, feeling six eyes fixate upon them both.

Typical of her nature, Leigh responded first to Cristeen's entrance. She sprang from her chair, fairly flying across the room to fling herself on Cristeen. The force of her momentum pushed Cristeen off balance; only Matt's steadying arm across her back kept her from falling.

"Oh, Cristeen!" Leigh was breathless with excitement. "I just knew you were alive. Are you okay now? Where have you been? Why didn't you contact me sooner? Tell me everything."

Matt began to think he was invisible, although he could feel Uncle George's examining gaze. As Leigh poured her questions out, not giving Cristeen a chance to answer, her eyes at last turned to him.

"Who's this?" Leigh asked her sister.

Leigh's greeting felt more like an assault. Cristeen had thought herself prepared for her sister's energy level. She was mistaken. The questions tumbled out with the same force as Leigh's embrace. Cristeen felt herself stagger, as much from weak and overworked muscles as from the emotional barrage. She fell back against Matt, who had the presence of mind to stand close, concealing her fragility.

Caroline Edwards came to the rescue. Ever the diplomat, she effortlessly guided Leigh back to her chair, giving Cristeen space to move.

"Leigh," Caroline's voice held a soft lilt, "give your sister a chance to breath. Only then will she be able to answer all your questions." Placing a hand on Cristeen's, Caroline added, "Come dear, you must be tired after your journey. Sit here."

Caroline tactfully maneuvered Cristeen across the room to the sofa. Despite there being another chair available for seating, Caroline instinctively recognized Cristeen's need for the support of her companion.

Cristeen stared at the sofa, then at her aunt. Any social grace she might have possessed was lost. Matt rubbed her arms encouragingly. It seemed impolite to sit without first introducing themselves, though Leigh had done a fair job of announcing her. She looked to her uncle, half expecting to see disapproval on his face.

"You look just like your mother," his voice was deep, warm, and friendly. "Don't you think so, Caroline."

"The resemblance is amazing." Caroline reached up to touch Cristeen's hair. "Tall, too, just like Bridgett. She always said I was the pixie in the family."

Caroline Edwards laughed warmly with the fond memory. Cristeen liked this woman who put her at ease instantly with the tender expression in her eyes as she remembered. Hot tears stung Cristeen's eyes.

"I was afraid you wouldn't like that similarity."

Caroline smiled, "You are Bridgett's first born. I would love you even if you were hideously deformed."

Cristeen glanced up at Matt, who reflected Caroline's smile. He gave her a gentle push; Caroline met her half way. The women embraced; tears fell freely from Caroline's eyes while Cristeen held hers back. When at last Caroline released her, Cristeen stood back and glanced at her uncle.

"Hello, Uncle George."

He didn't give her a chance to hesitate. His hug was enveloping, well deserving the description bear hug. He was a big man, as tall as Matt and a bit broader. He concluded the hug as abruptly as it began, holding her at arms length to look her over. Her apprehension returned, only to be quashed by a hearty laugh from her uncle.

"You surely are a sight for sore eyes," he laughed. "Had us all a bit worried. Wouldn't you agree, Caroline?"

Cristeen liked the way her aunt and uncle deferred to each other, their love showing in every action. Having made it past this first hurdle, she realized all three of her family members were waiting expectantly for an explanation of Matt's presence. What did she tell them? She certainly didn't want to down play his importance in her life, yet she had never actually told him how she felt.

Uncle George cleared his throat. "Well, young man, I suppose it is to you we owe a debt of gratitude."

His statesmanship was apparent. Matt stepped around Cristeen to shake George Edwards' hand.

"The pleasure has been all mine, Mr. Edwards. Your niece is a very charming lady."

Cristeen felt the heat on her face, and was thankful that Leigh could not see her. Caroline could, however; she smiled knowingly at her niece.

"May we at least have the honor of your name?" Caroline asked demurely.

Matt gallantly took her hand in his, giving a gentle squeeze. "Matt Donovan, Ma'am."

"Donovan, eh?" George was thoughtful. "From

Glenpark? Any relation to Peter Donovan?"

"My father, sir."

"Good man, Peter. Sorely missed, sorely missed."

Cristeen began to relax. Her aunt and uncle readily accepted both her and Matt. She felt foolish now for ever having doubted they would. With the formalities over, she sank onto the sofa, pulling Matt down to sit beside her. Caroline moved to the other vacant chair while George remained standing. Cristeen looked to Leigh; her sister sat despondently.

"What are you upset about?" She felt herself slipping into the role of elder sister. "You got your wish. I'm alive and I'm here."

"You were ignoring me."

"I can't escape you, Leigh, how could I ignore you?"

The younger woman giggled.

"And I have a bone to pick with you."

Leigh looked concerned. "I'm sorry. I won't ever talk about money in public again. And -"

Cristeen cut her off, "I don't care about that. The past can't be changed, and I'm not sure I would want to change it." She glanced slyly at Matt and was rewarded with a surprised grin.

"No, I'm a bit upset that you've been calling me Cris."

"Oh, that." Leigh looked chagrined. "I told Mike you hate it. I'm sorry, Cristeen."

"You can go back to calling me CeeCee, as you always have."

"Deal!"

A spark lit her eyes. Matt recognized it; Leigh was more like Cristeen than Cristy realized. They had different hair and eye color, Cristeen was more lithe, and Leigh more outgoing. Yet that same mischievous light danced in their eyes. On Leigh, though, the mischievousness showed plainly in all her facial expression.

"Now, CeeCee, fess up. Who's this guy?"

Enough time had passed for Cristeen to prepare for that question. "Leigh, may I present Matthew Donovan. Matt, this is Leigh Latham."

Leigh was indignant. Matt poked Cristeen in the side. "Oh, all right," Cristeen chuckled. "It is to Matt's ranch that Sky carried me, and there I have stayed for these past two months. Happy now?"

"Nope," Leigh grinned. "But I'll save the real hard questions for later, when we're alone."

Cristeen groaned.

"Go easy on your sister, Leigh," Caroline chastised. "Cristeen, I'm sure you would like to retire to your room and get some rest. First, we would like to hear just how well you are healing. Leigh was quite fearful of your injury."

Injury, singular? Oh, that's right, Cristeen thought. *Leigh doesn't know about the shoulder wound as that happened later.*

"My injuries are healing well, Aunt Caroline. The doctor assures me my leg is recuperating as well as he expected, if not better."

A bit over simplification, she thought to herself. Well, no need to go into the details. All they really needed to know was that she had been injured and was nearly recovered.

Caroline orchestrated the rest of their conversations. She kept the reunion short, obviously concerned that Cristeen would become faint with fatigue. The concept was amusing to Cristeen, but she went along with it as a means of avoiding her sister's more personal questions. When prompted by her aunt to do so, Cristeen took leave of her family, Matt trailing behind.

"Delightful family," he commented as he escorted her out.

"Hmmm," she grimaced, "Leigh's going to be torturous later."

Matt stopped, halting her as well. "What are you going

to tell her about me?"

"The less I tell her, the better off you'll be."

"I'm serious, Cristy." He pulled her against him. "I want to hear you say it."

She smacked her open palm against his chest. "It would be easier if you weren't teasing me."

He cupped her chin, lifting it and looking into her eyes. "I'm not teasing. I love you."

Her breath caught, and her heart seemed to skip a beat. The words were only words; his actions had shown how he felt long ago. Yet hearing him say those three words, she felt lightheaded.

"I love you, too."

TWENTY NINE

I t was a plan born of revenge and nurtured by greed. He would make that she-devil pay for killing Hank, that much was certain. Not that Hank Crespin ever treated Evan with anything more than contempt. Still, he was the only friend Evan Marks had, and a cousin to boot. Kinship alone demanded revenge.

At first he had thought to simply kill her. In fact Evan believed he already had. Then word got around that Reardon had found the red-haired woman his deputies were searching for. Evan knew at once it was her. She had managed to live through the attack and somehow she had survived even his bullet. He saw it hit her, knock her forward; a well placed shot into her left side.

By all rights she should be dead. That she was here in Fort Rossiter, very much alive, proved to Evan that she was an abomination. Women had their proper place; riding the trail unescorted, dressed in men's clothing, just was not right. All the more reason to end her existence.

The first problem to overcome was that do-gooder sheriff. Generally, Reardon stayed away from the rail yards, leaving them to be policed by the railroad. Evan knew a guy; didn't cost him much to keep out of sight in one of the yard shacks.

With a fair supply of cheap whiskey and plenty of time on his hands, Evan Marks stewed. He grew weary of hiding. What could Reardon do to him anyway? That dark-haired girl didn't remember him. Evan tested that by bumping into her one morning while she was shopping. She apologized, never batting an eye in recognition. She was harmless to him.

That redhead, the one called Cristeen, she was the source of his troubles. She'd gone to the courthouse with Reardon. Evan saw the wanted poster the next day, tacked up just outside the train depot of all places. Despite its dire purpose, he was flattered by the likeness. Yes, something must be done about Cristeen. Her sister, now, she could be valuable. George Edwards' nieces. An interesting twist.

He discovered the warehouse later that same day, while skulking about in a drunken rage. It was on the edge of the rail yard, the farthest building from the mill to which it belonged. Secluded in the middle of a bustling city. Perfect for the plan he was hatching.

* * *

Matt stepped into the Rossiter House foyer. Considering it was still early on Sunday morning, the level of activity in the hotel surprised him. Through an arched doorway to his right could be seen the main dining room. Many of the tables were occupied, with guests filing in at a steady pace.

He was only mildly surprised when Leigh approached him, coming out of the dining room still holding a teacup. A waiter trailed behind her, apparently accustomed to her habit of finishing meals on the go. Where Cristeen tended to first consider her words and actions, moving as cautiously with people as she would a wild horse, Leigh tended to rush into situations, her boisterous energy unrestrainable.

"Good morning, Mr. Donovan," she smiled warmly.

"A fine morning to you, as well, Miss Latham."

"Are you going to church with us?"

"It would seem that way." Matt had thought to be accompanying Cristeen only.

Leigh noticed his eyes stray to the dining room. "Uncle George will be out in a moment. Cristeen is upstairs with Aunt Caroline."

"Is anything wrong?" his tone was laden with concern.

"No, she'll be down soon enough. I don't know how she tolerates being cooped up in this building." Leigh paced.

Matt chuckled, "You simply can't keep still, can you?"

Leigh stopped pacing just long enough to consider his words. With a shrug she continued moving about the foyer. "Perhaps. I am curious, though; why is she so placidly following your instructions?

"You think Cristy is being placid?"

Cristeen complained to Matt at every evening meal these last three days. Mostly about inactivity.

"For CeeCee, yes." Leigh stood looking out the window. "She has always hated being told what she should do, and more so what she cannot do."

Matt frowned. "Maybe she just didn't like who was doing the telling."

Leigh glanced sidelong at him. "Oh, she's told you about Daddy."

An awkward silence threatened. Matt clenched his jaw, biting back his anger. Cristeen's father was dead, it was wrong to judge. He just couldn't help himself; the man had caused Cristeen so much anguish.

Leigh noticed with mild amusement his tension. She watched as he flexed a fist. *Good thing Daddy isn't here, 'cause I think this man would finally put my father in his place.*

She crossed the room, smiling warmly to break the awkwardness. "That black suit and silver vest will go well with CeeCee's dress."

Matt blinked. Leigh's restless energy popped up in the most unusual ways, like this leap in topics. She was laughing at his disorientation.

"See for yourself."

Cristeen was coming down the wide staircase, a vision of loveliness in a dress of pewter gray accented with black velvet trim on the lapel and hems. The short jacket bodice fitted closely, the long skirt fell nearly straight from waist to floor. The style lent itself well to Cristeen.

As nice as the dress was, Matt gave it little attention; his focus was on Cristeen's face. Her hair was drawn off her face to cascade in soft curls down the back of her neck. Tendrils wisped free, framing her face. The gray of the dress brought out her pale blue eyes. Matt crossed the room, abandoning Leigh without further thought.

"Good morning, pretty lady." He was pleased with the pink hue his greeting brought. "You had me a bit worried."

"Aunt Caroline insisted on fixing my hair." She broke eye contact, softly demanding, "Stop staring at me."

"I can't, you look stunning." He caught her hand, drawing her arm through his. "May I have the honor of accompanying you to church?"

"Can we walk?"

"Yes, it's not that far from here. You have to promise you'll let me stay on the street side, though."

She made a face. "Why don't you let me walk right down the middle of the street. That way if Marks is still around he'll be lured into making a move, and then Mike can arrest him."

"Do you seriously think I would allow you to risk that?" Matt stopped to open the front door.

Cristeen kissed his cheek; "Just checking."

She started through the open door only to be tugged back by his unmoving stance. She looked up at his pleasantly astonished expression and smiled. "Didn't expect that, did you?"

"You never cease to amaze me, Cristy."

Leigh brushed past them. "Uncle George is getting his

hackles up."

Matt heeded the warning. "Please do try to be respectable, dear."

Cristeen slapped his arm lightly.

Just as church was letting out, Mike caught up with them. Cristeen guessed from his attire that he was also in attendance for service. A young boy of about six years tagged along closely. She could see his resemblance to Mike and decided this was one of his children.

"Hi Uncle Matt," the boy enthusiastically greeted.

Matt bent and scooped him up. "Good morning Nick. Did you help Mommy this morning, like we discussed?"

Nick nodded his head vigorously. Matt was staying with Mike and Suzanne, as was his custom when in Fort Rossiter. Cristeen was seeing a new side of Matt; he was a very loving uncle.

"Did you extend the invitation?" Mike was asking.

"Not yet."

"Can I ask, Dad? Please?" Nick smiled shyly at Cristeen as he pleaded with his father.

"Sure, if it's okay with Uncle Matt."

Matt nodded approval.

Cristeen was curious. Nick came to stand before her, now nearly overcome with shyness. He looked at his feet and said something so quietly she could not understand him. Crouching down to his level, she asked him to repeat himself.

"Momma wants to know if you'll come to dinner at our house." Nick looked up at Cristeen with his eyes only.

He was so cute, dressed in a suit just like his father and asking so sweetly. Cristeen bit back her laugh, lest he mistake it for ridicule.

"I would be delighted, Nick."

The boy's shyness left him as he happily flung his arms around her neck. She rocked backwards, unprepared for his embrace, which ended as quickly as it had begun. Nick ran off to find his mother; Cristeen threw her hands out behind her to keep from sitting on the ground. Both men laughed as Matt helped her back to her feet.

"You two were troublemakers growing up, weren't you?" She accused, brushing the dust off the back of her dress.

"He was," each pointed a finger of blame at the other.

When he had recovered from the laughter, Mike elaborated on little Nick's invite. "Suzanne and I would like for all of you to come to dinner."

The Edwards and Leigh joined them as Nick sprinted away. Uncle George regretfully declined the invitation, explaining that he had already agreed to dinner with the mayor.

"I'm sure His Honor won't be offended if the girls do not accompany us, though," Caroline added.

"What about security, Sheriff?" George was ever pragmatic.

"Already thought of that," Mike smiled. "Rory will be watching out for any signs of trouble."

"I should have stayed at the ranch," Cristeen mumbled.

Matt heard her words. "Feeling smothered? Soon enough it will be over."

Cristeen thought about those words during dinner later that day. She watched Matt play with Mike's three boys, Richard, Nick, and Ben. At three years old, Ben was just beginning to assert his independence, keeping Suzanne busy. Matt's quarterly visits were clearly something the boys cherished. The sentiment was mutual; Matt romped in the yard with all three children, wearing them down before mealtime.

During dinner, Leigh was the one to entertain the boys. Cristeen was not surprised; Leigh had always enjoyed taking care of children. With the boys and Leigh preoccupied, conversation amongst the remaining adults focused on Cristeen. Suzanne's curiosity seemed insatiable.

It wasn't until afterwards, while helping with the dishes,

that Suzanne finally got around to the subject she hinted at throughout the meal. The men took the boys outside, Leigh brought Rory a plate of food. The door was just closing when Suzanne began speaking.

"Matt seems very fond of you," she stopped working to look at Cristeen.

Cristeen continued washing the plate she held. Only a slight hesitation in her hand movements showed she heard Suzanne. She willed herself to keep moving, give away nothing.

Suzanne took another tack. "You really like it up there in Glenpark? It is a very quiet community."

"Guess that's what I like most."

"I could never understand why Matt stays there, when he could live down here quite comfortably."

"Because he loves the land. And everything about ranching."

Suzanne smiled, "I suppose you are right. I never cared much for that kind of life."

"You are lucky to have a husband who likes his job here in the city."

"Yes," Suzanne turned back to drying the plates. "It is nice when a husband and wife enjoy the same environment. Do you like ranching, Cristeen?"

Cristeen laughed. "You're worse than my sister. I can't keep anything from her these days, either."

"Does that trouble you?"

She shrugged. "I'm not sure. Sometimes I prefer she not know what I'm thinking."

"Yes, little sisters can be bothersome." Suzanne thought for a moment about all the times her sisters had voiced that exact complaint. "You didn't answer me; do you like ranching?"

Cristeen dried her hands and moved to look out the window.

"Yes," she answered softly.

It was too simple an answer for so complicated a question. Being on a ranch put Cristeen at ease; living at Matt's ranch went beyond her ability to describe.

"What will you do when Mike arrests this Marks fellow?"

"I will testify against him, of course."

"No, I mean after it is all done and over. Will you go to Denver with your sister?"

It was the question Cristeen had been asking herself frequently over the last three days. She still had no answer. Although Matt said he loved her, he had not pursued the subject further. Cristeen could live in Glenpark, even without Matt asking. Nonetheless she wanted for him to ask, to say he wanted her there. Regardless, Denver was not for her.

On the ride from Nebraska, Cristeen had given little thought as to what she would do once Leigh was safely in Denver. She only knew that she did not desire to live in or even near the city. After leaving Julesburg, the mountains had loomed ever closer and began to dominate her thoughts. Now she knew for certain that was were she belonged.

While at the ranch, the subject of her remaining or leaving had never been brought up. Though Matt made it clear he loved her, he still did not talk about her going back to the ranch. Cristeen was fairly certain why. Matt liked that she enjoyed the ranch, but the fact remained that she was not wife material. Housekeeping was not her forte. Trying to follow a recipe with Katie had been like learning a foreign language. And she had no idea what other things a woman needed to know to keep her house in order.

Suzanne was watching her; Cristeen felt uncomfortable under her watchful gaze. This woman was the kind of wife Matt would compare her to: organized, patient, a good cook and housekeeper, a loving mother.

"I'm going outside," Cristeen opened the door.

"Is Rory out there?" Suzanne called after her.

"Yes, he's on the porch." Cristeen smiled at Rory and shuffled off the porch.

* * *

"Ollie-ollie-oxen-free!" Matt called loudly. He had given up trying to find Richard and Mike. He knew where Nick was, but let the boy think he had fooled his Uncle Matt. Ben had been easy to find; like most toddlers, he figured if he couldn't see Matt then Matt couldn't see him.

"Uncle Matt gives up too easily," Mike's taunt floated out from the carriage shed.

"Uncle Matt wants dessert," Matt retorted. That brought both Richard and Nick from their hiding places. Matt watched the shed closely, as he had checked there first. Mike swung down from the rafters, laughing at his successful job of hiding.

The men and boys tumbled into the house. Mike swept the front room with his gaze, concern mounting as he walked to the kitchen.

"Where's Ben?"

"Out on the porch with Rory," Suzanne answered without breaking her stride. She was already slicing the pie.

Matt glanced out the window. "Where's Cristeen?"

Suzanne's hand stopped in mid-cut as she looked up at him. "With them, isn't she?"

Matt stepped quickly back to the front room where he had removed his gun belt before going out to play with the boys. Suzanne's eyes widened with fear. Matt pulled the pistol from its holster and stepped onto the porch. Leigh glanced up at him.

"Where is your sister?"

"Right there," she pointed, then jumped up. "She was on the swing a moment ago."

Growling at Rory to keep Leigh on the porch, Matt moved across the yard. Mike's house backed up on an expanse of wheat fields. Marking the rear boundary was a stately old pin oak, from which hung a bench swing. Matt's eyes scanned the empty yard. Fear gripped him, twisting his gut. He was torn about calling for Cristeen, fearing that Marks might kill her instantly if he realized she was missed. He decided to risk it.

"Cristeen!" His voice carried across the wheat.

"Matt," Mike spoke quietly at his elbow.

Matt turned to look where his friend was pointing. At the corner of the carriage shed was a hint of gray cloth.

"I'm fine," Cristeen's voice never sounded so sweet to his ears. "Nobody's gonna hurt me; let me be."

Matt recognized that tone; this time he wasn't going to wait for her to come to him. He spun the pistol to hand it butt first to Mike. Then he strode decisively towards the shed.

Cristeen heard his footsteps approaching and turned, intending to walk away. She had been crying, did not want to be seen that way, particularly by Matt. She had not counted on his resolve being greater than hers.

"Leave me alone," her voice came through clenched teeth as his hand clamped around her arm.

"No," he pulled her around to face him. His anger washed out when he saw her puffy red eyes. He looked her over; there was no sign of physical injury. "You said you were fine."

"I am. Now let me go."

Matt cupped her chin, forcing her to look up at him. "You just scared ten years off my life. I think I deserve some sort of explanation. Why did you pick today to break security?"

Cristeen pulled her face away from his hand, though not before he felt her jaw clench. With eyes turned away from his, she gave a weak answer, "I just did, that's all. I'm sorry, I'll behave from now on. Let me go, please."

He groaned. *It's me, she's upset with me and isn't willing to let me know that.* Aloud, he pushed for the answer. "Cristy, please tell me what I've done that has upset you."

"Nothing, you've done exactly nothing," she spat out hotly.

Matt released his hold on her arm and let her stomp past him back to the house. Walking much more slowly, he rounded the corner of the shed in time to see Cristeen brush aside Leigh's comforting gesture. Leigh turned a baleful glare on Matt before following her sister inside. He stumbled to the swing, barely noticing Mike still standing in the center of the yard.

"What did you do, Matt?" Mike asked sympathetically.

"I have no idea," he glanced up at his friend. "She says I did nothing. Will I ever understand her?"

Mike chuckled softly. "We aren't meant to understand them, my friend. We are simply doomed to love them."

"You sound more like Ty every day."

Sitting down beside his friend, Mike set the bench to swinging gently. The branch creaked in protest; it was used to the boys and occasionally Suzanne sitting on the swing. The weight of two grown men threatened to overwhelm, yet it held.

"What were her exact words? Perhaps I can translate."

Matt stared at the house. "I did nothing, exactly nothing." He threw his hands up in exasperation. "How in the world do I send her into tears when I've done nothing?"

The door opened and Suzanne came out, sending Rory inside. She crossed the yard, pained sympathy on her face. With but a look, she let Mike know it was her turn to talk with Matt. Mike patted his friend's arm in parting; Suzanne took his place.

"I've always liked this swing." Suzanne pushed with one toe, picking up the momentum. "I owe you an apology, Matt."

"You didn't do anything wrong, letting her go outside."

"Well, I'm afraid I may have set the course for her tears. By the way, Rory is driving both of them back to the hotel."

Matt started to rise; she stopped him with a hand on his arm.

"What will you say? Hear me out first."

She had a point. "I'm listening."

Suzanne pushed again as the swing slowed. She considered her words before going ahead. "You do love her? Of course, that's obvious to everyone."

Matt was a bit startled that his love for Cristeen was so obvious. Suzanne smiled maternally at him.

"Have you by chance mentioned this to Cristeen?"

"Yes." He felt his face growing warm. Was he ever grateful she had sent Mike away before having this conversation.

"Oh, that changes things." She was silent for a few moments. "No, it doesn't really. Depending on exactly what you've said to her."

There was a question in Suzanne's eyes that Matt was unwilling to answer. "It was a private conversation."

Shaking her head she muttered, "Men."

Matt snorted, "Women!"

They each laughed.

"What I said before she went out into the yard is, I believe, what has Cristeen so agitated," Suzanne continued. "I thought it was because she was uncertain of your feelings for her."

"Tell me what you said," Matt felt a glimmer of hope. He did understand Cristeen more than he let on to Mike.

"I asked her what she was planning to do after this was all over, and suggested maybe she would go to Denver with her sister."

He thought about that for a long while. Seemed harmless enough a question on the surface. Cristeen was far too complicated to assume she'd take the question at face value.

"She'd hate Denver," was the only response he thought of.

"Why? It's a beautiful city." Suzanne loved Denver.

"Exactly. It's a city. Cristy loves the mountains. Loves being outdoors, working with the horses, playing with the dogs, even just sitting. So long as she is outside...." his voice trailed off.

"What? What's wrong?"

Matt leaped off the seat, setting it swinging erratically and scaring Suzanne.

"Matthew Donovan, you get back here and help me down!"

Malcolm confirmed that Miss Cristeen had retired directly to her room upon return. Would Mr. Donovan care to have a message sent up to her? No, Mr. Donovan would deliver the message himself! Matt took the stairs two at a time, ignoring the protests of both Malcolm and the front desk clerk.

Leigh answered his knock. "She doesn't want to talk to anyone right now." Her eyes spoke the loathing she kept out of her voice.

"You tell that obstinate sister of yours that I won't be sent away." Leigh stood firm, keeping the door barely ajar. "Tell her, Leigh. Now."

"I can hear you perfectly well on my own, thank you." Cristeen pulled the door open. "What do you want?"

You! his mind screamed. *I want you in my life, today and for the rest of my years.* It was a conversation meant for Cristeen, not Leigh. He turned his gaze to Cristeen's sister, hoping she could take a hint; she could.

"If you need me, CeeCee, I'll be in my room. Right over here," she made a point of letting Matt know she would be listening for any sign of trouble.

"You are a good sister, Leigh." He shut the door.

For all her bravado, Cristeen was scared. Matt could see it in her eyes, the way she back away from him, stopping only when her legs hit the chair by the dresser. He forced himself to remain standing at the door despite wanting to take her in his arms and reassure her of his love. She sat, unexpectedly, in the chair she had bumped.

"I'm going to move over there," he pointed to the bed. "I'd like to sit down. I'm not going to do anything to you."

You already have, Cristeen thought. She ground her clenched teeth. *Stop it, Cristeen, you are being foolish. You will not cry. You will not!* Whatever else, Matt had been a good friend, nothing could change that. If she could stay rational she just might be able to hold on to that friendship.

"Cristy, did your father ever say he loved you?"

The question surprised her, "What does that have to do with anything?"

"Who taught you that those words aren't worth a plug nickel?" She sank against the chair as if he had hit her. That wasn't the reaction he was going for.

"People say things that at the time they mean." She hesitated, emotion choking her words. After deep breath to regain control she went on, "How you felt Wednesday has no bearing on how you'll feel next week, or next month, or whenever this ordeal is over."

"I love you, Cristeen. I've been falling in love with you since the first time you spoke to me. I didn't know anything about your past then, and it did not matter. I don't care that you've lived in more places than I have even traveled through. Or that you spent more than half your life trying to be the son your father never had."

He got up, paced to the door. "I absolutely love that you talk to your horse. You are perhaps the most unique woman I have ever met. In fact, I had given up hope of ever actually finding a woman like you."

She sat in stunned silence while he spoke. When it was clear his intensity was spent, she risked a question. "What do you mean, a woman like me?"

Matt sank onto the bed, drained by his own tirade. He fell back, staring at the ceiling while collecting his thoughts. When he sat up again, he found Cristeen looked less withered as well as less defensive. Well, at least he was making some progress.

"My mother did not particularly enjoy ranch life," he began his explanation.

"Katie told me. For your father's sake, she endured the hardships."

"Gradually she came to love the people but she never really loved that ranch. Or even those mountains. In her heart she dreamed of Virginia."

"It's hard to imagine anyone living for so long at the foot of such glory and never appreciating its splendor."

"There, that's what I mean by a woman like you."

"What? That I like the mountains? That doesn't make me unique, even amongst women."

"It's part of it, though. You absolutely adore ranching, don't you?"

A slow smile spread across her face. "Yes, I reckon I do." A wistful look came into her eyes. "I like those Highland cattle you raise. They're much cuter than the longhorns in Kansas."

Matt breathed a sigh of relief. He was winning this battle, though he wasn't sure he liked the idea of raising cute cattle. "Cristy, can I come over there now?"

Her jaw clenched, she still didn't quite trust him. But she assented, nodding her head. He crossed the small room and held out his hands, pulling her onto her feet and into his arms.

"Suzanne talked to me after you left." She went still. "I never meant my silence to hurt you. I guess I assumed you understood what I meant when I said I love you."

"What did you mean?"

"That I can't imagine not having you in my life," he paused. "Now I realize it's deeper than that. I don't want a life that doesn't include you. I love you, Cristy, and I want to spend the rest of my life with you."

"I'm a horrible housekeeper."

"I can hire a housekeeper, that's not what I was looking for. I want a heart-keeper," he felt her silent giggle. "How about it, can I trust you with my heart? Will you come back to the ranch with me when this is over?"

Cristeen wrapped her arms around him and held on as if he might vanish. "I thought you'd never ask."

THIRTY

Evan Marks cursed at himself. He should just kill her and get it over with. But greed had finally won out over his desire for vengeance. He would grab both women, let that pompous Edwards believe they could be bought back. By the time anyone found them, Evan would be on a train hundreds of miles away. He didn't even care if Leigh lived. Cristeen must die.

He toyed with this idea, then another, of how to get both of them into the warehouse. Reardon, and that Donovan character, had finally loosened up their tight noose of security around the she-devil. He'd seen her on the street with her sister, unescorted, only just this morning. Now was the time, before anyone got antsy again.

The final plan came together more by happenstance than design. Leigh became separated from Cristeen purely due to each woman shopping at different stores. Evan grabbed Leigh, knocking her unconscious before she had the chance to scream. Come to think of it, he owed her that for the vicious knock to the head she had dealt him. He was careful to leave little clues by way of a trail for the she-devil to follow. He felt certain she would simply look for her sister, rather than go for help. This was, after all, an upscale merchant neighborhood.

Unfortunately for Cristeen, she did just that, believing Leigh had wandered off to look at another shop. She was approaching the mills before she realized how far she had gone. Seeing the run-down row houses against the backdrop of larger than life grain elevators gave her pause. She looked around, everything was unfamiliar. She was lost. Leigh was probably back at the hotel by now.

Cristeen turned to leave, feeling confident she could backtrack her own path. She'd just come down that alleyway over there, hadn't she? The sun seemed to shine brighter at the other end of that alley. If she couldn't negotiate her way back to the hotel, at least she could strike out for Matt's office. She took a step in that direction, a sense of fearful urgency growing in her belly.

Evan got the first one into his warehouse, tying her quickly to a support beam. He made it back to the row houses in time to see Cristeen hesitating. She was going to leave. No! His plan would fail. His hand went for his gun of its own accord. He forced himself to stop. A shot now would attract unwanted attention.

The alleyway was shadowy. Cristeen had never felt this nervous. Must be the closed in feeling, she thought. There was a rushing sound behind her. She whirled around just as Evan Marks reached her. Her outcry was cut short by the pipe striking her head. She crumpled.

Ha! So much for the mighty she-devil.

* * *

The outer office door banged open loudly. Matt was mildly annoyed, but left Booker to deal with it. His young financial manager could use some experience dealing with people hungry to get at his wealth. Some of the schemes these people came up with...he laughed, remembering a few of the more ludicrous ones.

Booker, or rather Dalton Avery, for Booker was just his nickname, did indeed go to meet the forceful visitor. And immediately escorted him into Matt's office. The knock at his door startled as well as irritated Matt. When it was Mike standing at the threshold, his irritation fizzled, to be replaced by cold fear.

"They're gone," Mike's face was pale.

"When? Where?" Matt was on his feet at once. There was no need to ask who they were; Mike would be here for only one reason. Cristeen.

"Leigh took Cristeen down to Linden Street, to window shop she said," Mike moved into the room. "That was at ten this morning. When they didn't return for lunch at the agreed upon time of one o'clock, George sent for me."

Matt glanced at the clock. It was ten past three.

"We searched Linden, then Mountain and Willow. Three of my men are still out there," he shook his head as he spoke.

"What is it you aren't telling me?"

"You need to come with me now."

"Mike, tell me."

Mike started out of the office. Matt grabbed at his gun belt, knocking over the coat rack in the process. Booker stared after him.

Generally, Mike tried to keep traffic to a jog or slower on his city streets. Today, Mike loped his horse eastward down Jefferson Avenue. He didn't wait for Matt, knowing his friend would follow. They crossed town, ending their journey on Mason Street, at the railroad depot.

Mike leaped off his horse, trailing the reins to ground tie the animal. Remotely Matt noted traffic was unusually light. Waiting passengers seemed to be gathering along one side of the platform in back. The fear gripping Matt's heart squeezed tighter as Mike crossed the double set of tracks, striking out for the freight yard. Once there he angled southward towards a yard shack.

"A switchman discovered it this morning." He held open the shack door. "Took a while for the information to get to me. Too late, unfortunately."

Inside, the little building seemed to be wallpapered with Evan Marks' wanted poster. On the little table that stood in the corner was the piece of evidence that disturbed Mike. One of the posters was face down, and scrawled across the back, in what appeared to be dried blood, were the words, "She Must Die!" Beneath that, in a neat hand that seemed out of kilter, was printed: Cristeen Latham, Rossiter House, Room 214.

"He knew where she was staying. He hadn't disappeared at all, just went to ground."

Matt couldn't breath. The little shack seemed to spin. He staggered back out into the daylight, gasping for air. The sun shone too brightly. He squinted and realized he had forgotten his hat in the rush to leave the office. As his breathing returned to normal there was a hubbub back at the platform.

Rory was running across the tracks, calling out to Mike, "Boss, you better come quick."

"You gonna be okay?" Mike asked of Matt, who simply nodded. "It's not her blood, you do realize that much? Too old."

Rory was standing before them. "Edwards just sent a runner to the office," he panted. Rory was a man who liked to work from his saddle. "They got a note."

"A note?" Mike queried. "What kind of note?"

"Askin' for money."

Matt's eyebrow shot up. "Ransom? Seems out of character."

Mike shook his head, pointing a finger back at the shack, "Guy's deranged, Matt. I always thought Marks was a few cards shy of a full deck."

They began walking back to their horses. "I hope you aren't trying to comfort me, because you are woefully bad at it."

Mike laughed, "I'll save my half-truths and illusions for

the Edwards."

The ransom note was written in the same neat handwriting as Cristeen's name and address on the poster at the rail yard. The message was simple; he was holding them both, to be release only after a payment of $20,000, details for the money drop would follow. As proof that he did indeed have Cristeen, Marks included with the note her Celtic cross pendant.

Caroline clung to the cross, beside herself with grief. "It was my mother's, my sister gave it to Cristeen. She was to give it to her daughter, continue the tradition."

George did his best to comfort his wife. "She's not dead Caroline. You must believe that now as firmly as you did when she was lost."

Matt gently took the pendant. A doctor arrived to administer a sedative to Caroline, who was then escorted away by one of the maids. George remained behind, though he obviously wanted to go with his wife.

"Whatever it takes, Sheriff, I want both girls back alive." He paused, glancing around as if to be sure no one else listened. "And I want that monster dead."

Mike watched him leave. "I don't guess you will be arguing against that dead monster thing?"

When Matt didn't answer, Mike turned to check on him. Matt was staring at the cross lying in the palm of his hand.

Feeling Mike's eyes upon him, Matt finally replied, "I thought he was gone. I told her she would be safe, that the shops on Linden are popular and Marks wouldn't try anything in such a public place, even if he was still around."

"It's not your fault, Matt."

Matt turned a tortured gaze on his friend. "She trusted me, Mike. After all these years, she finally trusted someone and she chose me."

Mike became alarmed, seeing his friend going to pieces. He did the only thing he could think of, short of actually smacking some sense into Matt. "Snap out of it, Matt.

Cristeen still trusts you. She's counting on you to get her out of this."

Matt glowered. Mike couldn't know if Cristeen were still alive. He closed his eyes, squeezing his hand around the cross at the same time. *Lord, please watch over Cristeen and Leigh. Keep them safe and lead us to them swiftly. And Lord, please wreak justice on this monster, Evan Marks.*

* * *

"CeeCee?" Leigh's whisper seemed like a shout in the empty warehouse. "Are you awake?

Cristeen moaned, despite her efforts to remain quiet. "I'm awake," she croaked. "Where are we?"

"In some sort of warehouse, I think."

Sunlight filtered through windows high up the wall. "Is it still today?"

Leigh snickered. "How hard did he hit you? Yes, it's still the same day."

There was a shuffling sound from the room adjacent to the large empty space. Evan Marks suddenly filled the doorway. Cristeen shut her eyes. When she opened them again, Marks was normal size once more. She had a screaming headache, her shoulder felt ready to dislocate, and she was almost certain her leg was broken again. Other than that, things looked good.

"Shuddup out there!" Marks yelled, then disappeared once more.

"He's going to attract more attention than we ever could." Leigh smirked. "Let's get him so mad he screams and brings down the whole city sheriff's department."

"Not a good idea, Leigh."

Marks stormed back into the room. Though it was Leigh doing most of the talking, he went immediately to Cristeen, kicking her right leg and sending a wave of pain through her that threatened to steal her consciousness away.

"Leave her alone!" Leigh cried loudly, apparently going forward with her plan.

Marks stepped around the post to slap her roughly. Satisfied for the moment, he stomped back to the little office room.

Leigh waited until Marks stopped ranting. When no more noise issued from the office, she again whispered to her sister. "Cristeen, are you alright?"

"No," Cristeen answered through clenched teeth. "Now stop talking before he comes back and does more damage."

What Cristeen wanted most right now was to lie down. With her back pressed against the pillar she had no way to get comfortable. Her head throbbed, her leg pulsed. In a detached part of her mind she wondered if the two were in concert, throbbing and pulsing to the beat of her heart. *I must be delirious,* she told herself. At least her warning to Leigh was being heeded; for the time anyway. Leigh wouldn't keep quiet long. If only Cristeen could lie down and rest her head.

She must have blacked out. The shadows had grown long when she looked around again. She wiggled her fingers, gratified to feel Leigh's back. Her sister squirmed, squealing in fear. Cristeen hissed a hasty *shh,* to no avail; Marks was at the door.

"I see I gotta gag you if'n I want quiet."

Surprisingly, he only gagged Leigh. Cristeen wondered at that. He came around to study her then; his face wavered in and out of focus.

"Cracked you good, didn't I?"

His laugh was maniacal. She shivered.

"Ya, that's right girlie, you best be afeared of me."

Then he was gone again. Cristeen couldn't be sure if he left or she passed out. Cold and hunger woke her. It felt quite late, but then she hadn't eaten since breakfast that morning.

Was it still the same day?

"Leigh?" A muffled reply reminded her that Leigh was gagged. "I'm sorry, Leigh."

There was a flickering light in the office window. Did he sleep? So what if he did, they were both tied and she was certainly going nowhere. Where was Matt? Was he looking for her even now?

A chill ran down her spine. If Matt found her, would Marks kill him as well? They were all doomed. She was powerless to save them this time. A sob escaped her; she heard Marks' deranged laugh. The sound steeled her resolve.

Lord, I know you're there. I know you are listening and that I can trust you. Please, Lord, please bring us safely out of this. And please don't let Matt get killed.

* * *

The light was blinding. Dawn, a new day. Cristeen opened her eyes, tried to rise. Her shoulder muscles protested painfully. And it wasn't dawn. Evan Marks cackled as he held the lantern in her face. He grasped her hair, forcing her to look up at him.

"Can't let you sleep, she-devil."

He stood straight, moving the lantern, giving her a glimpse of his face. She was frightened by what she saw—a mad man. He released her with a flick of his wrist, slamming the back of her head into the thick wooden pillar. He cackled again, so pleased with himself he forgot to kick her as he left.

The darkness quickly enveloped Cristeen once more. Her head smarted where it had hit the post; tears welled in her eyes. She bit her lip, holding back the sound of her sobbing. She would not give him the satisfaction of hearing her cry. As the tears rolled freely down her face, she felt a hand rub against her back. Leigh, mutely trying to comfort her. Cristeen cried.

THIRTY ONE

The second note was delivered just after nine p.m., brought to the hotel by a young boy. The boy described Marks perfectly, but had no idea where the man had come from or where he disappeared to after paying the princely sum of three bits for the requested task.

George Edwards read the note, detailing the exact location where he was to leave the ransom. The money was to be put inside a satchel, such as used by many workers to carry their lunch and trade tools to and from the workplace. The satchel was to be placed behind a rainwater barrel, near the employee entrance to the flour mill, located near the rail yards.

"I shall have the monies ready, gentlemen," George told Mike and Matt. "I would gladly part with twice the sum, so long as you promise me both Leigh and Cristeen can be safely secured from the hands of this mad man."

They were once again in the private parlor at the Rossiter House. Caroline rested fitfully upstairs. Mike toyed with the idea of lying outright, dismissing the thought upon looking into the steeled eyes of Edwards. The man would not be fooled with false hope.

"I can promise nothing, Mr. Edwards, except that I will find Marks and bring him to justice."

Forced to accept that reality, George retired from the room. Matt slammed his fist against the wall, cursing at the lack of any leads.

"You," Mike pointed to his friend. "Come with me."

Following Mike blindly had become second nature to Matt on this day. It was now more than six hours since Mike burst into his office; the odds of finding either Cristeen or Leigh alive were getting slimmer.

Mike was silent as they crossed the streets, heading back to the courthouse and his office. He empathized with Matt, in fact felt frustrated himself when each new lead failed to pan out. Inaction was going to eat away at his friend, until he went mad.

The cramped office was busy tonight. Rory was orchestrating the activity, freeing Mike to oversee activities outside and at the hotel. Matt sat on the deacon's bench, adjusting his belt as he did so to keep from sitting on his own pistol. Mike perched on the edge of his desk; his holster was tied down at the bottom, securing it to his leg. Matt considered that for a moment, the distraction a relief for his over-anxious mind. As Mike hooked his leg over the corner of the desk, the pistol stayed in place. Furthermore, strapped to his leg as it was, Mike could free the weapon quickly in time of need.

"Hello! You still with us, buddy?" Mike waved a hand across Matt's line of sight.

"Huh?" Matt blinked, "Sorry, guess I'm a little out of it."

"Numb, that's what I'd call it," Mike smiled sympathetically. "Pay attention now. I've got a gut feeling we're missing the obvious."

Rory had tacked up a city planning map on the wall. Though it was nearly three years old, and showed the site of the newly finished city hall as proposed, the streets were accurately laid out. Using pins dipped in various colors of paint, they began marking the map with the facts.

"Let's start with Linden," Mike instructed Rory. "Cristeen was last seen in front of the Red Lion china shop."

Rory stuck a pin through the map into the wall, approximating the store's location on Linden Avenue. Mike looked at Matt, deciding a little ribbing might ease the strain.

"Anything particular she might've been looking at?"

Matt frowned. "She's been looking for a wedding gift for Katie."

"Ahh," Mike winked at Rory before turning back to Matt. "And what about Gordon Jewelers? What could she possibly get Katie in there?"

"Cristeen was shopping in the jewelry store?" Matt was surprised.

"No, Leigh went in there, and from eyewitness accounts it sounds like they separated at that point."

"You oughtta consider vistin' Gordon's, Matt."

"Rory, I don't need you encouraging Mike. Especially since I already got an earful from Suzanne two days ago."

Mike laughed. "That's my girl, always the match-maker."

"Can we get serious again?"

Rory picked up a pin. "The trail leads from here, on Linden, over to Lemay. Lucky for us Cristeen sure is notice-able."

After an hour, the map resembled a colorful porcupine, and still they were no closer to finding Cristeen and Leigh. Matt began to pace. Rory left the room to get coffee. Mike continued to stare at the map, convinced there had to be a pattern. The pins all led to the same area, ending near a neighborhood of row houses. Those buildings were being searched.

"There has to be something we're missing," he mumbled, mostly to himself. Suddenly he jumped off the desk, picking up the pins and positioning himself at the map. "Matt, where is the money being dropped off?"

Matt spit out the mill address. Mike speared a pin into the wall. "Hand me that spool of thread, would you?"

The pins had come from Suzanne's sewing basket, along with a supply of threads and needles. Matt brought the thread to Mike, his curiosity roused. Mike anchored one end of the thread to the pin marking the rail yard shack. Tracing a thread trail across to the row-house pins, he seemed to backtrack Marks' movements.

"Would you look at that," Mike's amazement puzzled Matt. "He must have grabbed Leigh first. All the witnesses reported seeing a red-haired woman, Cristeen, walking alone."

Matt nodded, beginning to see the pattern Mike had been certain they would find. "He leaves enough of a trail to lure Cristeen into his trap, right about here," he tapped the map where the pins congregated.

The string went from there to the rail yard, snagging on the mill pin along the way.

"The mill is conveniently close to the trains."

"Grab the money and run," Matt finished. "What about Cristeen and Leigh?"

"He must be holding them close by. Can't afford to travel far, risk being seen."

They stared at the map, each trying to locate a possible · hiding place. The plot map clearly indicated the grain elevator, but showed the mill yard as a vague collection of buildings.

"What's really out there?" Matt tapped a finger on the map.

"The mill complex is a couple of large buildings. There's some miscellaneous sheds, a siding track, a bunch of warehouses."

"Sounds promising," hope lit Matt's face, giving him an air of boyish eagerness. "Best be discreet as we check it out."

* * *

Cristeen sagged against her bonds. Marks made it an hourly ritual to awaken her; she knew the time intervals simply because he told her. Scuffling footsteps alerted her to another hour having past. He went by her, going instead to Leigh. She heard Leigh muttering through her gag, then quite clearly she heard Leigh cussing at him. Marks laughed. Another sound - water splashing from a bottle?

"I like you're fire," he was saying. "Maybe I'll take you with me. For a spell."

Leigh's response was choked off as her gag was once again stuffed into her mouth. She coughed; Marks laughed more. Cristeen tried to push herself straight again, anticipating what was to come. She was too weak to succeed. Marks grasped her dress at either shoulder and hauled her into a sitting position.

"No rest for the wicked," he cackled. "No water either." He sloshed the bottle to emphasize his point. "Demons belong in the fire pits of Hell, don'tcha know."

He had been drinking. Cristeen felt her stomach pitch with the realization. He was drunk, insane, and completely in control of both her fate and her sister's. *No, this lunatic is not in control of my life! Lord, I'm trusting in you to save us.* Cristeen still had a little bit of determination left and her gaze held steady as Marks moved the lantern close to her face. He swore profusely.

"I'll break you, devil spawn," he proclaimed, loudly hissing in her ear. "Then I'm gonna kill you."

Cristeen closed her eyes and tried to turn away at the last moment as his fist smashed into her face. The blow struck her cheek, driving her head back into the post yet again. As he stood to leave he half-heartedly kicked at her leg, missing it altogether without noticing. The light grew fainter; Cristeen let herself sag once more. This time she managed to twist around and was able to lay her head on the floor.

Matt, where are you?

There were no more tears to fall.

* * *

"There, the building furthest back," Mike whispered as he pointed.

Matt took the spyglass. A light shone through the windows that ran the length of the building, high up near the roofline. He glanced at the sky; no moon, no stars. The light was coming from inside the building.

"We need to get a closer look."

Mike made a low bird whistle. Rory appeared from a nearby shadow. Speaking not a word, Mike conveyed their intent, finishing with a raised palm to tell the deputy to stay put. Rory nodded comprehension.

The building was a warehouse, one of many belonging to the mill. It was close to the tracks; on that side of the building a platform showed where sacks of flour were loaded onto waiting train cars. Gravel crunched underfoot; silence dictated a snail's pace. Steps led up to a small porch-like entryway, beside which was a lone first floor window.

Matt ducked back around the building. He whispered to Mike, "Light in the window. Office."

Mike nodded. He moved past Matt to peer around the corner. Then he pointed to a building further away. They moved over there, where a whispered conversation could be had.

"What time is it?"

Matt pulled out his watch. "I can't see. Reckon it's around three, or there 'bouts."

"The money's to be left at six in the morning." Mike looked back towards the central buildings. "Marks is counting on blending in with the work crowd."

Matt reviewed the mill yard in his mind's eye. "Won't be hard for him to slip back down here. You don't by chance know the train schedule."

"This is my city, remember? There's a freighter pulls in around five; not usually on time, so I can't be precise."

"Headed which way?"

"South," Mike looked at Matt, just barely making out his

grim expression. "He could have gotten clear out of the state without us even realizing he'd left."

"Could have," Matt agreed. "And he won't be stopping once he's got that money. We've got to act now."

"No need for anything rash, Matt. We've a few hours before the money arrives."

"He's got to kill them first, then creep up here undetected. Time is running out."

Assuming Marks had not already killed them. Neither one put that fear into voice. Mike slipped away to signal for Rory. There wouldn't be time to mount a large-scale rescue, and it was probably unwise to do so anyway. It would be just the three of them. The odds were in their favor.

THIRTY TWO

M att drew his pistol, carefully sighting down the barrel. A hand pushed his arm down; he glared angrily at Mike. With a nod of his head, Mike sent Matt back out of the building.

"What are you doing? I had a clear shot."

"Did you, now? In the dark, you were absolutely certain you'd hit only Marks?"

It was a hissed, whispered conversation. Mike's words gave Matt pause. Rory jumped in, voicing another objection.

"Even if you did hit only him, what if you didn't kill him with the first shot? He's armed, only needs an excuse to shoot."

With a frustrated groan, Matt conceded their points. "So what's the plan?"

* * *

Four a.m. Cristeen did not bother to raise even her head as the footsteps approached. She sensed time was running out; Marks was becoming increasingly agitated, his nerves winding him tight. His boot prodded at her chin, rolling her head limply off the floor.

"Aha!" Marks cried victoriously. "Broken at last."

His foot lifted, as if intending to smash it down onto her face. Her eyes caught a movement in the pre-dawn shadows at the far end of the room. Something seemed to melt out of the office, moving behind a stack of pallets.

Marks' foot set gently on the floor beside her. Cristeen risked a glance upwards. He saw the movement as well. His liquor soaked mind was having difficulty finding an explanation. Yet he was clearly suspicious. Muttering a string of profanities, he swung a vicious kick into her midsection, then stomped to the office. Something seemed to hold his attention; Cristeen couldn't see well enough to know if it was to his liking or not. He disappeared into the room. She saw him a moment later, taking a long drink from his bottle of whiskey.

The shadows moved. She closed her eyes and opened them again. Giant rats scurried along the wall. *Rats! Oh Lord, please not rats.* She struggled to sit up; Leigh pushed against her hands. Why was Leigh making it so difficult? She tried to shove her sister aside. It was no use, she was simply too weak.

Cristeen collapsed back onto the floor with a whimper. Gray light filtered through the high windows. Shadows pooled along the edges of the room. The rats were beyond her line of sight. She thought she could hear them scurrying across the room.

Leigh's body moved away from her hands. She must have seen the rats also.

Something brushed Cristeen's hands. Something warm. *A rat!* She whimpered loudly, trying to move her hands away from the teeth she felt gnawing at the ropes. Unexpectedly, a shadow coalesced into a person crouching beside her.

"Hush, Cristy," a familiar voice told her.

Matt? She tried to speak.

Matt peered anxiously at Rory as the deputy cut the ropes binding Leigh. A quick glance over his shoulder confirmed Mike's position outside the office door. They would at least attempt to take Marks alive; accidents happen. Rory began slicing at Cristeen's fetters. When Evan Marks realized what was happening and the shooting began, the women should be out of the line of fire.

Matt looked down at Cristeen. Rage blurred his vision; he willed himself to keep calm. Her lips were moving, trying to form a word. The last strand of rope gave way; Rory helped Leigh to her feet. Matt cautiously slipped his arm under Cristeen's shoulders, drawing her close to him.

"I knew you would come." Her voice could barely be heard.

"What the—" Marks shouted in alarm. He hesitated only a moment when he felt the muzzle of a gun against his skull. He was a dead man now, but that she-devil was going to die with him.

Marks got his gun clear of its holster, diving to the side as he did so. Mike cried out a warning and began shooting.

Matt hunched over Cristeen, shielding her from the bullets Marks managed to send her way. One creased across Matt's shoulder before plowing into the heavy wooden beam. A second splintered the side of the beam, was turned in its path and went harmlessly into the empty space of the warehouse. Matt held Cristeen tightly, even when the gunfire stopped.

The room was growing brighter as dawn tiptoed across the land. Cristeen closed her eyes, listening to the beating of Matt's heart, feeling the warmth of his embrace spreading through her cold and painful body. She couldn't remember a time she had ever felt so loved. Nevertheless, she had to move.

"Can't feel my arms," she squeaked.

Matt eased away from her. "What, honey? I can't understand you."

"My arms."

He set her down gently and vigorously rubbed her arms to get the blood flowing in them again. She felt the tingling sensation as life returned to her limbs. She tried to look at Matt, confirm he was really there. Opening her eyes hurt; two Matts wavered before her. Closing her eyes once more, Cristeen moaned in pain.

Matt stopped massaging her arms, scooping Cristeen back into his embrace. In the brightening light he saw the welt on her cheek, the goose egg bump at her temple. Tenderly he kissed her wounds, wishing he could take away the pain.

"You're hurt," Leigh's gentle concern drew a quick glance from Matt.

"It's nothing, a scratch."

She touched his shoulder and he winced. "More than a scratch, Matt."

Rory crouched on his heels, getting eye level with Matt. "We'll have a carriage here in a few minutes. I'll take you both to the doctor. Mike says to tell you the monster is dead."

* * *

Cristeen opened her eyes. Gradually details registered to her mind; the soft pillow under her head, the light blanket drawn up under her arm, the vase of flowers on the dresser. She was in her hotel room. The hand holding hers was Matt's.

He had fallen asleep resting his head and arms on the mattress beside her. She watched him as he slept, his shoulders gently rising and falling with each breath. For the first time she noticed the fine lines radiating out at the corners of his eyes. A smile twitched at her lips; she had never before seen him sleeping. All his cares seemed to have melted away, leaving a serene expression. A warm contentment spread through her. Ever so carefully she slid her hand out from under his, intending to sit up.

Matt's eyes snapped open as his hand clamped on hers.

It took him a moment to realize she was awake; his grip relaxed. He helped her sit up, propping pillows behind her back, then sat beside her. Worry etched his face once more.

Cristeen smiled, "It's like deja vu."

He returned her smile. "How do you feel this time 'round?"

"My head hurts," she touched her temple.

"You had a concussion. The ache will go away soon."

"How long have I been sleeping?"

He glanced at the mantle clock. "Nearly ten hours."

"How long have you been here?"

"I never left," he smiled tenderly. "We brought you straight here. Uncle George had a doctor waiting."

"And Leigh?"

"She's a little stiff and sore, but otherwise unharmed." His grin turned quirky. "She's got a bit of mother hen in her, you know."

"How so?"

"Wouldn't let me stay unless I let the Doc patch up my shoulder."

Concern leapt into Cristeen's eyes, reflecting the fear in her heart. "You were hurt?"

"Barely," he patted her hand. "I've had worse scrapes, believe me."

She closed her eyes and shuddered. "I don't think I want to know about the worse ones."

After a short quiet, she asked what was really on her mind. "Is it over then?"

"Yes, Marks is dead."

His flat tone opened her eyes once more. There was an expression of grim satisfaction on his face. In fact, he seemed almost pleased that her tormentor was no longer in this world.

Noting her searching gaze, Matt gave her a slow, sad smile.

"Nothing less than Marks deserved."

He caressed her temple, eliciting a wince. "Sorry," he softly kissed the bruise.

Cristeen closed her eyes again, content to simply feel his touch on her face. His hand lingered long before dropping to reclaim her hand. There was still a dull aching throb behind her eyes, the last remaining symptom of her concussion. With each pounding rush of blood through her head she remembered a little more about the previous night. So much seemed unreal; what was reality?

"What happened?" Cristeen opened her eyes again. "He wanted to kill me. What was he waiting for?"

Matt shrugged, "Can't know for sure. Mike suspects Marks was waiting for the train. In case the shot was heard."

Recalled to mind was Marks' foot, poised to crush her skull; she shuddered. "I'm not sure he intended to use a gun, or at least it would not have been the deciding factor."

His hand squeezed around hers and for a moment she saw pain in his eyes. The breath he released before speaking shook with emotion.

"I'm so sorry I didn't get there sooner."

"You got there at just the right time," Cristeen smiled to reassure Matt.

Memories of that last hour filled her mind with an otherworldly quality. Moving shadows, birdcalls, Matt materializing as if by magic. Trying to make sense of it all made the pain in her head jump sharply. With a groan she touched her forehead.

"I remember, but I don't," she turned a troubled gaze to Matt. "Does that make any sense?"

The pained guilt flared in Matt's eyes as he answered. "You were barely conscious, Cristy. I'm amazed you remember anything."

"Make sense of it for me, please," she pleaded. "I saw something in the shadows. Was that you?"

"Yes," he traced a finger along her jaw line. "You were frightened, weren't you? Why?"

She smiled sheepishly, "I thought it was rats."

"You don't like rats?" He was surprised; of all the scary things she had faced in her life to be afraid of an overgrown field mouse seemed somehow silly.

Cristeen grimaced. "That would be putting it mildly."

"Hmmm," he grinned, "I'll have to remember that; Cristy is afraid of rats."

"Don't you dare torment me with that!" Her giggle was cut short by another wave of nauseous pain. Matt gently covered her eyes with his hand; the darkness did seem to help.

"Did you, that is," her words faltered. "You told me Marks is dead. How?"

"God's justice."

She smiled indulgently.

"Mike shot him."

Mike emptied his gun into the man, but Cristeen did not need to know that. With all his heart, Matt wanted Cristeen to forget about the whole ordeal. Her imagination did not need fuel for those disturbing dreams she seemed prone to. Let her cling to the memory of being rescued, of finally being free from her fears.

"What's the last thing you remember?"

"Listening to your heart beating."

He was caught off guard by her answer. Had she even heard the gunfire? Cristy was choosing to remember something pleasant amidst the terror. She was ready to move on, put this ordeal behind her and get on with living. Her eyes held his as a soft smile tugged at her lips.

"I knew you would come for me. I prayed for that, and for God to protect you. He didn't let me down."

"I'm glad you trusted Him," Matt wrapped her in his arms.

Cristeen rested her head on his shoulder. She could hear

his heart beating, feel him breathing. His hand stroked her hair, his chin rested on the top of her head. She closed her eyes and absorbed the love.

"I want to go home," she whispered.

Matt kissed her forehead. "There's something we need to do first."

"What?" Cristeen looked up at him.

"Get Katie a wedding gift. Something she's always wanted."

Cristeen was puzzled only for a moment. Slowly a shy smile spread across her face. "A sister?"

He grinned as he nodded, "That is, if you still love me."

"Oh, I do love you!"

"Then marry me and make me the happiest man in Colorado."

"Only Colorado?" Her eyes sparkled with humor.

In response, Matt bent his head and kissed her. His intensity tempered with tenderness took her breath away. When he at last pulled away, Cristeen swayed against Matt.

"In all the world," he whispered.

Printed in the United States
1304000002B/49-255